Women's Studies and Culture

A feminist introduction

EDITED BY
ROSEMARIE BUIKEMA AND ANNEKE SMELIK

Zed Books
LONDON AND NEW JERSEY

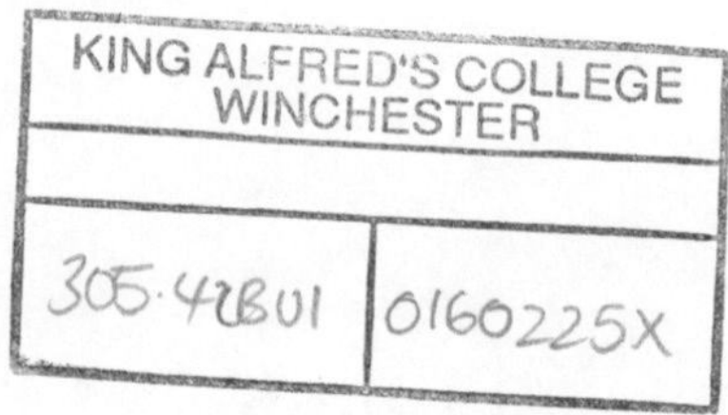

Women's Studies and Culture: A feminist introduction was first published in Dutch under the title *Vrouwenstudies in de Cultuurwetenschappen* by Dick Coutinho BV, Slochteren Laan 7, 1405 AL Bussum, The Netherlands in 1993 and in an expanded edition, with a new chapter on lesbian sexuality and a new epilogue by Rosi Braidotti, in English by Zed Books Ltd, 7 Cynthia Street, London N1 0JF, UK and 165 First Avenue, Atlantic Highlands, New Jersey 07716, USA, in 1995.

The extracts reprinted on pages 20, 24, 29–30, 34, 36, 38, 41, 48, 56, 60–1, 66–9, 71, 74–5, 79, 80, 86, 88, 91, 101–3, 111, 119, 127, 129–33, 135, 137, 142, 144–6, 148, 155–60, 172, 176 and 180 are from *The Color Purple* by Alice Walker, published in the United Kingdom by The Women's Press Ltd, 34 Great Sutton Street, London EC1V 0CX in 1983.

Cover designed by Andrew Corbett.
Set in Monotype Ehrhardt by Ewan Smith, London.
Printed and bound in the United Kingdom by Redwood Books, Trowbridge, Wiltshire.

A catalogue record for this book is available from the British Library.

US CIP data is available from the Library of Congress.

ISBN 1 85649 311 3 cased
ISBN 1 85649 312 1 limp

Contents

About the authors

ROSI BRAIDOTTI is professor in the Department of Women's Studies in the Arts at the University of Utrecht. Her publications include *Patterns of Dissonance: A Study of Women in Contemporary Philosophy* (1991) and *Nomadic Subjects: Embodiment and Sexual Difference in Contemporary Feminist Theory* (1994). She is currently working on a study of constructions of different bodies in bio-medical discourse since the eighteenth century.

DÉDÉ BROUWER is author of *Gender Variation in Dutch: A Sociolinguistic Study of Amsterdam Speech* (1989). She is currently working on variation and change in the use of dialect of women and men in Amsterdam.

LIESBETH BROUWER is assistant professor of Frisian literature and feminist semiotics in the Department of Agronomic Historical Studies at the University of Groningen. She is completing a book on early nineteenth-century constructions of national identity in Frisian literature.

ROSEMARIE BUIKEMA is assistant professor in the Department of Women's Studies in the Arts at the University of Utrecht and is a researcher in the Department of Literary Studies at the University of Amsterdam. She is author of *De Loden Venus* (1995), a study of textuality in biographies by daughters of famous women including Margaret Mead, Vanessa Bell and Milena Jesenká. She is currently working on a study of the mother–daughter relationship in literature by women immigrants.

JOKE DAME teaches at the University of Amsterdam and the University of Utrecht. She is author of *Het Zingend Lichaam* (1994), a study of the gendered meanings of the voice in Western classical music. In her current study on vocal masquerades, she applies the notion of 'listener response' to opera.

JOKE HERMES is assistant professor at the Department of Communication at the University of Amsterdam. She is author of *Reading Women's Magazines: An Analysis of Everyday Media Use* (1995). She is currently working on feminism and popular culture.

RENÉE C. HOOGLAND is assistant professor in lesbian cultural studies at the University of Nijmegen and post-doctoral researcher in comparative literature at the University of Amsterdam. She is author of *Elizabeth Bowen: A Reputation in Writing* (1994) and is currently working on a study of lesbian sexuality in contemporary Euro-western culture.

MAAIKE MEIJER is associate professor in the Department of Women's Studies in the Arts at the University of Utrecht. Her publications include *De Lust tot Lezen* (1988), a book on Dutch female poets and the literary systems and *In Tekst Gevat* (1995), an introduction to a critique of representation. She is currently working on a history of Dutch literature since World War II.

PAMELA PATTYNAMA is assistant professor at the Department of Literary Studies at the University of Amsterdam. She is author of *Passages* (1992), a study of female adolescence as story and discourse in post-modern women's literature and is currently working on (post)colonialism and gender in a study of cultural representations in the Dutch East Indies.

MIRIAM VAN RIJSINGEN is assistant professor at the Art History Institute of the University of Amsterdam. She is completing a book on the portraits of women by Anselm Feuerbach.

MIEKE VAN SCHERMBEEK teaches at the Department of Theatre Studies at the University of Amsterdam. She is completing a book on sexual difference and identification in the narrative structures of drama texts.

ANNEKE SMELIK teaches film studies at the Department of Women's Studies in the Arts at the University of Utrecht. She is author of *And The Mirror Cracked: A Study of Rhetoric in Feminist Cinema* (1995) and is currently involved in a project on cultural representations of gender and ethnicity in the media.

BERTEKE WAALDIJK is assistant professor in the Department of Women's Studies in the Arts at the University of Utrecht. She is author of *Het Amerika der Vrouw* (1995), a comparative study of the gender and history of social work in the United States and the Netherlands. Her current project aims at developing a feminist philosophy of history.

Preface

ROSEMARIE BUIKEMA AND
ANNEKE SMELIK

In *Women's Studies and Culture* we discuss the history of women's studies as it has developed in the arts and humanities in Western universities over the course of the last twenty years. Although 'women's studies' has gained a place within the humanities in not much more than twenty years, unfortunately its position is far from unproblematic. Women's studies is still only on the periphery of academic life. With this book we hope to strengthen and extend the place of women's studies in the arts and humanities. It has been written explicitly with a view to teaching. This overview is meant to provide an introductory course for teachers and students of women's studies within the wider and more diverse field of cultural studies in universities (and also possibly beyond). The picture of feminist cultural studies outlined in this book is composed in such a way that it is both an introduction and a basis for further study. In order to stress the diversity of the research presented and the broad applicability of the book as a whole, we have chosen the term 'culture' in the title.

Women's studies is strongly supported by the government in the Netherlands, and consequently knows a high degree of institutionalisation, which has allowed for feminist curricula to be developed in the universities. *Women's Studies and Culture* has grown out of our experience over many years of teaching an 'Introduction to Women's Studies' course at the Faculty of Arts of the University of Utrecht. The Netherlands have long been a small country at the heart of Europe, and due to this geographical factor, have functioned as a point of intersection. At the crossroads of Europe's women's movement, Dutch women's studies therefore maintains a persistently international outlook (Braidotti, 1991, 1993). This book reflects this awareness of international literature, coupled with local traditions of feminist practice.

Women's studies is characterised by its interdisciplinary nature. This makes it a rich and fascinating field in which all kinds of interconnections between disciplines, theories and scientific movements arise. However, this very interdisciplinarity demands knowledge extending beyond each individual discipline, as well as a critical look at the discipline itself. In other words, the interdisciplinary nature of women's studies, and the rapid developments within it, impose great demands on teachers and students. In this book we have attempted to deal with both the interdisciplinary approach and feminist criticism.

The book is divided into two parts. Part One contains introductions to each of the disciplines involved, in order to provide a clear overview of the field of cultural studies. Each chapter is structured around three different approaches which, in our view, characterise the main developments within women's studies: theories of equality, of difference and of deconstruction. This structure provides a common thread within the disciplinary introductions and illustrates interdisciplinary connections. In chapters 2 to 9 we show what knowledge and which new questions these developments have produced within feminist history, literary theory, linguistics, media studies, film studies, theatre studies, art history and musicology. This sequence is more or less representative of the order in which these disciplines have been introduced into women's studies. Naturally, not every field of study has evolved in the same way. The various disciplines differ greatly in the way in which they have welcomed and incorporated feminist theory. In particular, the deconstructive perspective has met with varying degrees of success and has a higher profile in some fields of study than in others. In order to understand the development of feminist thought in each discipline, the book begins with an introductory chapter in which we discuss extensively the aforementioned theoretical perspective. Chapters 2 to 9 should be read against this theoretical background.

In Part Two the three areas of equality, difference and deconstruction are also reflected. These chapters explore certain political and theoretical backgrounds that have been crucial for the development of a differentiated feminist critique of Western science: lesbian studies, black studies, semiotics and psychoanalysis. Part Two can serve as study material for advanced students and for teachers who wish to go more deeply into the subjects in the disciplinary introductions of Part One.

The guiding thread weaving through the book is an analysis of the novel *The Color Purple* by Alice Walker. In our teaching we have found this novel to be very suitable as illustrative material for theoretical texts. *The Color Purple* is a novel so rich in material that diverse themes can be studied within each discipline. In this way we hope to make the theory accessible and more easily understood. *Women's Studies and Culture* may in fact be best used for teaching in conjunction with *The Color Purple*. It is a popular novel, which students enjoy reading and is readily available. Because a film has been made of the novel it is also possible to study visual and auditory aspects; a video of Steven Spielberg's film *The Color Purple* can easily be obtained. The page references used in this book are taken from the Women's Press edition of *The Color Purple* (London, 1986).

Even though the book generaly follows a chronological order, it is not necessary for the chapters to be read in order. Because of the interdisciplinary nature of the subject, it is suggested that students should for the clarification of particular concepts, trends and developments cross-read different chapters. We have made some simple suggestions for cross-reading in the text.

A number of practical aids are included to assist both teachers and students with the teaching material. At the end of each chapter there is a short list of literature recommended for further study. A complete general bibliography can be found at the back of the book. At the end of this bibliography we have listed literature making particular reference to *The Color Purple* and other publications by Alice Walker.

At the back of the book there is also a set of student assignments for each discipline, in which students are encouraged to tackle the subject matter independently and creatively. We have included a glossary which explains once again the central concepts within feminist cultural studies used in this book. Readers are advised to consult this glossary where necessary when reading the chapters. These aids should allow for a flexible course which is adaptable to different formats.

We thank students who have taken part in our 'Introduction to Women's Studies' for their enthusiastic and critical response to the teaching material. We hope we have converted their comments into a useful book.

This book has also come into being thanks to the material and moral support of the Department of Women's Studies in the Humanities at the University of Utrecht, to which we therefore offer our heartfelt thanks.

Part One

I

Windows in a round house: feminist theory

ROSEMARIE BUIKEMA

> I wanted to build me a round house, says Shug, but everybody act like that's backward. You can't put windows in a round house, they say. But I made me up some plans anyway. (Alice Walker, *The Color Purple*)

Introduction

In surveys of women's studies at Western universities feminist academics generally distinguish three different perspectives in the development of feminist theory: theories of equality, of difference and of deconstruction. These feminist perspectives refer to different strategies and theoretical positions in the debate about the significance of sexual difference (Stimpson 1984, Brügmann 1990, Braidotti 1994).

In this book we will go more deeply into the interaction between these three perspectives within women's studies in general. In addition, particular attention will be paid to the kind of questions that are investigated within feminist cultural studies. We describe the process of the development of academic women's studies, which is characterised by a gradual differentiation of the category 'woman' into colour, class, age, sexual preference, etcetera.

Within the general paradigm of equality, feminist studies in the humanities have aimed both at eliminating the disadvantage that women authors, directors, composers and visual artists have with regard to their male colleagues, and supplying missing historical information about women. In addition feminist studies signal and analyse sexist images of women in work produced by men. This so-called 'critique of sexism' generates a line of research that can be looked upon as representative of theories of 'sexual difference'. Within the paradigm of sexual difference, feminist studies focus on establishing a female aesthetics independent of the cultural norms and values set by men. Eventually we see the development of feminist cultural studies that is inspired by post-structuralist and deconstructive theories. These studies challenge binary oppositions such as man/woman, white/black, equality/difference. Within this paradigm feminist critics analyse the meanings that are attached to concepts such as 'woman' and 'femininity', and whiteness and blackness, on the basis of the notion that meanings are produced in a complex interaction between text and context.

The different perspectives within feminist theory distinguished above – striving for equality between the sexes, emphasis on the differences between the sexes, or transcendence of the equality/difference opposition – will first be elucidated in this introductory chapter. In chapters 2 to 9 these feminist perspectives are further elaborated within the various branches of cultural studies. Of great relevance for the development of feminist research in the humanities are the fields of study of lesbian studies, black studies ('black' is used here as a political term which does not literally refer to skin colour but to a marginalised social position on the basis of ethnicity); psychoanalysis (as the theory of the unconscious) and semiotics (as the study of signs and symbols). In return feminist theory has greatly influenced these fields. This is why chapters 10 to 13 concentrate on the interaction between feminist theories and the development of these fields of study. Like the chapters in Part 1 the final four chapters explicitly illustrate the basic link between theory and politics within women's studies.

In the course of its existence feminist cultural studies has gone through internal changes under the influence of black, lesbian, psychoanalytic and semiotic criticisms. It is therefore important to note that the various theoretical approaches that can be distinguished in feminist theory and in the resulting feminist studies (equality, difference, deconstruction) do not follow each other chronologically in the sense that the birth of one theoretical framework marks the death of the other. Once initiated the various types of research develop simultaneously and for the greater part in relation to each other.

Equality

The theory of equality involves the kind of feminism that is directed towards removing social and cultural differences between women and men. The main political objective is women's demand for equality with men as regards opportunities to realise their ambitions, as well as the demand that women receive equal pay and cultural recognition. Within this framework women represent an undervalued and oppressed group. In relation to men, women, as Simone de Beauvoir put it, are the second sex (Beauvoir, 1960). Within this analysis of the inequalities between the sexes, white feminists do not hesitate to compare women with blacks, as both being oppressed groups. This analogy, however, reveals the implicit whiteness of academic feminism: if women are the 'niggers of the world' as John Lennon expressed it, then what is the position of black women? The analogy between women and blacks obscures the different kinds of oppression and it also relegates black women to invisibility. However, the interrelation between racism and sexism was to become an issue for academic feminism only much later.

Feminists who in the course of the seventies followed Beauvoir in her struggle for emancipation wanted to bring it about from a social and cultural perspective, so that women too could gain the status of the first sex. As in the work of de Beauvoir, however, the struggle for social and cultural equality may involve different political objectives. It may be inspired by emancipatory ideals about equality for all people as well as by radical strategies concerning criticism of sexist thinking and action. In the first case the emphasis falls on the position of women as individuals; in the second case the central focus is on the analysis of structures that oppress and harm women as a group.

These different political aims affect the object of feminist thought. Equality-minded feminist critics establish that the canon, whether it concerns historiography or the categorisation and assessment of a cultural corpus, musical work or visual art, consists mainly of work produced by men. This cannot possibly be an accurate reflection of the cultural activities developed in Western culture. Consequently, feminist critics assiduously start tracking down forgotten female historical figures, authors, visual artists, playwrights and composers to add to the existing canon. The result is a large number of monographs and biographies indicating that women have indeed been culturally productive, although their work has not managed to penetrate the canon and has sunk into oblivion.

At first this line of approach, in which individual women are rescued from obscurity, does not lead to a fundamental cultural analysis. Feminists try to win a position for women within the dominant social and cultural structures. At a later stage the criticism expressed by radical feminists is generally adapted by emancipation-minded feminist critics. Filling the gender gaps in history and art is then accompanied by a reflection on the masculinistic, hetero- and ethnocentric construction of cultural values as such.

To be able to identify the development and various stages of feminist cultural studies some attention should be paid to the concept of the subject on which the various approaches are based. Emancipatory theories of equality initially proceed from the notion of a coherent, rational, autonomous and universal subject that precedes her or his social and cultural environment. In this view, in which the human subject in a certain sense commands her or his own thoughts and actions, one has control over human development and social change. De Beauvoir is a typical example of an emancipatory theorist who assumes a universal, autonomous human subject. She argues that it should be possible for women to lead the kind of life men do. If that is what women want they should dedicate themselves to this cause, specifically by not allowing their social ambitions to be smothered in motherhood. Again, this position can be criticised for its implicit assumption of a white female subject's perspective. Many black feminist critics have pointed out the different functions of motherhood and family for white and black women (see e.g. Carby 1984). But, as we pointed out before, within institutionalised feminism, the necessary reconsideration of the implicit whiteness of the feminist subject is to be developed later.

I have already mentioned that de Beauvoir combines two feminist strategies which, logically speaking, are not entirely compatible. She emphasises the autonomy of the subject and at the same time criticises the social and cultural structures that turn the subject into who and what she or he becomes. In this line of reasoning the subject is not autonomous, but dependent on a social and cultural context for her or his becoming. Think, for instance, of de Beauvoir's famous statement: 'One is not born, one becomes a women.' In other words, if society changed, the subject would change with it. If sexist structures could be abolished, women and men would have the same opportunities to realise their ideals.

Within the perspective of equality, then, de Beauvoir on the one hand takes the position of an emancipatory feminist when she emphasizes that women are responsible for their own lives, while on the other hand she presents herself as a radical feminist in her analysis of the way in which women are represented as the Other in a patriarchal society, that is to say as objects and not as subjects. Emancipatory feminists as well as radical feminists presuppose a universal human subject. In the emancipatory feminist view, however, the subject is autonomous, whereas in the radical feminist view the subject's identity is determined by the structures in which she or he exists. Inspired by de-Beauvoir-related radical feminist social analysis, the critique of sexism is developed within feminist cultural studies. Feminist critics demonstrate that images of women created by men are produced in texts and social practices as universal representations. The more the experience of real, living women was left undiscussed in the public sphere, the more fictitious women became as the subject of art produced by men.

In this way a society and culture have developed abounding with images women cannot identify with. Absent as they were from public life, women functioned as a screen on which any male fantasy could be projected. The circulation of this kind of projections, as if they were realities, is considered to be an important reason for the absence of real women in social and cultural life. The assumption is that sexist texts and social practiees influence the way women think and feel about themselves.

Feminist cultural critics have challenged and analysed this use of women as a projection screen in male art. Feminist film critics have revealed how the script available to women invariably ends in marriage or death. Feminist literary critics have exposed the pleasure with which women are described as sex objects by male authors. Feminist theatre critics have examined the limited interpretation of female roles in the theatrical world.

According to these studies, we find ideologically biased representations of the world surrounding us in literature, in film, on the stage and in visual art which create a one-sided impression of what is desirable, valuable and true and what is not. Early radical feminists at first analysed representations of women in relation to the lives of real women. According to these theorists texts are more or less faithful reflections of reality. Examples of this kind of criticism can be found in the work of Kate Millett (1969). Like their emancipation-minded sisters, these radical feminist texts complained about the non-realistic cultural status of women and images of women, as well as the lack of possibilities for identification which this textual economy offers them (Fetterley, 1978). At a later stage critiques of sexism emphasised not so much the general untruthfulness of sexist representations of women, as the effect these representations have on women's lives. Black feminists, moreover, have emphasised the specific constellation of inequalities for black women. Authors like Barbara Christian, Audre Lorde, Hazel Carby, Alice Walker and bell hooks, to mention just a few, have discussed the many oppressions (racism, sexism and capitalism) to which black women are exposed. Their studies represent a critical phase in which, in contrast to the radicalism of de Beauvoir, the demand for equality does not exclude an affinity with theories of difference.

Difference

In feminist academic work the emphasis on the differences between the sexes led to a political–theoretical strategy that advocated a specific type of research. Rather than trying only to make established social and cultural structures accessible to women, feminist critics proposed also to strengthen women's cultural and social position by combining forces and promoting women's interests. Within feminist cultural studies, for instance, the equality project had drawn attention to increasingly more literary, musical, theatrical and visual art by women. On the basis of theories of sexual difference feminist critics subsequently raised the question of a specific female aesthetics.

The metaphor of the voice is generally used to refer to this female aesthetics. The female voice can in this context be seen as representing essentialist ideas about femininity as well as the investigation of specific female cultural traditions. In the latter case studies focus on texts and other artefacts produced by women. These artefacts are not primarily related to potentially similar work by men or to movements particular to a certain historical period. They are mainly compared with each other. This feminist tradition involves a political detachment from dominant standards of what is beautiful, interesting and important. It is therefore not concerned with adding biographies and work of women artists and/or historical figures to the male canon, but concentrates on the construction of a structured corpus of texts, of a different canon: a female canon.

The idea which underlies this particular interpretation of the female voice is that women take up a different position both in public and in private life. They look at and experience life from a different perspective and consequently produce a different kind of art and write a different type of stories about the past. Feminist literary theory has demonstrated, for instance, that the themes women write about differ from the ones men write about. In her study of Dutch women poets of the fifties, the literary theorist Maaike Meijer establishes a connection between the work of Ellen Warmond, Hanny Michaelis, Micha de Vreede and Lizzy Sara May on the basis of a number of common themes which Meijer refers to as The Great Melancholy. Meijer observes that this theme is entirely absent from, or present in a completely different form, in the work of (famous) male Dutch poets from the same period. She relates this difference to the social situation of women in the post-war reconstruction of the Netherlands (Meijer, 1988).

Sexual difference, as it is understood in the studies I have mentioned earlier, is a socially constructed difference. Feminist theorists criticise the universality of the subject as male and contrast it with a female subject. Within this interpretation of sexual difference, which is to be located primarily in English-language research, a distinction is made between sex and gender, in which 'sex' refers to the biological difference between women and men, and 'gender' to the identity as well as the social position which accompany this biological difference in a particular culture. The sex/gender issue will be dealt with more extensively in the chapters on feminist history and psychoanalysis. Already at a fairly early stage feminist cultural studies were confronted with criticism of their unequivocal interpretation of the category 'woman'. The emphasis on the difference between the sexes has consequently been extended to include differences within the sexes. This criticism was expressed predominantly by black and lesbian women. In many respects their experiences are different from the experiences of the group of white, often heterosexual women who initially determined the feminist agenda through publications in professional journals and contributions to conferences. By now it has become generally accepted within women's studies to think of women as a group of individuals who do not share the same social experience. Black, white, lesbian, heterosexual, older and younger, more and less educated women are not in every respect concerned with the same struggle. As mentioned earlier, for many black women living in a society dominated by white values, the private sphere is on the one hand a shelter from racism and on the other hand a possible site for sexism whereas early white feminists unanimously declared the family the breeding ground of women's oppression (Carby, 1984).

A second elaboration of the metaphor of the female voice emerged from the practice of French feminists such as Hélène Cixous and Luce Irigaray. Cixous and Irigaray practise a female writing, an *écriture féminine*, in which gender is not so much put in a historical context as considered to be an embodied difference which affects entry into culture. This approach is based on feminist reinterpretations of psychoanalysis on the one hand and structural linguistics on the other.

Psychoanalysis, originally ridiculed by feminists, appears to serve the study of a sex-specific aesthetics extremely well. Psychoanalysis was one of the first theories to attempt to assess the construction of male and female sexuality. One of Freud's great merits is that he makes a distinction between the conscious and the unconscious. He convincingly expounds his theory that a subject's actions are to a large extent determined by unconscious motives. He seriously undermines the notion of an autonomous subject by stating that s/he does not control her or his own actions. Feminist criticism of psychoanalysis generally focuses on the fact that in the development of his theory Freud always presents man as the norm and woman as a deviation from this norm. Freud describes how the little girl, at first active in her sexual drives (the little girl is then like a 'little man'), is forced, through the Oedipus complex, into sexual passivity; this process will be discussed in greater detail in the chapter on psychoanalysis.

Écriture féminine takes from psychoanalysis a metalanguage, a set of instruments for reflecting on the role of the unconscious in the development of girls and boys as well as in the development of a culture. Without taking the male process as the norm, Cixous and Irigaray adopt the psychoanalytic view that the sexual development of girls differs from that of boys because their anatomy and their position in the Oedipus complex is different. As a result, the sexual desires of girls and boys follow divergent tracks; girls and boys thus experience different desires and different fantasies with regard to themselves and the other. Following Lacanian psychoanalysis, the authors of the *écriture féminine* speak in this context of libidinal economies, which allows them to refer to the relation between sexuality and politics (see Chapter 12 and/or the Glossary). In Cixous's view the masculine libidinal economy is characterised by castration anxiety, interpreted as the fear of losing something important, of becoming deficient. This fear incites the drive to collect things (for instance, important works of art in a canon) to avert the experience of a potential lack.

The feminine libidinal economy, on the other hand, is free from this fear of loss and consequently free from the need to collect, to retain. Cixous emphasises that women must find and develop a voice of their own following a strategy which she indicates with the French word *voler*, meaning 'to steal' as well as 'to fly'. The female voice must steal because women do not have a share in the dominant culture. It can fly because women are not tied to demarcations of genre and fixed structures of meaning (Cixous, 1976).

I have already mentioned that the concept of subjectivity for *écriture féminine* forms at the same time the basis for a critique of language and of subjectivity in structuralism. This critique involves, among other things, the structuralist idea that meaning is produced through binary oppositions. Binary oppositions are opposite positions that exclude each other. Masculine is set against feminine, black against white, homosexual against heterosexual, subject against object, body against mind, active against passive, etcetera. The poles of these oppositional pairs are nevertheless structurally related. 'Masculine' can only acquire meaning through its opposite 'feminine', 'white' through its opposite 'black', 'heterosexual' through its opposite 'homosexual', 'citizen' through its opposite 'strange', 'us' versus 'them'. Feminists like Cixous and Irigaray point out that the semantic opposition between the binary opposites is not a real opposition, because in language each term is hierarchically related to its opposite. One of them is better, more desirable, more appreciated than the other. It is for this reason that theories of sexual difference radically reject emancipatory theories of equality. In the struggle for equality the feminine will disappear behind the more highly valued masculine norm. Within this interpretation of sexual difference the feminine exists predominantly as the negative of the masculine, as that which is not represented, that which has no cultural form. The feminine is known to us only through the projections of men. In other words, the feminine in our culture says something about the male unconscious. But what about the female unconscious? This question is raised in the practice of the *écriture féminine*. In this writing of the feminine, femininity is represented positively, as something that can be represented in culture.

Initially the often misunderstood writing practice of *écriture féminine* was received as an exploration of female aesthetics. However, when European and American feminist theory started to incorporate the views on the relation between text and identity on which the *écriture féminine* was based, their writing was interpreted by a number of critics, not as an essentialist practice (Moi, 1985), but as a theoretical practice which has changed the consensus about the very meanings of femininity and masculinity in Western culture (Whitford, 1991).

In terms of textual analysis *écriture féminine* can be understood as a post-structuralist practice which, in my description of the development of feminist cultural studies, represents a link between theories of sexual difference and theories of deconstruction.

Deconstruction

'Deconstructivism', 'post-structuralism' and 'post-modernism' are the terms often used to refer to the research which in feminist cultural studies develops from criticisms of structuralism and psychoanalysis. Although in general academic usage these terms are used as synonyms they are in fact not. Nevertheless, they share two fundamental points of departure, namely that thinking in terms of binary oppositions can be transcended, and that views about the possibility of an autonomous subject are no longer valid. The latter refers to 'the death of the subject', a phrase that is often used in this context. (For an excellent introduction to deconstruction see: Culler, 1983; Johnson, 1994.)

For an introduction to feminist cultural studies the practice of deconstruction is of particular importance, because it demonstrates a specific method of textual analysis. The aim of feminist cultural studies based on deconstructive theory is still to put an end to the absence and/or subordination of women and the feminine in Western culture. But now the central focus is on the question of what terms such as 'femininity' and 'woman' refer to in a specific context.

Deconstructive feminists see reality first of all as a discursive reality. Within deconstruction there is no division between discourse and reality. We cannot think and talk otherwise than through language. In other words, our reality is discursive. Consequently, language does not refer to reality but is the means by which reality becomes intelligible and meaningful. The illusion of the human subject as an autonomous signifying centre of the world who has the capacity to express her or his most authentic experiences is thus exposed. This involves a relativisation of the status of the subject as it is understood in theories of equality, and also, though sexually differentiated, in English-language theories of gender. For theorists of deconstruction the subject does not precede language but is decentred, incorporated in language, acquires significance in language. Within this approach words derive meaning, not from how things could actually be, but from each other, from the fact that one word differs from another. Something acquires meaning in its constant reference to something else. The word 'woman', for instance, refers to a network of meanings that are attached to the word 'woman' in texts.

Derrida, one of the founders of deconstruction, uses the idea of a trace to illucidate his staggering theory of language. Every word grafts itself into the text carrying with it a load of meanings. Every notion of a fixed identity is put into perspective, as a result of which the oppositions on which Western thought is based are also stripped of definite meanings. Derrida observes that the system from which the oppositional pairs derive their meaning is a normative system. Every system of meaning is based on an ideology that gives preference to certain meanings. Man/woman, white/black, culture/nature, mind/emotion: these are not real binary oppositions but oppositional pairs constructed in language. The interesting question in the practice of deconstruction is: what happens to the meaning of a text if we follow the trail of a seemingly insignificant detail in the text, of that which is marginal or left out? That which is neglected, put aside in the text, can be informative exactly because it can contain the reason for this marginal treatment. In feminist deconstructive practice this approach has been elaborated by various theoreticians, such as Mieke Bal, Barbara Johnson, Julia Kristeva, Gayatri Spivak, and many others. They observe that, for instance, the signifying sequence woman = emotional = petulant = capricious = unreliable can be found in innumerable cultural practices. Woman = reliable = self-confident occurs significantly less often. In this respect the chapters on literary theory and black studies, for instance, show that white people experience and describe black people as strange, terrifying and inferior, because in this way they can avoid experiencing what is really terrifying: the unknown within oneself. In a similar way it is possible to deconstruct representations of femininity.

Nothing could please the deconstructivist more than to expose the rhetoric which attempts to conceal the irrationality of the rational theory.

The consequence of deconstructivist thought for feminist theory is that femininity is disconnected from a specific female identity. Femininity can be regarded as a discursive construction and not as exclusively related to a specific biological or social group. An insight into the way in which positions of power are distributed in texts between the masculine and the feminine, and/or between white and black, can be a forceful instrument in the struggle against the one-sided and/or unequivocal cultural representations of femininity.

The general outline of feminist theory presented above is meant to serve as a stepping stone to the chapters following this Introduction, in which the experiences and results of twenty years of feminist studies in the arts and humanities will be considered for each discipline separately. Again and again new windows will be installed in the established house of knowledge, commanding a wide vista of areas to be entered by the reader. The first window will be installed by a feminist historian who will broaden the general outlook on history.

Literature for further study

Braidotti, Rosi (1994) 'The Subject in Feminism', in *Nomadic Subjects*. In this essay Braidotti sketches the development of feminist theory and of feminist ideas of subjectivity.

Brügmann, Margret (1990) 'Marilyn Monroe Meets Cassandra: Women's Studies in the Nineties'. Introductory article on the history of feminist cultural studies with examples from art and literature.

Carby, Hazel V. (1984) 'White Women Listen! Black Feminism and the Boundaries of Sisterhood'. Good introduction to feminist black criticism in which the intimate connection between racism and sexism is illustrated with analyses of the implicit whiteness of feminist discourse.

Moi, Toril (1985) *Sexual/Textual Politics: Feminist Literary Theory*. Good overview of the development of feminist literary studies, with ample space for French feminist theories. One could object to Moi's partiality against Cixous's (alleged) essentialism and in favour of Kristeva's constructivism.

Stimpson, Catherine R. (1984) 'Women as Knowers'. Short sketch of the intellectual and political climate in which women's studies developed.

Journals

Women's Studies International Forum. Pergamon Press

Differences: A Journal of Feminist Cultural Studies. Providence: Brown University.

2

Of stories and sources: feminist history

BERTEKE WAALDIJK

Introduction

The implicit assumption that history is a specifically male affair came under attack by feminist historians around 1970. Their outrage was both political and professional. It was fed by the need of the new feminist movement for a historical identity for women and by the professional pride of feminist historians who argued that mainstream history was one-sided, distorted and incomplete. Whether about an individual or a group, history books were full of men: generals and soldiers, thinkers and revolutionaries, inventors and workers, kings and farmers, emperors and slaves. Women appeared to have no historical significance. In most historical narratives they were either absent, of marginal importance, or an exception to their gender.

Women's history has formulated a multifaceted answer to this one-sided story. In the space of twenty-five years it has developed, within and also often outside the universities, into a specialised field that meant – in the words of Joan Kelly-Gadol – 'to restore women to history and to restore our history to women'. At first, interest lay primarily in the factual supplementation and correction of standard history. In the course of time, interest shifted from documenting specific women's traditions and culture to more theoretical considerations of the role of gender in the construction of history. In other words, the desire to demonstrate that women were historically just as important as men resulted in curiosity about the ways in which the history of women differed from that of men. Eventually women's history developed explicit critiques of historical knowledge.

This development reflects an analogous shift of focus to other areas of women's studies in the humanities. However, women's history has also strongly looked to its 'own' discipline, history. Thus, much time and attention has been spent on the question of whether women's history should strive for integration into general historical studies. Would the goal of women's history be reached when all historians pay attention to women and gender?

In this chapter I describe the development of women's history with regard to debates surrounding three themes. First of all I examine how the distinction between the public and the private became a crucial theme within women's history. This characterised the first attempts to classify relationships between the sexes historically. Then, with regard to discussions about equality and difference, I will describe how the idea of difference has resulted in extensive research into women's worlds and traditions of female experiences. Finally the recent deconstruction of the opposition between fact and fiction will be discussed. The linguistic turn in social and historical sciences has made it possible to see historical narratives primarily as stories. These three debates offer a possible framework for the development of women's history. It is important to note that with regard to both content and chronology they are not totally separated. The discussions about the category of 'gender' illustrate this point. The usefulness of this concept, originally a social sciences term, as an analytical concept for historians has been a recurrent theme in all debates in women's history described in this chapter.

A characteristic and attractive feature of women's history is the obstinacy with which the importance of the earlier themes of private/public and inequality/women's own traditions are defended. Both repeatedly received new impulses. This does not mean that women historians reject the third perspective of historical philosophical reflection. Rather this indicates the understanding that the emergence of new facts about women and their cultural traditions in itself forms a distinct theoretical challenge to a discipline where the activity of men has for so long determined the agenda of research. In direct interaction with theoretical reflection, women's history constantly provides an explosive production of knowledge about women who lived in the past.

Equality: public and private

Feminists in the 1960s and 1970s opposed the unequal division of roles between men and women. The idea that motherhood and housekeeping were pre-eminently a woman's destiny encountered opposition. In the period before that this middle-class idea had acquired unprecedented popularity, particularly in Western Europe and the United States. Women who had other ambitions, who wanted to devote their lives to politics, business, art or science, were considered abnormal (whether pathological or not). Even though it presupposed an economic well-being reserved for the middle classes, the ideal of the male breadwinner and the woman taking care of the house and children had assumed a timeless dimension of general validity. When people did not subscribe to this ideal on the basis of religious conviction, it was defended by referring to a natural tendency, a biological or psychological determination. Women's history has contributed immensely to the political critique of women's role by historicising this specific division of labour. It has made changes in the present and the future conceivable by describing changes in the past. Many different studies showed that historically the housewife who exclusively took care of her house and her children was the exception rather than the rule. Research on priestesses, for example, in classical antiquity, medieval abbesses, midwives in recent times and on the lives of women in the revolutionary movements of the nineteenth century, has supported the idea that in every historical period and in every society women accomplished considerable tasks beyond those of caring for a family. In addition, it has shown that housekeeping is anything but a static concept. In pre-industrial societies housekeeping involved, as well as the care of a house, husband and children, making clothes and implements, taking produce to the market and the supervision of staff. But even as factory work conquered nineteenth-century Europe and America, it seldom proved to be the preserve of men. Women contributed to industrialisation with their cheap labour.

The history of the unequal division of labour by gender has been related to the distinction between the public and the private sphere. By historicising this distinction, women historians have shown that its validity is limited in space and time. Moreover, women's history has revealed this distinction to be a hierarchical opposition. Why is the history of the public sphere of politics, finance, science and art well recorded, while the private sphere has evidently not been important enough to enter history books?

Questions about the historical origin of the distinction between the public and private spheres have produced a number of interesting studies. At first an economic approach dominated. Women historians adopted historical concepts such as 'industrialisation', 'modernisation' and 'capitalism' from socio-economic history and Marxism. They researched what these great transformations which have changed the world since 1750 have meant for women.

They established that through industrialisation women lost their traditional power over the production of goods. The status that women in agrarian societies derived from their ability to spin and weave, from their skill in making candles and soap, for example, and from their knowledge of medicinal herbs disappeared when factories took over these functions. From then on many women became merely consumers who bought clothes, food and medicines using money earned by their menfolk. The modern nuclear family is the result of a separation between the public world of production and the private sphere of consumption and reproduction, the bearing and raising of children. The work that women have done in the service of reproduction was unpaid and had a lower status than the work by which a man earned bread for 'his' family. According to this interpretation, the division between the public sphere and private life is a consequence of the capitalist industrialisation of Western life. This process has marginalised the work of women. Because a woman was supposed to have no responsibility as a breadwinner her work outside the house was less well paid.

In this view, women's role and labour are the product of social and economic factors, not the consequence of a biological tendency. In this context the term *gender* was introduced in women's history. This concept was used to indicate the social construction of differences between men and women.

The economic explanation of the inequality between the male public sphere and the female private sphere is, however, not unproblematic. Within this approach priority has been given mainly to the history of the white middle and lower classes in Europe and the United States. The experiences of other classes and other ethnic groups have not been taken sufficiently into account.

For example, the distinction between public and private spheres was meaningless for black Americans living in slavery. Hard, unpaid work on plantations was the rule for men and women alike. Marriages between slaves were neither recognized nor respected and there was no question of a sacred private sphere. Relationships between women, men and children who lived and laboured together were often stronger and sustained longer than those with absent or missing family members. After the Civil War and the abolition of slavery, most African-Americans lived in great poverty, without any civil rights. The ideal of a family with a housewife and a permanent male breadwinner who, moreover, did his duty as an active citizen remained, for many, an illusion (Jones, 1985; Horton, 1986).

Historians who study pre-industrial societies have emphasised that patterns of asymmetry between men and women have not been dependent on the advent of Western capitalism. Role divisions, whereby women especially have informal and men formal public power, date back much further (Pomata, 1987; Blok, 1995). These cannot be explained by socio-economic or political concepts such as capitalist industrialisation and liberalism.

Feminist cultural anthropology has provided an alternative. The study of slowly or hardly changing kinship relations, as well as the way in which these were symbolised, has offered more possibilities for explaining the place of women in pre-industrial societies. Cultural anthropological views also proved productive for the historical research of industrial societies. The idea that women could be symbols of male power, functioning as 'signs' in communication between men, sheds a new light on the exclusion of women from public life. As signs women cannot give themselves any meaning and their contribution to politics and science is therefore inconceivable (Rubin, 1980). In this perspective women's history should therefore not look for female exceptions in the public sphere, but rather new ways should be developed to describe the history of women's worlds (Pomata, 1983).

Thus, debates about the history of the distinction between public and private reveal a shift from socio-economic explanations to a structuralist approach.

Difference: the other history of women

Just as every emancipation movement since the nineteenth century has defended its right to liberation by referring to history, the modern feminist movement has also claimed its own history. Within women's history many took on the work of writing the history of the women who struggled to improve the social position of women. This story was almost unknown and revealed an endless number of women, organisations and precursors of modern twentieth-century feminism. Here, women's history has discovered a field that traditional history has mainly passed by (Jans, 1990).

Who before 1975 had ever heard of Christine de Pisan, who in 1405 made a plea for the recognition of women? Who had ever studied the relationships between the labour movement and the first feminist movement from a feminist viewpoint? Who knew of the struggle of women to be admitted to institutions of higher education? And who had ever heard of Sojourner Truth, the black female slave in the United States who had bought her freedom and preached against slavery and for equal rights for women? As early as 1851 she rejected the argument that women should be protected and revered instead of being given equal rights with the following historic words:

> And a'n't I a woman? Look at me! Look at my arm! (and here she bared her right arm to the shoulder, showing her tremendous muscular power). I have ploughed, and planted, and gathered into barns, and no man could head me! And a'n't I a woman? I could work as much and eat as much as a man – when I could get it – and bear the lash as well. And a'n't I a woman? I have

> borne thirteen chilern, and seen 'em mos' all sold off to slavery, and when I cried out my mother's grief, none but Jesus heard me! And a'n't I a woman? (Lauter, 1990)

Sojourner Truth was one of the first supporters of women's rights. The right to vote was introduced in most democratic countries in the first decade of the twentieth century, after a long struggle by an international suffrage movement (Banks, 1981), a fact that has received hardly any attention in the political histories of these countries. Historical research into the past of women's movements has reflected contemporary political discussions. During the 1970s, feminism became less and less associated with the struggle for equal rights. Feminists wondered whether they should not rather focus on the cultural, physical, and symbolic bonds between women. Should women, rather than demanding equality, instead explore difference? Feminism was not the only political movement in these years where the struggle for political equality shifted to questions of cultural identity. In the United States it was preceded by the black civil rights movement.

For the history of feminism this political shift has been particularly productive. It has created new concepts which make it possible to define the women's movement more broadly and to study the origin of feminist traditions further back in time. The demand for economic or political equality ceased to be the criterion for 'real' feminism in women's history. The empty space in which an individual exceptional woman seemed far ahead of her time with her plea for an improvement in the position of women (such as Olympe de Gouges (1979), who in 1791 drafted a declaration of the rights of women analagous to the Declaration of the Rights of Man) becomes filled with a history of women's cultural traditions. Women's history has evaluated and analysed cultural practices by women in a tradition of their own. Distinguishing 'real' feminists from 'traditional' women is no longer the object of writing the history of feminism and women's movements. The different cultural, religious and social traditions of women turned out to be as important for the origin of a women's movement as the explicit demand for equality and the right to vote.

The focus of the feminist historian has broadened to female artists, writers, nuns and witches. The history of the private sphere is no longer interesting because of the restrictions that it imposed on women, but because of the wealth of material which demonstrates that through the ages women have formulated their own culture and their own symbols. Forms of art and culture are discovered as expressive of female traditions: letters, songs, craft work, patchwork quilts, gossip, diaries, mystical texts (such as those of Hildegard von Bingen) have been rescued from oblivion and acquired historical importance as part of specific cultural traditions of women.

Thus, the accepted hierarchy of what is and what is not important in history is turned round: marginal issues become central. The description of that which traditional history had ignored signifies an implicit attack on the male norms which had consigned all those historical riches to the margins of history (Bosch, 1987). It is not a coincidence that precisely this trend within women's history sought a connection with feminist literary theory. After all, in that field, too, women writers have been rediscovered and women's traditions restored to visibility by an explicit rejection of male norms for literary values and canon formation.

Inspired by the idea that women in all ages had in common the fact that they were women, studies of every period, every region, every class and every ethnic group can examine the way in which women gave meaning to their existence, looked after their interests and aimed for change. Research into women's culture has contributed to the historical documentation of differences among women. This perspective within women's history shifted from women as victim to an understanding and (re)appraisal of their roles. In this way the experiences of lesbian women, of working women, of women in colonies are no longer judged solely from the perspective of victim. Witches were no longer seen only as victims of malicious misogyny; for some feminist historians they could embody female traditions of wisdom and natural healing.

Studies which describe the life of African-American women before and after the abolition of slavery in the United States can be seen as another example. Victims of racism and sexism, these women survived through their own cultural traditions. In her book *Labor of Love, Labor of Sorrow* (1985), Jacqueline Jones shows, for example, how black communities in the South combined an African cultural heritage with experiences of slavery. During slavery, these strong traditions of women were crucial for the survival of the communities of women, men and their children.

The rediscovery of the specific cultural traditions of African-American women has also formed a source of inspiration for the work

of Alice Walker. In *The Color Purple* she incorporates much of her historical knowledge and appreciation of the cultural traditions of black women. These sometimes go back to pre-slavery African history. The indestructible bond between the sisters Nettie and Celie is a hymn of praise to bonds between women which are stronger than slavery and marriage. Their close bond bridges the distance between Africa and America. The novel represents the different forms of African-American culture of women, such as quilts, African natural remedies, Blues music and family celebrations. The optimistic message of the book seems to be that slavery, metaphorically represented in the book by the early years of Celie's marriage to Mr. ——, cannot destroy a culture. It is possible to criticise this positive interpretation (see hooks, 1990b). In the novel the improbably happy ending is not conducive to historical credibility. The same criticism can be made of much historical writing which describes the richness of a separate women's world. Critics argue that only positive examples are selectively highlighted from the past, to serve as inspiration for the present.

Descriptions of differences among women confront women's movements and feminist historians with difficult and painful contradictions. The experiences and interests of different women often stand diametrically opposed to each other. Is the term 'women's history' broad enough to describe both the experiences of women slaves and that of the wives of the plantation owners (Fox-Genovese, 1988)? Is it fundamentally possible for the experiences of Jewish women under the Nazi regime and those of non-Jewish women to be explained within the same framework (Koonz, 1987)?

Which category of analysis can help us to understand all these differences? For many historians of women's traditions, the concept of gender is too vague and general. For them the strength of women's history is to put women at the centre. But what should be done when other historians consider this a cover-up of racism and class differences? Or when black feminist historians prefer to classify their history as black history rather than as women's history? These discussions about difference, both between men and women and among women, make women's history a dynamic field that will remain constantly in motion.

Deconstruction: women's history and the boundaries between fact and fiction

In 1974 Joan Kelly posed the question 'Did women have a Renaissance?' Her answer was negative (Kelly, 1987). Whereas for men of the emerging bourgeoisie a period of new opportunities arrived with the Renaissance, for women the political and cultural renewal in the fourteenth and fifteenth centuries signified a loss of power, independence and influence. What had been a historical fact for men seems to have had a completely different significance for women. Kelly's approach is exemplary of the desire of women's history for a revision of traditional historical knowledge. Apparently objective facts have been questioned and debated once more.

This has often drawn the criticism from male colleagues that women's history is subjective and is dancing to the tune of feminist politics. Feminist historians respond in different ways to this reproach. They emphasise professional academic rules for the writing of history. Their articles and books are exhaustively annotated and their general conclusions carefully drawn. Books with too general titles that end with 'sweeping statements' about the history of women and the future of feminism have made way for precise, detailed studies limited in time and place.

In this respect, it is crucial for women's history to refute the argument that the history of women cannot be written because there are no sources. Ingenuity and perseverance showed that the sources for women's history are inexhaustible. Covering a varied range from diaries to annual accounts, from registers of births to housekeeping books, from periodicals to student dossiers, from myths and fairy tales to legal sources – if the right questions are asked these sources can uncover suitable new data about women in the past. Special publications and archives have come into being for the collection, preservation and professional opening up of important sources for women's history (Hinding, 1979). To a significant degree they support the academic recognition of women's history.

These newly available sources are not only preserved but also disseminated in lectures, articles and books. Feminist historians have done ground-breaking work in the interpretation of primary sources. One problem with much source material is its prescriptive nature: educational reading material for girls, instructions for marriage and housekeeping, ecclesiastical rules with regard to sexuality, and regulations about paid work. Such material describes not so much how women lived but how men thought that women should live. Thus the abundance of advisory literature published after the Second World War which relegated women to house and home, may even have indicated the opposite: apparently many women did not follow this advice. Feminist historians have become particularly adept in reading the nuances and learning to look through the biased opinions about women with which so many sources are tainted.

The paradoxical consequence of demonstrating every effort to be objective about women's history is that feminist historians have become aware that historical objectivity in itself does not exist. They have realised that writing history is not so much the collection of objective facts as the construction of historical meaning and significance. The processes which determine whether something ends up in a history book, or whether a person or an event acquires historical significance, prove to be connected with gender at many levels. The origin of historical sources about women, the decisions about preserving and opening up this material, and the concepts by which they can be interpreted and evaluated: gender plays a role on all these levels. Therefore feminist historians cannot be satisfied with looking at the ways in which gender determined the lives of women in the past; they have to start to analyse explicitly what role gender plays in the construction of historical significance (Blok, 1995). One important theoretical contribution to this shift is provided by Joan Scott (1986), who suggests that the concept of gender is not used exclusively to define the social construction of masculinity and femininity, but also plays a primary role in ascribing meaning to relations of power. The intersection of race, class and gender has remained a challenge for women's history.

With this philosophical interest in the construction of historical significance, women's history links up with deconstruction. Not the truth of the facts, but the construction of their meaning has become central. Moreover, this theory has received an important impulse from the study of the role of women and femininity in the history of historiography. In addition to research into what traditional history has forgotten, feminist historians study the connections between gender and the norms which determine what will not be forgotten: the preference for the description of changes in the public sphere, the norms for historical objectivity, the historians' own perception of their task.

From this perspective it has become almost obvious that history is a male discipline in which women – not just as objects but also as writers of history – have played a marginal role. A study of the lives and works of women writing histories from the Middle Ages to the twentieth century shows how the exclusion of women from the public world of learning and politics has determined their writing of history and its reception (Davis, 1980; Grever, 1995). The historical interest of these women historians '*avant la lettre*' rarely fitted, with regard to content and form, into the historical categories of their times, in which economy, forms of government and high culture were designated as the public fields of interest (Pomata, 1993). Complete family histories, countless historical novels based on independent research, and a fascinating study of women's humour in the United States, for example, have remained unread and misunderstood by colleagues (Smith, 1984b). The facts presented in these studies by women did not fit into standard historical knowledge; the style in which they were written differed too much from accepted historical discourse so that for contemporaries the expertise of a female author as a historian was sometimes literally unthinkable.

Research into the historically marginal position of historiography by, about and for women can illustrate the fact that women's history does more than come up with new data about women who lived in the past. It increasingly questions – both implicitly and explicitly – the ways in which historical knowledge is produced. Women's history has gone beyond filling the empty pages in history books to become a form of feminist critique of traditional historical knowledge which also has much to say about the pages that were filled in the first place. To return once more to the question of whether women experienced a Renaissance: the importance of Kelly's negative answer lies simultaneously in the information she provides about women in fourteenth- and fifteenth-century Italy, and in the way in which she encourages readers to question the significance of an accepted historical concept such as a Renaissance. Or, to end with *The Color Purple*: for feminist historians the relevance of the novel lies especially in the construction of the text. Like feminist historiography, Alice Walker's novel does not present the events through the eyes of the powerful; her text refuses the right of the oppressor and the story is not told in his master's voice, but through Celie.

We will read in the following chapter what it means to put the perspective and the interests of women first within literary theory.

Literature for further study

Davidoff, Leonore, and Catherine Hall (1987) *Family Fortunes: Men and Women of the English Middle Class, 1780–1850*. A detailed study of the way in which the distinction between private and public spheres came into being in England during the Industrial Revolution. Through an analysis of diaries, correspondence, architecture, leisure activities, paintings and newspaper reports, the authors show the way in which 'gender' and 'class' are closely related.

Davis, Natalie Zemon (1980) 'Gender and Genre: Women as Historical Writers, 1400–1820'. Beginning with Christine de Pisan, Davis describes the few women historical writers known to European history in the period between 1400 and 1820. Davis makes a connection between the lack of women historical writers and the social position of women. For comparable studies, see Smith, 1984b, Grever 1995).

Duby, Georges, and Michelle Perrot (eds) (1991–1994) *History of Women in the West*. This publication consists of five parts – Ancient Times; The Middle Ages; From the Renaissance to Modern Times; The Nineteenth Century and The Twentieth Century – each consisting of a large collection of articles in which the result of twenty years of feminist historical research has been compiled and evaluated. The Eurocentric approach can possibly be criticised: 'Woman' refers to women in Western history.

Jones, Jacqueline (1985) *Labor of Love, Labor of Sorrow: Black Women, Work and the Family from Slavery to the Present*. A classic study of the cultural traditions of African-American women.

Pomata, Gianna (1983) 'La storia delle donne: una questione di confina'. Because women are constantly identified with nature, Pomata argues that it is necessary for feminist historiography to question the distinction between nature and culture. For her analysis of the biological and symbolic significations of the body she makes extensive use of cultural anthropology.

Scott, Joan Wallach (1986) 'Gender: A Useful Category of Historical Analysis'. This much quoted article describes the development of women's history through the theories feminist historians have used. The author formulates a proposal for using gender as a category for analysing the social position of women in the past. She also advocates research into the role gender plays in the construction of historical meaning.

Journals

Gender and History, Oxford and Cambridge: Blackwell Publishers.

3

A manual for self-defence: feminist literary theory

MAAIKE MEIJER

Introduction

Feminist literary criticism begins with the reader's choice for the perspective and interests of women. This choice leads to other text interpretations, different reading experiences, alternative literary theories and new literary histories. This choice is not tied to the historical period of feminism and therefore 'reading as a women' and the 'resisting reader' are of all ages. In the Middle Ages Christine de Pisan did this in her book *Le Livre de la Cité des Dames* (*The Book of the City of Ladies*) of 1405. I will first discuss this book in order to compare it later with the 1978 book by Judith Fetterley, *The Resisting Reader*.

Christine de Pisan begins her book – in the 'I' form – by relating how she is sitting in her study reading a book about the evil nature of women. Medieval literature and science indeed knew a popular misogynist genre, initiated by the church fathers, which was the litany against female vices. De Pisan wonders why:

> so many different men – and learned men among them – have been and are so inclined to express both in speaking and in their treatises and writings so many wicked insults about women and their behaviour. ... judging from the treatises of all philosophers and poets ... it seems that they all speak from one and the same mouth. They all concur in one conclusion: that the behaviour of women is inclined to and full of every vice. (Pisan, 1983: 3–4)

At first de Pisan does not recognise this terrible 'vice' in her own experience of women. Then she thinks that all these great scholars cannot be mistaken; she herself must thus be quite stupid and ignorant. Thereupon she plunges into a great sorrow 'for I detested myself and the entire female sex, as though we were monstrosities in nature' (5). She complains to God that He has not put her into the world as a man. While she sits with 'my head bowed in shame' (6) three crowned Ladies appear, who have come to comfort her. Their message is: trust what you yourself know for certain instead of what you only hear from others. These Ladies assign de Pisan the task of building an (allegorical) City of Women, 'so that from now on, ladies and all valient women may have a refuge and defence against the various assailants' (10), that is, de Pisan is to write a book which lists all the positive things said about women in all available sources. *The Book of the City of Ladies* is a work of defence: an encyclopedia of female inventions, learning and art, and a history of queens, army commanders, heroines and saints, who prove the stereotypical images of women to be untrue.

De Pisan's book is a medieval 'self-defence manual for the female reader', as Fetterley argues in *The Resisting Reader*. In Fetterley's book, a process is taking place which shows a striking similarity to the process outlined by de Pisan. Fetterley is not burdened by the church fathers, but rather by the American literary canon, dominated by male authors. The female reader drowns in these male images of the world, in which women and the feminine are often depicted as irritating and inferior. The texts are often constructed in such a way that every reader identifies her/himself as a matter of course with the lot and the view of the male characters. Women therefore constantly identify against themselves while reading, but do so unconsciously. They are programmed by these texts to be 'assenting readers'. As opposed to assenting and unconscious reading, Fetterly proposes a gender-conscious, resisting reading. Just like de Pisan, Fetterley discusses this in stages: first the phase of being intimidated by the authority of the male tradition; then the internalisation of its contempt for women; then the anger against the self-hatred which the culture instils in women, and finally the birth of the 'resisting reader'. Fetterley's resistance takes the form of arming women with different ways of reading the very same books. De Pisan's resistance, on the other hand, takes the form of looking for alternative texts, for different representations of women, for female subjectivity.

Christine de Pisan's feminism used the means of her time; like her medieval opponents, she wrote an encyclopedic work making use of all available sources, regardless of whether they were mythological or scientific, 'heathen' or Christian, legendary or historical.

Fetterley's resistance also uses the means of her times; she relies on the *reader-response* theory which emerged in the 1970s. Within dominant literary theory, attention was shifted from texts and textual structures to the ways in which different readers can give different meanings to a text. For Fetterley this opened up an opportunity to introduce feminist ways of reading which could no longer be dismissed as scientifically 'wrong'. The generation of feminist critics that preceded Fetterley (de Beauvoir, 1960, first edition 1949; Millett, 1969) found themselves in another, older paradigm of literary theory; the paradigm of the immanent interpretation, in which the text was considered to have a 'correct' meaning and a timeless value. De Beauvoir and Millett see the text as a historical and social mirror of patriarchy, thus they deplore the fact that the text does not represent women's experience. They are here availing themselves of a mimetic literary view – also adhered to by Marxists – as a result of which every text is, and/or ought to be, a reflection of reality. In the climate of the early 1970s the mimetic view was revolutionary, but in the 1980s it would be rejected both by feminists and by nearly all other literary theorists in favour of more constructivist and textual theories of literature: the text does not reflect reality but constructs one (Moi, 1985). In the 1980s feminists turned to the emerging theory of reading, and deconstruction was also welcomed by feminists and developed further. Feminist criticism thus has become possible within all forms of literary theory. Moreover, feminist thinking has exercised considerable influence on modern literary theory.

I distinguish three preoccupations within feminist criticism: the critique of sexism; women's writing; and (interventions in) theory. This list reflects a chronological order. From the end of the 1970s, however, work was carried out in all these three fields simultaneously. In all three the phases of equality – difference – deconstruction also stand out, yet for the critique of sexism the emphasis lies first on equality and later on deconstruction; for women's writing it lies on equality and difference, while feminist literary theories recognize all three phases.

Critique of sexism

The first object of study for the feminist approach to literature – which itself initially occurred mainly outside universities – is 'the image of women in literature'. Simone de Beauvoir, Kate Millett and many others began to deliver critiques of sexism in canonic texts by male authors, who often gave a discouraging and depressing picture of female characters. According to Millett, authors like Norman Mailer and Henry Miller take pleasure in describing women as objects who can be used at will, tortured and despised. Sometimes an old fear of women appears to lie behind this sexism.

A feature of sexist texts is that the narrator takes little or no distance from denigrating images of women. I will return to the crucial role of the narrator later. In the relationships and sexuality of male authors there is sometimes a tangible element of revenge, of the unloading of old hurts onto women. The way in which old hurts are metonymically visited on women can be illustrated, for example, in the Dutch novel

Kort Amerikaans ('Crew Cut') by Jan Wolkers. When the main character, Erik, is about to rape – he calls it seduce – 'his girl', he thinks:

> I'll cut you down to size, he thought. You'll give in, just like the Kraut. He recalled the German officer who had given him a slap in the face when, stepping off the tram next to him, he had trodden on his toes. (81)

Narratologist Mieke Bal analyses this passage (1988: 69–70). She is not so much concerned that this extract reflects sexism but rather with the way in which the text both reflects and produces sexism. Bal provides insight into the cultural mechanisms and textual devices – in this case metonymy – which both enable and naturalise rape:

> It is clear that this boy wants to revisit his humiliation by the German officer, a powerful man, on 'his girl'. This shift from the first enemy to the loved one can only be made on the basis of what the boy sees as a similarity between the two: evidently both seem equally fearsome and threatening to him. (69)

The main character of *Kort Amerikaans* persuades his girl (Ans) that she 'wanted' sex forced upon her and even 'enjoyed' it. We are not told what the girl herself thinks. Thus *Kort Amerikaans* alienates the female reader, because the male I-figure, Erik, constantly focalises the events, that is to say that the narrator reproduces only Erik's point of view. Access to Ans's feelings and thoughts is blocked, as it were, by Erik. If the female reader wants to finish reading the novel anyway, she has to remain identified with the male central character: the novel enforces that identification. That is an identification against Ans, and by implication against women.

Mieke Bal has shown that focalisation is crucial for the point of view and experience of the narrated events (1985). Her theory of focalisation has become an essential instrument for feminist literary criticism. Because the distribution of focalisation in a text is so crucial, to recognise sexist images of women alone is not enough. The point is how those images function in the text. In some texts it is a matter of embedded sexism, used to typify a character in a negative way. Obviously, a sexist character does not necessarily produce a sexist book. Thus in *The Color Purple*, Harpo and his father Mr. —— are often characterised by their sexist behaviour and ditto comments, while the reader's view of events is wholly obtained through Celie, the primary focaliser. Celie's position in the text sees to it that this sexism does not appear as obvious, as ironic or funny, but as problematic.

Through the transition from a mimetic to a more textual understanding of literature, the critique of sexism has become increasingly differentiated over the years. Protests against the unrealistic image of 'woman' in canonical literature have been modified by the attention on focalisation and other narrative processes. Studies have been made of the ways in which specific literary genres and gender ideology are intimately connected: just think of the inevitable romance in the genre of the novel, which traditionally smothers the female subject either by marriage or by death (Blau Du Plessis, 1985). Also, analyses of narrative structures in texts have proved very important, because they have shown the textual mechanisms that reproduce the man as a subject and the woman as object (de Lauretis, 1984). Furthermore, female readers are nowadays no longer being portrayed as victims of the all-powerful text. The feminist reader sees sexist texts not so much as assaults on her mental well-being, but rather as documents of the system that she wants to denounce. In a way a sexist text serves a reverse purpose. It playes a role in feminist–political discourse, as an illustration and demonstration which undo its misogyny. As a result the sexist effect of the text is diminished for future generations of readers.

Analysis of racism in texts is just as necessary as critique of sexism. They often go together: consider the stereotype of black women as exotic, sexy and purely natural, exploited in advertisements and advertising. For a critique of racism it is necessary to reflect on one's own position as a white and/or black reader: a black reader can bring her/his own experience and position consciously into play in order to decide whether to allow her/himself to become involved with a white text. A white reader should learn to recognise different forms of racism and should reflect on her/his involvement in the colonial racism which forms an integral part of Western culture and upbringing. A specific contextual knowledge is necessary for anti-racist criticism, but otherwise the methods of analysis used in critiques of sexism can also be used for the critique of racism. Until now critique of sexism has been motivated by the struggle for equality: analyses have been directed against the unequal treatment of women in texts. Deconstructive anti-sexism and/or anti-racism is connected with the view that sexist texts are not in fact about women, but about men, just as Western or Eurocentric texts are in fact about whites. This view could only be postulated if one assumes that literature no longer mimetically reflects reality. Even a realist text is biased by its verisimilitude, that is, the text only produces an illusion of reality. The text is always a symptom of the person, the culture or the discourse of which it is the result. That insight is one of the themes in *The Color Purple*. Shug explains it to Celie, who sees God as a big old man dressed in white.

that's the one that's in the white folks' white bible [says Shug]. Shug! I say. God wrote the bible, white folks had nothing to do with it. How come he look just like them, then? she say. Only bigger? – How come the bible just like everything else they make, all about them doing one thing and another, and all the colored folks doing is gittin' cursed? (166)

Shug here shows to be a 'resisting reader' who sees through the projected character of the image of God and the Bible. As a 'resisting reader', moreover, she puts her own text against it, just like Christine de Pisan: 'God ain't a He or a She but a It.' Shug's pantheistic theology is a projection of her life-force.

Toni Morrison (1992) compares a text with a dream and reminds us that the subject of the dream is the dreamer her/himself. Instead of indignation about sexist images of women (woman as a brainless temptress) or racist stereotypes (blacks as primitives), we would profit from exploring the purposes that such fantasies fulfil for those who called them into being in the first place. What do such projections tell us about the person and the culture which nourishes these fantasies? This question prompts Morrison to analyse the function of black characters in white American literature, and the fears and repressions of whites that sustain those representations, in her book *Playing in the Dark: Whiteness and the Literary Imagination* (1992). She shows how the construction of the 'American', the new white man in the 'heroically conquered land of infinite opportunities', depends on the presence of a black slave population. Thanks to the slaves whom he could control, whose labour he could expropriate, on whom he could blame everything that he despised in himself, the often vulnerable colonist could believe himself to be a superior American.

Just as female characters in men's texts often inhabit male fantasies, black characters in white literary texts are often figures of projection, necessary as contrast to give the white subject his identity and autonomy. In her analyses Morrison relies on theories of deconstruction. A deconstructivist exploits the tension between the manifest and the latent level in the text. The text is seen as an arena of contradictions, where culturally highly valued elements (rationality, abstract thought, domination, control, language, masculinity, whiteness) attempt to dominate over the 'other': the literal or metaphorical 'female', 'black', or that which is outside the male, white order. The effect of the literary text can be both to release and to repress the 'other'. Repression never succeeds completely. Thus the deconstructive reader is like a psychiatrist who asks questions of the resisting text, which nevertheless gives its unconscious away in slips of the tongue.

Morrison puts the principles of the different analyses into practice.

She observes, for example, that many American classics end with images of blinding whiteness (far-ranging snow-covered mountains, a glacier, a white boat, the peaks of Kilimanjaro), in combination with representations of blacks or native Americans who are dead, impotent or completely submissive. Thus Edgar Allen Poe's *The Narrative of Arthur Gordon Pym* ends with two white men, Pym and Peters, floating on a milk-white ocean. In their boat the Indian, Nu-Nu, dies and the boat shoots through the swirling white curtain of a waterfall, behind which a huge white figure rises up. The story then comes to an abrupt end. Such white figures often crop up after the appearance of a black figure, here the native American Nu-Nu. Their structural place in the story, their repeated appearance, and the suggestion of paralysis and incoherence which they convey, requires an interpretation which does justice to their ambiguity and their contradiction. On the one hand these images of whiteness appear to be a crushing counterweight against the black shadow figure, but on the other hand they also appear to say that whiteness is without significance, threatened, sterile, static, meaningless.

Women's texts, 'female' texts

From the beginning, feminist critics nursed great expectations about texts written by women. These expectations were fed by the idea of equality – women write just as well – and by the idea of difference – women write from a different world of experiences and feelings, and their voice until now has been insufficiently heard. The initial desire for non-sexist texts about the 'real' lives of women was punctually fulfilled around 1975, by a wave of fictionalised autobiographies by authors such as Anja Meulenbelt, Lisa Alther, Marilyn French, Marie Cardinal, Verena Stefan and many others, who recorded the lives of contemporary women. When that genre became established many women writers turned ostentatiously away from the realist text in order to start writing utopian, avant-garde or absurdist texts. On an international basis the 1970s were the cradle of a new generation of female authors, who for the first time unmistakably 'write as a woman'. Authors such as Adrienne Rich, Fay Weldon, Margaret Atwood, Christa Wolf, Elfriede Jelinek shed the scrupulous sex neutrality which their predecessors (for example Iris Murdoch or Marianne Moore) had displayed.

Écriture féminine set the trend in France. *Écriture féminine* refers both to the new associative, poetic, embodied writing style of authors like Hélène Cixous, Chantal Chawaf, Annie Leclerc and Marguérite

Duras, and to a post-structuralist theory of female aesthetics and female writing. That aesthetics was not only perceived as being socially and culturally determined, but was also seen as an aesthetics connected with the materiality of the female body (Cixous), or with the metaphorical 'feminine' as a subversive force in language (Kristeva). Cixous's fictional orgies in language are clearly an attempt to unchain the female 'other' in the text. In her aesthetic philosophy she endeavours to turn the binary man–woman opposition around. Cixous and Irigaray attempt to exploit 'the feminine' as a niche which preserves everything that 'phallogocentric' culture has repressed. 'Woman' is here both the literal site and the metaphor.

Such anti-realistic texts have served a new generation of feminist critics, which lay the emphasis more on the discontinuous relationship between text and reader than on recognition and reflection. Texts do not merely reflect but also construct meanings. Texts bring something about, precisely because they 'kidnap' the readers, seduce them and bring them into collision with their own internalised clichés and established concepts. In this connection I have spoken of the erotics of reading (Meijer, 1988).

In literary theory, the interest in women writers leads to a passion for rediscovering and reinterpreting historical female authors. Comparative rediscoveries are, for example, Charlotte Perkins Gilman, Djuna Barnes, Jane Bowles, H.D. (Hilda Doolittle), Zora Neale Hurston, Radclyffe Hall and many of the authors who have been republished in the Virago Modern Classics series. The reinterpretations carried out by feminists also shed a surprising new light on both familiar and less well-known female authors. Thus Emily Dickinson has been liberated from the stereotype of the unworldly maiden-like recluse, whose work had to be censored and 'corrected'. Virginia Woolf has been recognised as one of the founders of feminist literary criticism and as one of the most outstanding modernists. Woolf, too, had to be liberated from a stereotype: that of the fragile, frigid, apolitical, upper-class lady. Moreover, feminists developed new views on authors about whose work (often greatly reductive) interpretative traditions had already been established: the Brontës, Jane Austen, the German writers of the Romantic Movement, Sylvia Plath and many others. With respect to these rereadings it should be stressed that the great writers are not *Einzelgänger*, but are embedded in a tradition of women's writing. Thus these reinterpretations bring to light the 'lost continent' of women's literary traditions: the traces of women's culture in the Bible, female troubadours, medieval women's songs which had their roots in the oral tradition, the American sentimental novel of the nineteenth century, the English 'female Gothic', female travel stories, detective writers, feminist science fiction, autobiographical writings, the post-war Dutch female poets, as well as lesbian literature and the rich tradition of black writers and poets in the United States. Increasing numbers of publications in the field of women's literary history, made a wholly different perception of the traditional literary history possible. Examples are Elaine Showalter's *A Literature of Their Own* (1977) and Alicia Ostriker's *Stealing the Language* (1986). In addition a steady stream of anthologies of the work of female authors is appearing, of which Louise Bernikow's radical *The World Split Open* (1974) and Gilbert and Gubar's brilliant *Norton Anthology of Literature by Women* (1985) are representative. The work of black writers has been well represented in these overviews.

Black women's literary history and criticism started somewhat later and initially reacted against the Eurocentrism of the white feminist critics. Black critics more or less followed the same route: first they emphasised the continuity between black women's lives and their (simultaneously rediscovered and re-evaluated) texts; later they focused more on textual strategies in works by black writers. See, for example, Hazel V. Carby, *Reconstructing Womanhood* (1987), Susan Willis, *Specifying* (1987).

The Color Purple acquires another dimension when it is read in the context of the literary black women's tradition. That tradition begins with the so-called slave narratives, with the speeches of black abolitionists like Sojourner Truth, Frances Harper and Angelina Weld Grimké, with Blues singers like Bessie Smith and Gertrude 'Ma' Rainey. Just as white women's literary history shows how until the twentieth century women writers had to fight off the prejudice that women could not develop intellectually and could not earn money by writing, so black women's literary history reveals how black women's literature originated against a background of forced illiteracy (it was forbidden for slaves to learn to read and write) and in spite of poverty and racism. The importance of language for the ability to get a grip on one's own life is also a theme in *The Color Purple*. Celie's increasing grip on language, and the instrumental role of women in that process, runs through the story as a guiding thread. Celie learns to read and write from her sister Nettie, Shug and Mary Agnes. At the same time her growing command of the language is also shown in the novel: Celie's letters become longer and increasingly differentiated. Her growing subjectivity and her grip on the world go hand in hand with the ability to put her experiences, feelings and views into words. The importance for the writers themselves of genealogy, of continuity with their 'foremothers', is shown in Alice Walker's *In Search of Our Mothers' Gardens: Womanist Prose* (1983).

There she relates how and thanks to what she has been able to find a voice.

Alice Walker is no genius in isolation. The amazing flowering of black women's literature (think also of Maya Angelou, Toni Morrison, Paule Marshall, Ntokaze Shange) has a long history of continually building on each other's work and writing against oppression, as can be seen by reading the chapter on black criticism. Women's literary histories bring an insight into the continuity and relative independence of women's cultures, which largely fall outside the schools, movements and divisions of dominant literary history. In fact feminist literary historians claim the 'power of naming' and in their turn label schools, movements and stages in which women's literature is developing. One example of such a new movement is the 'Great Melancholy', the term under which I studied Dutch post-war female poets, who worked closely amongst themselves alongside the famous male poets of the same period (Meijer, 1988: 287–315). In fact feminist historiographers attempt to describe the women's cultures they have discovered as 'different-but-equal'.

However, the initial assumption that women's culture would form a completely different world has been quickly abandoned in favour of the view that women's texts are really 'bi-textual', in dialogue with both male and female literary traditions. In this connection see Showalter's essays 'Towards a Feminist Poetics' and 'Feminist Criticism in the Wilderness' (Showalter, 1986).

Female artists maintain a polemical relationship with the male tradition, which they both appropriate and undermine. This 'bi-textuality' was further complicated in the debate on difference in the eighties to become a multi-textuality: 'women's literature' is no monolithic whole, but is itself further divided into subcultures (ethnic, lesbian, popular cultures and different national cultures). The hypothesis of a relatively autonomous women's culture has nevertheless proved productive in collecting, reinterpreting and contextualising an invaluable quantity of material by women authors. That great and as yet incomplete task will be a condition for every future radical comparative approach, that is to say a truly bisexual and multicultural literary history.

Theory and theoretical interventions

Over the last ten years, after an initial resistance to academic theory, feminist critics have launched into great theoretical activity: they have made interventions in dominant theories, developed independent theories, and made strategic use of theories (narratology, semiotics, psychoanalysis) which are particularly suitable to feminist questions.

Interventions in dominant theories aim at introducing the category of *gender* into theories which pretend to be neutral or universal. For example, in order to be able to work with psychoanalysis, Freud's own prejudice with regard to the superiority of male sexuality and to the male super-ego needs to be dismantled. Theories of authorship – such as Harold Bloom's *The Anxiety of Influence* (1973) – cannot be directly applied to women authors. Bloom recognises in literary history an Oedipal conflict between literary fathers and sons who write and, by writing better texts, 'kill' their paternal predecessors. Women who write, however, have a completely different relationship to the tradition. They often experience a primary fear of writing: a fear that they will not be able to create, that they will never play the role of 'precursors', and that therefore the act of writing will isolate or obliterate them. Gilbert and Gubar (1979) formulated a feminist theory of female authorship, the 'anxiety of authorship', in which they argue that Harold Bloom's author is not as neutral and universal as he pretended.

I will go into more detail on the feminist use of *reader-response criticism*, because here the approaches of equality, difference, and deconstruction can be easily recognised. Feminists are making important contributions to a theory of reading by looking at the role played by *gender* in the reading process. The question is whether female readers read differently from male ones. On the basis of the equality theory, the answer to this question is a whole-hearted 'yes'. Feminists argue that the same text has different meanings for female readers and male readers, because women always 'automatically' approach the text from different life experiences and identifications. Female characters speak directly to the reader's self-image. Women reading Shakespeare, according to Carolyn Lenz (1980), will pay more attention to the complexity of the female characters. They will identify more readily with Cordelia than with King Lear, with Lady Macbeth than with her husband. By extension, a possible response to Walker's *The Color Purple* will depend on the identification which you as a female and/or black and/or lesbian reader are likely to have with Celie. Every woman has some experience of feeling belittled, ill-treated and trapped at some time in her life: through Celie they can relive that experience. With Celie the reader can find release from self-hatred. Within this kind of identification, women's texts achieve a more liberating effect than men's texts, as we saw in the previous section.

However, this unproblematic appeal to female experience was soon questioned, at which stage the theory of difference was introduced. Can the female experience be immediately available, wonders Shoshana Felman (1975), amongst others. Is it enough to be a woman in order to be able to read as a woman? Reading-as-a-woman is not an immediate effect of biological gender: it is rather a critical position, a difference, that has to be reproduced by women. Jonathan Culler indicates that distance in the second position by putting more emphasis on the word 'as' in 'reading-as-a-woman'. In her criticism of Culler, Modleski feels that this second position should rather be called 'reading-as-a- feminist'. The term feminist expresses the paradoxical relationship between being made into a woman and being born a woman. A feminist is a woman who has distanced herself from her allotted place in the gendered world. She is a woman polemically. Judith Fetterley (1978) also notes the shift from equality to difference by pointing out that women do not automatically read 'as a woman'. They may read just as men read. Women adopt the uncritical reading attitude which standard canonical literary works produce in their readers. According to Fetterley female readers are masculinised. The power of rhetorical structures of the text can only be broken down by resistant reading.

The third position can be referred to as deconstruction. Under the heading 'critique of sexism' above I defined the deconstructive way of reading as the search for the tension between the dominant, explicit, most articulated level of the text and the subversive elements active within it. The text is seen as the stage on which the struggle between the culturally dominant and the culturally repressed takes place. The reader tries to be receptive to those elements that subvert the openly disseminated message. A classic example is Felman's (1975) reading of the short story 'Adieu' by Balzac. It is the story of the nobleman Philippe, who is separated from his beloved Stéphanie in the Napoleonic war in icy Berezina. Stéphanie goes mad and dumb: she spends her life in the countryside and no longer speaks. On Philippe's return he spares no effort to induce Stéphanie to speak: in particular, she has to recognise him and call out his name. For this purpose he restages – in the dead of winter – the situation in which the parting took place. At the moment when the mad Stéphanie finally recognises him and speaks his name, she dies.

In contrast to male readers, who read 'Adieu' only as a realistic war story and treat the Stéphanie theme as an irrelevant digression, Felman reads it as a story in which the female figure, Stéphanie, has the central role precisely because she undermines the patriarchal world of men's wars. To that end Felman is reading symbolically rather than realistically. The war drives Stéphanie mad. Her madness signifies the 'other' of men's world of war. Philippe's fanatical desire to restore Stéphanie to her senses has an egocentric motive: after all, the sign of her recovery has to be that she recognises him and speaks his name.

Her normality will consist of reflecting him, giving him his identity. In this perspective, all Philippe can offer Stéphanie is a mirror function of the woman who makes him a man. Stéphanie refuses to be Philippe's 'other', however, in that particular way. Her death indicates that in patriarchy the only place for woman is derivative; as a function or part of the man. According to the French philosopher Luce Irigaray, there is in fact only one sex, the male, and the feminist task consists of discovering the yet unrepresented feminine as the other of patriarchy. The dead or as yet unborn feminine cannot exist as long as women fulfil the role of being men's shadows – this is what Felman reads with reference to Irigaray, in Balzac's fascinating story.

Conclusion

Feminist theory of reading has provided many new studies, of canon formation, periodisation, reception, literary criticism, genres and rhetoric etc. In general, feminist critics are not afraid of attacking established reputations and entering polemical debates with others and among themselves. In order to illustrate this I will end by referring to the polemical article 'Writing the Subject: Reading *The Color Purple*' by bell hooks (1990a), which does not go along with the general praise of Walker's book. After we have all given in to the overwhelmingly *happy end*, hooks observes that Walker weakens the subversive power of lesbian sexuality by making it compatible with the heterosexual order; for Walker sex cannot go together with power; Shug ends up as a vulnerable older woman who is afraid of losing her sexual power over men; Sofia, the woman who has never yielded to racist intimidation and sexist oppression, has become a tragic figure. Given the spectacular changes which take place in *The Color Purple*, hooks finds it problematic that Sofia, the revolutionary, takes no part in the happy ending. *The Color Purple* can be situated in different literary traditions: in the modern women's tradition of sexual confession and also in the line of the African-American slave narratives. The nineteenth-century slave narrative belongs to a genre from way back which, from the black perspective, gives a realistic record of the savagery of life in slavery and escape from it. This radical genre was meant to raise the political consciousness of black and white and to trigger a process of social change. hooks reproaches Walker that on the one hand she leans heavily on the slave narrative – the historical novel increases the social realism of the text – while on the other hand she depoliticises and romanticises it. Celie's liberation takes place separately from any collective social struggle and thus becomes a black female version of the old capitalist 'American Dream'.

This is a remarkable critique by a black woman who reads a black 'womanist' text as a resisting reader. Her position is thought-prevoking. Read for yourself and make up your own mind.

Literature for further study

Bal, Mieke (1985) *Narratology*.

Culler, Jonathan (1983) 'Reading as a Woman', in *On Deconstruction*. Clear and concise introduction to the development of feminist reading theory, criticised nevertheless by various feminists. See, for example, Elaine Showalter (1987) and Tania Modleski (1986).

Felman, Shoshana (1975) 'Women and Madness: The Critical Phallacy'. Outstanding analysis of the reception of Balzac's 'Adieu', relying on Irigaray's theory in which it is stated that 'woman' cannot be articulated in our culture. Balzac's text can be read as a forceful allegory of the exclusion of woman and the feminine.

Gates, Henry Louis Jr (ed.) (1990) *Reading Black, Reading Feminist: A Critical Anthology*. Collection containing authoritative articles in the field of black feminist literary criticism, including black lesbian criticism. Other important collections in the field of black criticism and literature are: Henry Louis Gates Jr (ed.) (1984) *Black Literature and Literary Theory*, and ibid. (1986) *'Race' Writing and Difference*. Also Houston Baker Jr. (1984) *Blues, Ideology and Afro-American Literature: A Vernacular Theory*.

Green, Gayle, and Coppélia Kahn (eds) (1985) *Making a Difference: Feminist Literary Criticism*. Good compilation of essays in the field of feminist literary criticism.

Mills, Sara, Lynn Pearce, Sue Spaull, Elaine Millard (eds) (1989) *Feminist Readings, Feminists Reading*. Good introduction with clear and practical examples of feminist methods of interpretation.

Showalter, Elaine (ed.) (1986 orig. 1985) *The New Feminist Criticism: Essays on Women, Literature and Theory*. Handy anthology with very important articles, by Annette Kolodny, Jane Tompkins, Nancy Miller among others. Also Showalter's influential essays 'Towards a Feminist Poetics' and 'Feminist Criticism in the Wilderness'.

Weedon, Chris (1987) *Feminist Practice and Poststructuralist Theory*. Accessible introduction to post-structuralist theory.

Journals

For a general and international overview see the monthly *Women's Review of Books*, Wellesly, USA: Wellesly College Center for Research on Women.

4

Language and gender: feminist linguistics

DÉDÉ BROUWER

Introduction

Linguistic studies into language and gender cover two different aspects of the phenomenon of language: the linguistic system and linguistic performance. According to Marxist-inspired theories, the unequal roles and positions of women and men are reflected both in the linguistic system and in linguistic usage. What is said about women and men, the ways in which they are addressed, how they talk and what role is expected of them in verbal interactions: according to linguistic studies this can all be traced back to the class- and sex-specific norms and values in society. Until now, studies into the ways in which meanings are constructed, and in particular into the construction of femininity and masculinity in discursive practice, have been left to semiotics. Within semiotics both the linguistic system and linguistic performance are understood as vital ways in which the subject creates a reality for itself. Within a semiotic view, the relationship between the subject, language and reality is one of mutual constitution. This will be discussed in more detail in the chapter on semiotics. This chapter will however maintain the – within linguistics traditional – distinction between linguistic system and linguistic performance.

The first part of this chapter discusses studies within the field of the linguistic *system*: language about women and men. The second section moves on to linguistic *performance*: language of women and men. Finally a few recommendations will be given for a differentiated form of language and gender studies.

Language about men and women: emancipation and equality

Studies of language about men and women are usually understood as studies of linguistic sexism. Linguistic sexism can be described as verbal signs which discriminate between people on the grounds of their gender. To the general public, linguistic sexism indicates the asymmetry and polarisation between the sexes (Vetterling-Braggin, 1981). In the 1970s in particular many linguists were engaged in the struggle for emancipation and equality in language (Miller and Swift, 1977; Nilsen et al, 1977). The idea was that an inventarisation of sexism in language would unmistakably show the subordination of women and could thus play an important role in consciousness-raising.

There are broadly two themes in these studies of linguistic sexism: the invisibility of women in language and gender stereotyping. Gender stereotyping often involves the degradation of the female variant in the form of either a negative or a sexual connotation (which is usually negative anyway).

Invisibility

The asymmetry between the sexes is shown most clearly in the invisibility of women in language. The most obvious example is the opening lines of letters addressed to women. Men are addressed as 'Dear Sir' or 'Dear Mr'. Very logical. Less logically, women are also addressed as 'Dear Sir'. This 'Dear Sir' approach is sometimes taken to absurd lengths, as I once experienced when I received a letter from the health insurance concerning a typical sex-specific minor surgery, in which I was nevertheless addressed as 'Dear Sir'. Women also become invisible in references such as 'mankind', or the generic 'he'. The one-sided use of the personal pronoun 'he' to refer to human beings produces the impression that women are ignored and passed over. Psycholinguistic research has demonstrated that texts which refer only to 'he' do not provide women with any opportunity for identification. Mind you, neither women nor men consider these texts to refer to women (Martyna, 1978; Silveira, 1980).

While women are often not addressed in texts, they are also treated differently from men in daily linguistic usage. Women are more likely than men to be called by their first name by their boss, an echo of the contact between adults and children (Wolfson and Manes, 1980). In *The Color Purple* Celie speaks to men, including her husband, as 'Mr.', while Shug, who has an equal relationship with her husband, usually calls him by his first name, 'Albert'. When, after her stay with Celie and Mr. ——, Shug decides that the time has come to go off into the world again, the following dialogue takes place between Celie (I) and Shug (she) about Mr. ——/Albert (he):

> He beat me when you not here, I say.
> Who do, she say, Albert?

> Mr. ——, I say.
> I won't leave, she say, until I know Albert won't even think about beating you. (66)

Only when Celie is independent and has developed her self-esteem does she write about Mr. —— as Albert. The white shopkeeper Alphonso, by whom Sofia is employed as a clothes saleswoman, usually calls black women 'auntie'. But he no longer dares to address Sofia in that way: 'First time he try that with Sofia she ast him which colored man his mama sister marry' (237).

Finally, women become almost invisible in names used for occupations. Since women are participating more intensively in social life and entered professions which had been more or less the domain of men, there has been a lively discussion in the Netherlands about the introduction and use of female occupational titles. Like in most languages, but unlike the English language, in Dutch the introduction of female occupational titles usually means a derivation from existing titles used for men, by adding a sex-specific suffix. Now what is really sexist? The use of the same occupational name for men and women, or the creation of separate terms for women?

Advocates of female versions of occupational names refer to the invisibility of women in language. In the 1970s the effort to make women visible sometimes took frivolous forms to function as an eye-opener: *her*story instead of *his*tory, *frau* for the German *man* (one), e*woman*cipated. Their point of view was then often illustrated with the following anecdote, probably well-known by now: 'A medical doctor is driving with his son. They have an accident. The doctor is killed on the spot. His son is taken to hospital, seriously injured. The doctor on duty enters the operating theatre into which the patient has been wheeled, looks at him, turns pale and says: "This is my son. I would rather not operate on him." Mystery: What is the family relation between the doctor on duty and the patient?' When this riddle was in circulation, only a few people could give the answer: the medical doctor in the hospital is, of course, the mother of the seriously injured child.

The use of female occupational titles would not only make people more aware of women in the work force, but also give girls and women the opportunity to deviate from the stereotypical expectations about their social roles. At the same time, it would disclose the male-dominated sectors and unequal access to key positions in occupational life.

On the other hand there are those who support the use of a single occupational name for men and women because it is irrelevant to make a gender distinction and the focus should simply be on 'human beings'.

Both linguistic and social arguments have been advanced to plead the case against female forms of occupational names (Brouwer, 1991).

According to this group, in which I also include myself, the very fact that conscious choices must be made about the construction of female forms of a word shows that this is no longer a part of our linguistic instinct. There are, in principle, seven suffixes in Dutch which can form female personal nouns. Only four do still have a certain function in modern Dutch. The number of female suffixes in Dutch has decreased in the course of time and so has their productivity. Central to the notion of productivity are the spontaneity and the lack of premeditation by which, in principle, an infinite number of new, in this case female, formations can be constructed. In this sense, only two suffixes, *-e* and *-ster*, can be regarded as being still productive in modern Dutch. Since people in the Netherlands have not systematically feminised personal nouns for such a long time, their feeling for it has almost been lost, which is reflected in insecurity about which suffix is to be chosen to feminise personal pronouns. It is often difficult, if not impossible, to make a choice. In addition, the Dutch language, like English, has a great number of nouns which refer to both women and men and from which it is thus unnecessary and usually impossible to derive female forms. The consequence of this confusion is that women will be made visible in occupational names in an inconsequential and inconsistent way, which seems hardly conducive to a truly equal treatment of women and men in occupational life.

As a rule a suffix does not have a clearly defined meaning. From the perspective of semantics, female derivations sometimes convey other, usually less valued, meanings. A suffix can easily carry over connotations from one specific formation to another. Female derivations run the risk of acquiring a lower value than the corresponding male forms. This is the more likely given the generally lower value of women in Western society, as a result of which an asymmetry can arise between the word that indicates the man and the female derivative. The meanings of pairs such as *secretaris–secretaresse* (a 'secretaris' refers to an official with high status, a 'secretaresse' is a secretary), gouverneur–gouvernante (governor versus governess) *kassier–caissière* (banker versus cashier) illustrate this unequal value. Semantic and connotative asymmetry of male and female forms is not confined to the Dutch language: in French there is a distinction between '*un homme public*' (a male official in a public function) and '*une femme public*' (a prostitute) or '*un professionel*' (a professional) and '*une professionelle*' (a prostitute) (Mortagne, 1981), and in English between 'bachelor' and 'spinster', 'governor' and 'governess' or 'master' and 'mistress' (Lakoff, 1975b). Because of semantic asymmetry, there seems to be a tendency to use the same occupational title for both sexes in French, although this language is largely characterised by grammatical gender. In the Soviet Union, too, a similar development is taking place towards the use of the same occupational title for women and men, especially for occupations with low social status (Comrie and Stone, 1978).

Since 1980, when a law on the equal treatment of men and women came into effect in the Netherlands, staff advertisements have indicated a strong tendency to use the same occupational titles for men and women. In almost all advertisements one title is used, which is accompanied by 'M/F'. In the discursive practice of the 1980s female forms were avoided and new, sex-neutral terms were invented, to which 'M/F' could then be added. This uniform 'M/F' advertisement policy has also been applied to new professions with English titles such as controller, manager, or programmer of which female variants in Dutch are difficult to imagine indeed.

Nevertheless, new female occupational titles may appear in the near future in order to make women more visible on the one hand, and to reveal their invisibility in certain sectors of occupational life on the other. However, in my opinion, the use of the same occupational title in Dutch for both men and women will win out, because of both the weak linguistic feeling for gender marking in Dutch and a tendency to follow the pattern of the English language.

Sex stereotyping

Stereotyping is the signification of someone's behaviour and personality in terms of characteristics which are considered to typify whole groups or categories. By over-generalising certain characteristics, individual differences are overlooked or denied, which is both simplistic and offensive to the one whom it concerns. It is mostly minority groups, people who are socially subordinated or stigmatised, who have suffered from stereotyping. Thus women, in the case of linguistic sexism, are more frequently stereotyped than men. Even though the social roles of women and men have changed enormously, stereotypical views and ideas about women and men continue to exist. They still haunt our minds and, often without our being aware of it, influence our attitudes towards the emancipation of women and men. Thus, women would gossip (women's talk) where men discuss (men's speech). Women should be kind and not too learned or they are called a shrew, battleaxe or bluestocking. When a woman is unmarried or has no partner, she is not independent, but she has missed the boat, or she is an old maid or spinster. Men have to be strong and tough or they are tied to the apron strings, henpecked or a wimp. Men can go through life quite well independently and/or without a partner; they have then got away scot-free or are simply called a bachelor. Such terms indicate the social expectations concerning the roles of women and men, while individual differences are ignored. Stereotypes are persistent but not ineradicable. A comparison of the last three editions of the extensive Dictionary of the Dutch Language (van Dale), reveals changes in views about women and men and their language. A dictionary is an excellent source for an inventorisation of linguistic sexism on a semantic level, that is to say on the level of meanings of words. We recognise the asymmetric relation between the sexes in the definitions of women and men, in the choice of adopted compounds with the words 'woman' and 'man' and also in the choice of example definitions. In many editions, women appear to be defined more negatively than men; they are dependent and they are reduced to the body and physical appearance. A dictionary not only illustrates the state of affairs within a language community, but it also has a normative influence. By describing and referring to a specific ethnic group in a mostly negative sense, stereotypical views and prejudices are repeatedly confirmed and established. In each new edition of the Dictionary of the Dutch Language we see a trace of emancipatory changes. But equality is still a long way off.

In 1976 and 1984 a boy was a 'male person in the period of life between man and child; not yet elderly male person'. In contrast, a girl was described as 'marriageable, unmarried, young woman; sweetheart, esp. fiancée; prostitute, tart'. In 1992 'marriageable' was omitted from the definition of '*girl*'. In all three editions a man is an 'adult person of the male sex'. A woman is an 'adult person of the female sex'. So far, so good. But '*woman*' also denotes a 'female person who is no longer a virgin' while a man is not interpreted as a 'male person who...'. A male is just a 'man, male individual', while a *female* only refers to a woman contemptuously, just as *women* and *womenfolk* mostly have a disparaging connotation. The following examples refer to compounds; in Dutch, nouns can be extended into compounds which remain separate words in English, joined by an apostrophe. In 1976 *women's talk* was described as 'chatter of women'; in 1984 it was changed into 'talk of women (sometimes with a negative connotation)', and in 1992 '(sometimes unfavourable) talk of women'. The compound *men's talk* is not given. A number of example phrases in which women are saddled with the negative characteristics of the whole of human nature were replaced in 1992, occasionally allowing a 'he' to be the subject of a lowly deed or bad characteristic as well. In the previous edition, the following example was added to 'popular': 'she was a popular piece of meat', compared with 'he is very popular in company'; it is true that in the latest edition the first example has been retained, but 'she' is also the subject of the second one instead of 'he'. The compounds 'woman's leg' '-thigh', '-face', '-skin', '-knee', '-lip', '-ear', '-foot' had disappeared in 1992, just like 'woman's whim' and 'woman's chatter', 'woman's gossip'.

In addition to a more balanced relation between women and men, we may also find another social emancipation in the dictionary. The example phrases for the entry '*dishes*' underwent the following changes over the course of time. Three editions ago the example given was 'the maid is doing the dishes'. In 1976, when fewer ladies could afford to keep a maid, this was replaced by 'she is doing the dishes'. In the last two editions it is 'he is doing the dishes' and 'he has again left the dishes in the sink'. For stereotypical compounds referring to Jews the comment 'insulting' has now been added.

Linguistic performance of women and men: difference

At the beginning of the 1970s, the emergence of sociolinguistics (the study of linguistic usage in the context of society and culture) stimulated empirical research into linguistic differences, which focus on linguistic variation according to class, region, age, and ethnicity, as well as on gender differences in linguistic performance. One of the main questions is whether there is a 'women's language' and a 'men's language'.

Anthropological findings from the beginning of this century point to absolute linguistic differences between the sexes in some non-Western languages in which 'male' forms are used exclusively by men, 'female' forms exclusively by women. Such sex-exclusive differentiation was found in Native American languages, the Eskimo language spoken in Baffin Land, Chukchee (spoken in West Siberia), and African and Australian Aboriginal languages (see for an overview Bodine, 1975). Languages of European origin know no forms of language used exclusively by women or exclusively by men. The terms 'women's language' and 'men's language' should thus not be regarded as absolute concepts, but as a matter of degree, that is to say that one gender uses a form of language more often or less often than the other. Empirical studies of gendered linguistic performance resulted from the dissatisfaction that women began to express at the beginning of the second feminist wave. A much-heard complaint within this and other contexts is that communication from woman to woman is so very different from that between women and men. At the time, two American linguists, Mary Ritchie

Key and Robin Lakoff, each published a book on women's language: *Male/Female Language* (Key, 1975) and *Language and Woman's Place* (Lakoff, 1975). Their statements are based on their own intuition and on incidental observations of the linguistic usage of acquaintances. Their observations on the choice of words differ somewhat from those of male linguists at the beginning of the twentieth century, for example Otto Jespersen, who speculated that woman's language naturally arose from the supposed nature of women. Women would, in accordance with their female nature, express themselves more chastely and sensitively than men (Jespersen, 1922). With respect to syntax, both Lakoff and Key observe that women are more uncertain and polite than men. Women would rather pose a question than make a definite assertion, and seldom would they give direct orders.

The difference between Jespersen on the one hand and Ritchie Key and Lakoff on the other is that the linguistic differences between women and men are no longer explained on the basis of innate characteristics, but on the basis of different education and socialisation, and on the basis of unequal social positions. The starting point of female linguists in the 1970s was that the linguistic differences between women and men did not reflect so much their character or natural temperament as their different upbringings and unequal social positions. By explaining linguistic differences within a sociological framework, they open up the perspective that knowledge of the differences can contribute to consciousness-raising, which in turn can contribute to change.

The few, mostly small-scale, studies reveal a much more diffuse and more complex picture than stereotypical statements would lead us to believe. In some studies specific gender differences in linguistic usage were indeed established, while they did not surface in other studies. Moreover, linguistic differences do not appear to be connected exclusively with the gender of the speaker: the age and status of the speaker or the situation and the gender of the addressee also determine the use of a linguistic variant (Crosby and Nyquist, 1977, Brouwer, Gerritsen and de Haan, 1979).

Those studies have been mainly based on the speech of white women and men. Although one of the most striking examples of linguistic ethnic differentiation is the difference between the speech of blacks and whites, especially in the United States, this phenomenon has received relatively little attention. Labov (1972a) wrote a pioneering book on Black English Vernacular, studying the speech of blacks, that is black men, from eight to nineteen years old. With very few exceptions, black women's speech has not been the subject of linguistic studies (see Trudgill, 1983: 51-77, which also gives a short overview of the most frequently cited characteristics of Black Vernacular English; Edwards, 1989).

Ethnicity in a multicultural community is a particular kind of social differentiation and, as such, will often have linguistic differentiation associated with it. The term 'Black Vernacular English' is generally used to refer to the non-standard English spoken by lower-class blacks in the urban ghettos of the northern part of the United States and elsewhere. The term 'Black English' has the disadvantage that it suggests that all blacks speak this variety of English, which is not the case. Each language knows a number of varieties. When 'standard' language or variety is mentioned below, it refers to that variety of a language which is usually used in print, in schools and in courses for non-native speakers learning the language, and which is normally spoken by educated people and used in news broadcasts and other similar situations. Because language as a social phenomenon is closely tied up with the social structure and value systems of a society, different dialects are evaluated in different ways. A so-called standard language usually has much more status and prestige than any other dialect.

Pronunciation and syntax

Most linguistic studies of the linguistic performance of women and men have focused on phonetics, that is, on pronunciation. There are several reasons for the focus on pronunciation. First, features of pronunciation are easier to study than choice of words or syntax. Even a short extract of spoken language features many possible sounds, while specific words or specific sentence constructions may not occur at all. Moreover, differences in pronunciation can easily be compared and an average score of pronunciation of one sound can thus be calculated, because a different pronunciation of a word does not change what the word refers to. The text of *The Color Purple*, written in Celie's social dialect, the black vernacular of the Southern part of the United States, does not detract from the signification, but actually provides more information about her social position and background. Second, social judgements about differences in pronunciation are generally more clear-cut than, for example, about different syntax. A couple of words usually suffice to position someone regionally and socially. Consciously or unconsciously, people judge someone in the first instance by the way he or she speaks. Thus, pronunciation functions as a visiting-card and plays a role similar to that of other attributes, for example, clothing. In *The Color Purple* Shug is in many respects a woman of the world – self-assured, a successful Blues singer (Queen Honeybee), big house, smart clothes – eloquent. When Celie has set up her own sewing workshop, her help Darlene wants to teach her to talk 'properly':

> You say US where most folks say WE, she say, and peoples think you dumb. Colored peoples think you a hick and white folks be amuse. _Think how much better Shug feel with you educated, she say. She won't be shame to take you anywhere. (183)

Sociolinguistic research has frequently demonstrated that women use the standard variants more frequently while men use the social (and regional) dialect variants. Correspondingly, women and men differ in their ideas and feelings about language varieties: women have a more positive attitude towards standard language, men towards non-standard or dialect. It also turns out that a shift towards standard language takes place as the formality of the speech situation increases, and that women show a relatively greater shift than men. Most of these studies concerned North American urban varieties of English in cities like New York or Detroit (Labov 1972b). Wolfram (1969) found that black women within each social class in Detroit used forms closer to standard norms than men. This was partly explained by the fact that women more often than men had jobs as domestic servants, waitresses or salespersons, which would encourage them to practise standard language (Hannerz, 1970). A similar linguistic pattern was also found in Canada, in cities in Britain such as Norwich and Glasgow, for Australian English in Sydney, and for Dutch in Nijmegen and Amsterdam.

In spite of this consistency, the gender pattern is not always as marked as might be expected. Sometimes, differences between the sexes are slight: in some cases the gender pattern does not involve all the socially sensitive features; in other cases the gender pattern fails to occur at all, as in a study of the black working class in Washington DC, which did not find women to use more standard forms than men (Fasold, 1972). Nevertheless, considering the amount of sociolinguistic evidence the gender pattern needs to be explained.

Explanations for the linguistic variation between women and men are mainly speculative, which is hardly surprising given the descriptive nature of most of the studies. Many older studies assumed a direct causal link between gender and language performance by claiming that language usage is connected with sex-specific roles. Two, partly conflicting, explanatory role orientations are postulated. First, it is suggested that women may speak more correctly than men because their role is generally assumed to be raising the children, which would make the women feel that they should set an example. Second, the influence of employment on language performance is proposed as an explanation.

Since most women do not have paid work, they cannot acquire status through their occupation or earning power. It may be, therefore, that they have to be judged on their appearance and that they try to derive their status from other signals of status, including speech. This last explanation is contradicted by studies in West Germany; there, it is women in employment who adapt more to the standard norm, presumably because of their more insecure position on the labour market and the sharply defined gender expectations at work.

Several more recent studies suggest an indirect causal relationship between gender and speech, using the intermediary concept of social network. A study of a black population in South Carolina showed the influence of the type of work on speech: women, who worked more frequently than men in white-collar occupations, consequently had a different social network from men and moved faster towards (syntactic) standard forms (Nichols, 1980). Similarly, the results from an investigation in a bilingual, German-Hungarian community in eastern Austria pointed to the importance of social network, in this case its 'peasantness', and the linguistic attitudes and aspirations involved. Women, averse to becoming peasants or marrying them, used German more often than did men (Gal, 1978). In the report of a study carried out in Belfast it was suggested that the degree of participation in a social network affects speech behaviour. The more people were part of a close-knit vernacular network, the more they expressed their group identity by conforming to the language norms prevailing in that group. Women, generally less embedded in such networks than men, adapted more to the standard pronunciation (Milroy, 1980).

These studies show that any correlation between an isolated social variable such as gender and a linguistic variable is insufficient evidence for the thesis that differences between female and male speech are markers of gender. In addition, the gender pattern may vary cross-culturally. In the Merina culture in Madagascar, strong value is placed on speaking indirectly and avoiding open confrontation. In this community, it is women who are seen as norm-breakers, associated with a direct, impolite manner of speech, expressing anger and giving negative information (Keenan, 1974). In a study of Swahili in Mombasa, Kenya, women seemed to preserve the vernacular rather than standard features (Russell, 1982).

Until now, explanations for gender differences in linguistic performance have been put forward within an academic framework in which men's behaviour is taken as the norm and prototype. As a result the explanation of gender variation in language amounted to explaining the 'deviant' linguistic usage of women. Even though they regularly use standard pronunciation, the linguistic usage of women needed be explained rather than that of men, whose speech in fact deviat... from the (standard language) norm. The gender bias in sociolinguistics is thus quite illogical: after all, speaking standard language is generally considered desirable in Western society and is hardly ever thought of as being abnormal. The question 'why do women talk so correctly?' should in fact read better as 'why do men talk so vulgarly?'

In addition to linguistic performance, linguistic attitude is also an object of study. The denominator 'linguistic attitude' includes thoughts and feelings concerning linguistic variations, linguistic behaviour and language users. The interest of the study of thoughts and feelings about linguistic variations lies in its value in explaining and predicting linguistic variation and linguistic change. By testing linguistic attitude, one can find out how speakers think about their own linguistic performance and how they generally judge linguistic variations and those who use them. Self-evaluation tests emphasise the norms within which women and men operate with regard to their own linguistic performance. Women are more favourably disposed towards standard language, men towards social dialect; women are more negative towards the use of swear words, men more positive. Language functions as an important indicator of social status and female and male characteristics: standard pronunciation is associated with high social status and femininity, social dialect with lower social status and masculinity. There is definitely a double standard with respect to social status: in a study in Amsterdam, female speakers, irrespective of their pronunciation, were assessed less highly than male speakers (Brouwer, 1989: 90).

Verbal interaction

The earlier mentioned gender differences in choice of words, syntax, and pronunciation were mainly based on interviews with or observations of individual women and men. But language is used in a variety of situations, mostly in conversations between one or more people. A conversation is a social event and shows a specific structure. Someone begins the conversation, the conversation continues in a particular way and finally ends. As a rule the succession of utterances is fixed by social rules and not every reaction is socially acceptable.

Studies of verbal interaction between women and men initially concentrated on linguistic differences between the speech of women and men. These studies assumed that the gender differences found in linguistic strategies used by women and men reflect their socially unequal positions. In conversations, men apparently dominate women by taking the floor: they interrupt women more often than they do other men, whereas women do not interrupt men (Zimmerman and West, 1975). In most cases it appears that men also determine the subject of discussion, while women mainly do their best to allow the conversation to run smoothly, an effort which the American linguist Pamela Fishman has called 'interactional shitwork' (Fishman, 1983). Women mainly stand out as good listeners and focus completely on the interests of the male, constantly encouraging him to talk by emphasising their attention with words or gestures (for example,'right', 'do you think so?', 'really?' or by always looking at him attentively, smiling), at the cost of their own contribution.

The picture that emerges from these studies contrasts sharply with the widespread belief that women talk more than men. It is highly probable that the comparison 'women are more talkative than men' falls short. Actually, it is more likely that a separate standard is applied for women which comes down to silence (Spender, 1980). When silence is the norm women can of course easily be accused of chattiness. It is not far-fetched to assume that the cultural norm demands women to keep their mouths shut most of the time. Despite results from sociolinguistic studies, stereotypical ideas about women's language as 'chatter, gossip, prattle' do live on. Even though the linguistic behaviour of women and that of men does not conform to this stereotype, it is still perceived as such. In studies in Britain, students listened to tape recordings of dialogues between women and men, in which both sexes had equal speaking time. Asked about the share of women and men in the conversation, all the students, male and female, thought that the women talked more (Cutler and Scott, 1990).

Some studies have been made of the way in which women talk amongst themselves and how men talk amongst themselves (Tannen, 1990). In connection with their different environments, the private and the public sphere, women are more intimate and approachable in their contacts and men are more practical and competitive. This is proved, among other things, by the nature of the subjects under discussion and the extent to which a subject is talked through. Amongst themselves, women pay more attention to others and the way in which they function in relation to others. They focus more on acceptance and recognition and they exchange more personal experiences. In their conversations they show attention through, for example, frequent use of 'mm' while the other speaks. Amongst themselves women do regularly interrupt each other. They don't do this in order to bring up a different subject but to show their sympathy by acknowledging or supplementing what the other is saying, even by sometimes finishing off the sentence for the other. Usually, a different subject is introduced after a natural silence.

Amongst themselves men are more distant from each other. They undertake joint activities rather than discussing their problems with each other. They do the latter more often with women. Their conversations are aimed at expounding or resolving something. They are keener on hierarchies and avoid displaying weakness. Conversations among girls or boys also reveal that girls are more cooperative and boys more competitive. A similar pattern was found in conversations of same-sex groups of black working-class children in Philadelphia (Goodwin, 1980). The girls' group showed a fluid hierarchy, their directives were often proposals for future activity, while the boys' group was more hierarchical, with status enacted through giving commands, contradicting each other, and usurping speaking time. Boys bragged about achievements, girls talked about appearances and relationships.

Some linguists have suggested that women and men belong to different subcultures (Maltz and Borker, 1982). Especially in the period between five and fifteen years of age, when girls mainly relate to girls and boys to boys, sex-specific manners and conversation are learned. The result is that in conversation men and women can misinterpret each other's behaviour. When, for example, a woman presents a problem to a man, because she wants his moral support by discussing it with him in more detail, a man thinks that he is supporting her by immediately and efficiently providing her with a solution. Women interrupt each other more supportively and men interrupt each other more competitively. In mixed discussions women are put off by interruptions by men, which they experience as aggressive, and consequently fall silent. And men then think that women have nothing of interest to report.

Differentiated studies

Every linguistic community shows, in addition to regional, social and ethnic variation, situational variation: not all people speak in the same way and a person does not speak in the same way in every situation. There are differences in linguistic performance between people from lower and higher social classes, from different ethnicities, between young people and adults, and between women and men. Furthermore, individual speakers vary their linguistic performance according to the formality of the situation. At home, for example, people are more at ease than during a job interview, which results in a more informal and more formal style of speaking respectively. Linguistic variation can be found at different levels – pronunciation, choice of words, syntax, interaction. It is unlikely that the different patterns of variation can be traced back to a single underlying aspect. As discussed above, studies of linguistic performance are not void of complications. Intensive research often produces only a few results about one linguistic level, one socio-economic group (often the middle class), one ethnic group (often the white Westerner), in one social situation.

The majority of studies of linguistic performance by women and men have been made from the perspective of difference. Women and men are thus considered as two polarised yet homogeneous categories. Usually the similarities between women and men and differences among women and among men are passed over. However, gender is not a statistically intrinsic individual feature, but is established in concrete historically changing social relations. A comparison of the linguistic performance of women (and men) of different ages, social backgrounds, ethnicity, sexual identity and (sub)culture would shed more light on the social construction of gender. Sociolinguists and conversation analysts have demonstrated in their empirical studies that linguistic performance is socially determined. Their research focuses mainly on the interaction between people in everyday language. It is generally performed on the basis of one discipline, usually linguistics. Therefore the understanding of 'situation' or 'context' has been underdeveloped. Over the last few years conversation analysts, who are mostly sociologists, have argued in favour of a theory in which language is understood to construct a social structure. Such a theory could be developed on the basis of a study of the micro-politics of communication. Also in the domain of linguistics the universality and the autonomy of the subject should be problematised in order to understand how gender is constructed and can be deconstructed in everyday conversations (Todd and Fischer, 1988). At the beginning of the third decade of studies of language and gender, an interdisciplinary collaboration between sociolinguists, conversation analysts and semioticians seems desirable for a more complete understanding of linguistic performance, gender and social context.

Literature for further study

General introductions

Cameron, Deborah (1985) *Feminism and Linguistic Theory.* Theories of feminist lingistuic models inspired by semiotic approaches to language and text.

Coates, Jennifer (1986) *Women, Men and Language.* Study of linguistic performance of women and men. Partly dedicated to sociolinguistic study of the acquisition of sex-specific linguistic behaviour and the linguistic interaction between adult and child.

Graddoll, David, and Joan Swann (1989) *Gender Voices.* Study of linguistic sexism and linguistic performance.

Anthologies

The following anthologies give a good overview of approaches and studies in the field of language and gender:

Coates, Jennifer, and Deborah Cameron (eds) (1989) *Women in Their Speech Communities: New Perspectives on Language and Sex*. This anthology emphasises a transcultural perspective.

Philips, Susan U., Susan Steele and Christine Tanz (eds) (1987) *Language, Gender and Sex in Comparative Perspective*. Also focuses on a transcultural perspective.

Thorne, Barrie, Cheris Kramarae and Nancy Henley (eds) (1983) *Language, Gender and Society*. Contains annotated bibliography which takes up nearly two hundred pages. This bibliography is a practical starting-point for further study, subdivided into nine headings: introductions, linguistic sexism, stereotypes and linguistic perception, linguistic performance (equality and difference), verbal interaction, genre and style, children's language, cultural and ethnic variation, non-verbal communication.

Todd, Alexandra D. and Sue Fischer (eds) (1988) *Gender and Discourse: The Power of Talk*. Focuses on a discourse analysis of language.

Journals

Finally there are the following periodicals about gender, language and text, published twice a year.

Women and Language, editor: Anita Taylor. Communication Department. George Mason University, Fairfax (VA 22030) USA.

Working Papers on Language, Gender and Sexism, editors: Dédé Brouwer, Anne Pauwels and Joanne Winter. Department of Linguistics, Monash University, Clayton (Vic 3168) Australia.

5
A perfect fit: feminist media studies

JOKE HERMES

Introduction

The Color Purple provoked fierce reactions, especially from black men. In particular, the film directed by Steven Spielberg has been slated by the black community and is seen as insulting to black men who, according to black critics, are depicted as rapists and tyrants. Celie's stepfather rapes her. Mr. —— only wants Celie when she takes her cow along with her, and he treats her like dirt. The only black man depicted in more-or-less friendly terms in the book, Sofia's husband Harpo, is a wimp in the film.

The emotions of black men in response to Spielberg's film are analogous to the indignation which the feminist movement and feminist theory have displayed in relation to popular culture. The way in which femininity is represented in popular culture has been discussed intensively in the women's movement. Some feminists oppose popular culture because women are depicted as second-rate citizens in popular films, television advertising and newspapers, which is supposed to have disastrous consequences for their self-image. Others take the view that feminists should in the first place have respect for the wishes of women and thus also for any pleasure that they derive from television, women's magazines and other popular media (Hermes, 1995).

Popular culture as villain

The first feminist discussions about popular culture were the bestsellers *The Feminine Mystique* (1963) by Betty Friedan and *The Female Eunuch* (1970) by Germaine Greer. Both books are landmarks of feminist media criticism and argue for equal treatment of the sexes. Friedan and Greer are concerned with the self-images which the culture (literature just as much as women's magazines and the *Harlequin* or Mills and Boon romances) imposes on women and by which inequality between women and men is maintained.

Betty Friedan, herself a former editor of women's magazines, gives them in particular a hard time. She compares their editors with Frankensteins who create a female monster using the image of the 'happy housewife heroine':

> I helped create this image. I have watched American women for fifty years try to conform to it. But I can no longer deny my own knowledge of its terrible implications. It is not a harmless image. There may be no psychological terms for the harm it is doing. But what happens when women try to live according to an image that makes them deny their minds? What happens if women grow up in an image that makes them deny the reality of the changing world? (Friedan, 1963: 59)

Germaine Greer, in her turn, criticises the genre of romance, which is specially written for a female audience. In these light romances the arrogant, brutish type of man is invariably glorified.

Although Friedan and Greer differ in their backgrounds (Friedan relies especially on sociological studies; Greer draws more on classical psychoanalysts like Freud, Horney and also Reich), their work echoes the dictum formulated by Simone de Beauvoir in 1949: one is not born, one becomes a woman. Academic studies of popular culture rest initially on the assumption that women and men are really equal and that differences are the result of upbringing and socialisation in the family, at school and especially through the media. The anthology *Hearth and Home* (1978), compiled by Gaye Tuchman, about the involvement of the media in images of women is a striking example of this.

For Gaye Tuchman the mass media are the most important cause of the reproduction of patriarchal relations between the sexes. She refers to studies which assess the number of women appearing in different genres and what role they play. Even in a television genre such as the soap opera with many women characters and many female viewers, men appear systematically to have a better education, more prestigious jobs and higher incomes. Tuchman is concerned about the effects of this outdated representation of society. She is an author who believes unconditionally in the equality of men and women. The danger of these outdated images of women's role is that girls will imperceptibly internalise them. As television viewers they will model their behaviour on that of women on television.

Tuchman's anthology illustrates the main objectives of early feminist media criticism. The texts are sharp and polemical and target the alleged causes of the false consciousness of women and the disgusting ways in which femininity and women's bodies are depicted as stupid, inferior or as objects. The reputation of a feminist critique of popular culture was established with these early texts. The media seduce the viewer into a false image of reality. On the issue of the interaction between popular culture and social reality, two unfounded assumptions underlie equality-minded media criticism. First, popular media texts consist of transparent, unequivocal, unrealistic messages about women. Second, women and girls will passively absorb these messages as (wrong) lessons about real life. Both these assumptions have been challenged.

Critics who do not stop at equality but adopt a difference approach stress the ambiguity of texts and raise new questions, including some about the pleasure that stereotyping and conventional media texts apparently offer women. The central issue is not social inequality but the popular text itself. Structuralism, psychoanalysis and semiotics offer insights and methods for analysing text mechanisms. Within this approach, media texts offer a multiplicity of opportunities for female and male identification that the text can render significant for its readers and viewers.

Popular culture as a source of pleasure

Feminist critics like Tania Modleski (1984) and Cora Kaplan (1986) are particularly interested in the specific attraction of popular genres for women. Modleski's analysis follows Marxist lines. With sensitivity to the specificity of texts, she explains the pleasure that women may experience from popular texts in terms of a connection between housework, the social position of women and genre rules. Modleski distinguishes the narrative structure of the American soap opera through a number of characteristics: there are many main characters and many plot lines which are not always, or not at all, completely resolved; there is more scope for 'bad' manipulative women than in other genres; people who are believed to be lost crop up regularly and relationships which seem to have no future at all are given a second chance. Modleski concludes that the narrative characteristics of the soap opera produce a textual position for spectators which can be compared with that of an ideal mother:

> The subject/spectator of soap operas, it could be said, is constituted as a sort of ideal mother: a person who possesses greater wisdom than all her children, whose sympathy is large enough to encompass the conflicting claims of her family (she identifies with them all), and who has no demands or claims of her own (she identifies with no one character exclusively). (Modleski, 1984: 92).

According to Modleski's analysis, the question is no longer how soap opera reflects stereotypical images of women, but how the text actively produces a symbolic female identity by constructing a specific subject position – that of the ideal mother – in the narrative structure. The viewer/mother, who identifies herself with each of the characters in turn, sees the 'greater whole' and sympathises with sinners and victims. By repeatedly serving up the many aspects of a case, by never coming to a permanent conclusion, the soap opera undermines the viewer's capacity to form a clear judgement. The privileged position of the mother is pleasurable, suggests Modleski, because the text temporarily displaces fear and anxiety about the collapse of the family (a day-to-day North American and Western European reality).

Modleski takes the position of the objective academic who, however committed to the female viewer, never acknowledges her own position as a viewer. On the other hand, Kaplan takes her own pleasure as a starting point and puts it in the context of the norms and values of popular culture which dominate feminist circles.

Kaplan's essay about the bestseller and television series *The Thorn Birds* begins with a confession. As a teenager Kaplan loved scenarios of the type 'boy meets girl and they live together ever after'. Fortunately for Kaplan, a child from a left-wing family, such stories are also available in 'real' literature and not only in pulp fiction:

> I read with heart pounding and hands straying, reducing the respectable and popular to a basic set of scenarios. *Peyton Place, Jane Eyre, Bleak House, Nana*: in my teens they were all the same to me, part of my sexual and emotional initiation, confirming, constructing my femininitity, making plain the psychic form of sexual difference. In my bookish, left wing but rather puritanical household I kept the secret of my reading practice pretty well; after all it was precocious and respectable, was it not, to read all of Dickens at thirteen, to have a passion for Zola a year later? Only I knew that I read them for the sentimental and sexual hype. Physically I developed late; before I swelled, curved or bled I had, psychically speaking, read myself into womanhood. (Kaplan, 1986: 117)

Her secret pleasure in reading is discovered when Kaplan reads a 'wrong' book, the racist and conservative *Gone With the Wind*, and is completely carried away by it. Her mother's reaction and the shame that afterwards overtakes her make her withdraw from such romances. This leads Kaplan to conform for a full fourteen years to left-wing and feminist norms which declare popular culture taboo.

Then Kaplan is moved by a television episode of *The Thorn Birds*, an Australian family epic about the love between a young woman and a priest, the ideal mother-man with whom any form of sexual relationship is of course taboo. According to Kaplan the attraction of *The Thorn Birds* has everything to do with the fact that the book establishes instead of denies the conflicting and ambiguous place of women and femininity in gender relations. Greer and Friedan suggest that popular culture seduces women into a false consciousness with which they go along uncritically. Modleski explains the attraction of the *Harlequin* series and of soap operas by the way in which these genres accommodate the 'real' position of women. Kaplan, on the other hand, supposes that fantasy offers a subject the opportunity to escape from fixed, gendered rules and norms. The attraction of texts, then, is not necessarily related to identification with specific positions but can also be the effect of the transgressions of the text; of the appeal of that which is forbidden yet thrilling, exciting and dangerous. The incest taboo, the daughter seducing the father figure (a priest, at that); breaking the vow of celibacy; the racist fear of miscegenation; the loss of status for the mother who has a child by a Maori; all this stirs up excitement in the viewer/reader. Kaplan analyses how the text breaks taboos at the level of fantasy. Fantastic scenarios allow the reader to exceed boundaries, to violate norms. There are many indications to suggest that readers do not always identify 'correctly' and remain within expected conventions.

From this perspective *The Color Purple*, too, can be read as a transgressive text which evokes a number of tensions. Instead of giving main roles to principally men and whites, as usual, both book and film focus on black women. The violent relationship between Celie and Mr. —— evokes (especially in the film) the relationship between slave and master. The racism which the black community has to endure appears to be partially displaced to man–woman relationships. The lesbian relationship between Celie and Shug, finally, is a powerful metaphor for female bonding. The short kissing scene in the film suggests enough for experienced spectators (who are perhaps also acquainted with the much more explicit text of the book), but it also symbolises the black community as a harmonious 'womanist' (the term is Alice Walker's, 1983) community. *The Color Purple* plays with conventions like colour and sexual preference. The success of the film seems, however, to lie particularly in the combination of this challenge with Walker's sentimental form. The pedantic letters from Celie's sister Nettie, the improbable but moving 'happy end', the good that finally triumphs make the film easily recognisable as a standard Hollywood melodrama. Since a melodrama always suggests that pain and suffering are everywhere and a constant part of the human condition, it is not so difficult for white viewers to let Celie, Shug and the others 'bleach', as Kaplan suggests. Perhaps it is also the case that the sentimental nature of the film facilitates for white spectators a catharsis of feelings of guilt and unease about the generally poor position of blacks and their own privileged position. After all, it is essential for the genre to wallow in all kinds of pity. For black spectators things are obviously different; below, I will come back to black responses to *The Color Purple*.

Popular culture and the construction of femininity

With the analysis of the large role played by popular culture in the construction of sexual difference, the question of deconstruction of femininity becomes crucial. In feminist studies of popular culture the focus on femininity as a construction marks a shift from mechanisms in the text to the reception of the text. The central question here is what meanings media texts may have for consumers. One possible answering can be found in in-depth interviews with women readers and viewers. Janice Radway's research into the reception of *Harlequins* heralds the beginning of this sort of study of readership, based on open interviews. In *Reading the Romance* (1984) she argues that analysis of an isolated text should be supplemented by a study of reading as a complex, social and everyday event. Meaning, according to Radway, cannot be derived just like that from the structure of the text. Reading is an active process of negotiation which engenders both meaning and pleasure.

Radway interviewed a group of women in a small American town and asked them to draw up a top ten of good romances and a top ten of bad ones. She used both lists to study the texts of successful and bad romances and to bring up salient differences. Thus, the ideal romance features a hero who is in a position to take care of a heroine. The heroine is intelligent and energetic. As far as there are any villains in the story, they are clearly distinguishable from the hero. The villain should be a rapist, not to be trusted and, moreover, bad through and through. In disappointing romances heavy-handedness on the part of men is not exclusively the preserve of the villains. Here, the profile of the hero is not easily distinguishable from that of the rapist. Books not qualifying as successful do not lend themselves to a possible re-interpretation of male behaviour and forsake their intended duty of (temporarily) dispelling the fear of rape and other male violent abuse.

Radway concludes that the women she interviewed use romantic novels as a 'declaration of independence' in relation to the position they have in patriarchal discourse on the family: the position of the always available, caring mother and housewife. While reading they are not be disturbed nor are they available. At the same time they do submit to conventional discourses of femininity by investing energy in the imaginary reconstruction of masculinity. Because that is how women read these romances: as stories about the transformation of insensitive machos into loving and almost maternal human beings.

One and the same practice – reading romances – can contain conflicting positions and investments which, according to Radway, nevertheless result in the reproduction of traditional female subjectivity. For her study Radway chose to interview a single group of women. No attention is paid to how class and ethnic differences affect the reception of this genre. In reaction to Radway's work, others have attempted to systematise difference among women and to show that femininity and pleasure can take different forms in relation to popular culture. Below I discuss two examples which remarkably enough conflict with each other.

Seiter et al. (1989) conducted extensive interviews with day-time soap opera viewers in the United States. They established that Modleski's position of the ideal mother is indeed confirmed by the answers of better-educated middle-class informants, but on the other hand is fiercely rejected by the majority of working-class informants. The researchers conclude that the viewing position indicated by Modleski as that of the 'ideal mother' presupposes a specific social identity – that of a middle-class woman with a husband who brings home the money. Such a viewing position is not open to working-class women who are often critical of the way in which the soap opera represents women's problems. These are in fact identified by some women as typically upper- and middle-class problems. Women from the working class in particular resist the soap opera. In contrast to middle-class women they criticise the lack of realism and the escapism which the text produces. This reception analysis establishes that women are not a homogeneous category; class does make a difference. But how valid is the distinction made by Seiter and her colleagues? And does class always make the same difference?

In Andrea Press's interviews with women who follow the prime-time soap opera *Dynasty*, it is precisely middle-class women who are critical. Women from the working class do not consider the differences between the *Dynasty* characters and themselves to be relevant. According to Press that is because they think the *Dynasty* text is realistic. Her respondents from the middle class, on the other hand, refuse to allow themselves to be bamboozled by the conventions of realism which characterise this television series, as most prime-time programmes. Press concludes that there is a difference between middle-class women, who draw on ideologies of femininity and the family 'in order to criticize the show's characters', and working-class women, who 'invoke [such categories] to affirm the depiction which they view' (Press, 1990: 179-80).

This finding is in direct conflict with the conclusions of Seiter et al. that it was women from the working class who were most critical of the discrepancy between textual representation and their own experiences. It is difficult to understand what has caused this difference in research results. It may possibly have to do with the way in which the notion of class has been deployed in both research projects, with the interview locations or the differing codes of day-time and prime-time soap opera. It is clear that the female subject positions prescribed in a text are not adopted by viewers just like that. Class, gender and race play a role in processes of production of meaning. It thus appears to be incorrect to assume that the meanings are already established in advance.

Along the lines of the study by Janice Radway, Jacqueline Bobo (1988) studied the criticism of *The Color Purple* and held an interview with a group of black women. They were quite unanimously impressed by the film – 'Finally, somebody says something about us' – and felt strengthened by Celie's triumph. They thought the criticism of Walker and of the film, particularly on the part of black men, completely unjustified. The women do recognise that the film stands with one foot in the tradition of the racist represention of blacks. Spielberg has not succeeded in making a credible character out of Harpo – in the book a gentle, friendly man – and characterises him as a buffoon. Spielberg's interpretation of Sofia is also not quite successful. Bobo argues however that, as black spectators, the women are by sheer necessity used to filtering out offensive racist images and codes from what they see in the theatre and the cinema. Also, the recent visibility and popularity of the work of black female writers enables spectators to read and interpret *The Color Purple* as part of their legacy, as establishing who they are and what they want.

Bobo's analysis can be read alongside Michele Wallace's (1990) response to the film. She describes herself as a black woman and teacher in rural America who saw the film in her home town among a white audience who simply accepted it as a sentimental tale. They hardly seemed to notice that Celie was black. Wallace left the cinema in a bad mood. The second time she saw the film, in New York with a mixed audience, she was amused by a small marital dispute which arose between a black woman and a man. The woman said: 'Shit, I wouldn't take that mess' when Mr. —— treats Celie badly. To which the man replied: 'It's a movie baby, you know, *just* a movie!' Wallace's message is that spectators will interpret stories differently in different places and contexts. Sometimes stories inspire the spectator into a hope or anger which far exceeds the text and can only be understood if one takes into account relevant contexts, discourses and the cultural competence of the spectators. In the case of *The Color Purple*, the context varies from historical and contemporary discourses on the position of blacks in the United States to literary discourses on black literature in which women have no place; from the reputation of the director to the personal life histories and knowledge of viewers and readers; from recent feminist literature to the codes and structures of Hollywood films.

The following chapter will introduce the multi-layered meanings in film and the position of the female spectator which lie at the heart of feminist film theory.

Literature for further study

Ang, Ien (1985) *Watching Dallas*. Ang confronts *Dallas* with feminism and discusses the difference between 'male' and 'female' popular culture. On the basis of letters from viewers she reconstructs the pleasure that they experienced in watching the soap opera *Dallas*, by using notions such as 'melodramatic representation'.

Brown, Mary-Ellen (1990) *Television and Women's Culture*. A recent collection of articles on women and popular culture. Brown stresses the symbolic resistance of women in their viewing pleasure when watching different women's genres. Some quiz shows for example make a spectacle of what are normally private and invisible housewifely qualities.

Friedan, Betty (1963) *The Feminine Mystique*. A classic in which women's magazines are harshly ridiculed. Can be considered as one of the books which gave the initial impetus to the second feminist wave.

Gamman, Lorraine, and Margaret Marshment (eds) (1988) *The Female Gaze: Women as Viewers of Popular Culture*. Essays on all kinds of popular genres read and viewed by women (crime fiction, blockbusters, *Dynasty*) and a couple of contemplative articles, including an analysis by Andrea Stuart of the reactions to *The Color Purple*.

Geraghty, Christine (1991) *Women and Soap Opera: A Study of Prime Time Soaps*. Geraghty assembles feminist studies of soap opera. On the basis of structural characteristics she makes an original distinction between patriarchal American soaps and matriarchal British soaps.

Greer, Germaine (1970) *The Female Eunuch*. Another classic. Stimulating, sarcastic essays on the way in which women are represented in 'high' and 'low' culture.

Hermes, Joke (1995) *Reading Women's Magazines: An Analysis of Everyday Media Use*. An example of recent ethnographic research investigating the use of women's genres. Not only female readers, but also male readers, are interviewed.

hooks, bell (1990b) *Yearning: Race, Gender and Cultural Politics*; *Black Looks:*

Race and Representation (1992) and *Outlaw Culture: Resisting Representations* (1994a). Critical essays on various cultural subjects, linked by a political tone, personal recollections and a post-modern theoretical perspective.

Kaplan, Cora (1986) *Sea Changes: Culture and Feminism*. Contains a variety of essays, including those referred to in this chapter, 'Wild Nights' and '*The Thorn Birds*'. Kaplan writes of *The Color Purple* that it is probably easier for non-American spectators to 'bleach' the film. The essay concerned is called 'Keeping the Color in *The Color Purple*'.

Modleski, Tania (1984) *Loving with a Vengeance: Mass-produced Fantasies for Women*. Modleski has a keen eye for very different 'women's genres'. This book discusses *Harlequins*, female horror, the Gothic novel and soap opera.

Wallace, Michele (1990) *Invisibility Blues: From Pop to Theory*. Wallace writes fascinating essays on questions of colour, meaning and authorship. Includes pieces about the position of black women writers; about famous texts by black women in the United States, including *The Color Purple*; and about the phenomenon of Michael Jackson.

6

What meets the eye: feminist film studies

ANNEKE SMELIK

Introduction

The Color Purple is one of those films which never fails to carry me away: my handkerchief always gets wet while watching and the happy end is met by my sigh of relief. In spite of this Kleenex experience, I am also irritated by the way in which one of my favourite novels has been filmed. The film does away with many of the trenchant political questions of the novel and establishes prejudices about race and gender. This conflicting viewing experience indicates a tension which is characteristic for feminist film theory: the friction between pleasure and politics.

Two quotations from famous articles which heralded the beginning of feminist film criticism reproduce this contrast well. Laura Mulvey wants to break down the conventional pleasure of patriarchal cinema:

> Women, whose image has continually been stolen and used for this end, cannot view the decline of the traditional film form with anything much more than sentimental regret. (Mulvey 1989/1975: 26)

In the same vein Claire Johnston writes that if a women's cinema is to emerge it should be 'paving the way for a radical break with conventions and forms' (1973: 4). Yet, such a revolutionary strategy can also embrace visual pleasure:

> In order to counter our objectification in cinema, our collective fantasies must be released: women's cinema must embody the working through of desire: such an objective demands the use of the entertainment film. (Johnston 1973: 31)

The tension we see here between politics and pleasure has been particularly productive if we consider the stormy development of feminist film theory and film practice. This chapter aims at making the reader familiar with the sometimes inaccessible labyrinth of feminist film theory; where possible I shall apply the theory to the film *The Color Purple*.

Equality: images of women

Because of the feminist movement women started to look at films with different eyes. At women's film festivals women rediscovered forgotten women's films, women directors, women screenwriters and actresses. At the beginning of the 1970s this brought about a 're-vision' of film history (Haskell, 1973). This historical and sociological approach looked for equality and emancipation in cinema. The criticism of these first feminist film critics concerns classical or dominant cinema: the Hollywood dream factory. Hollywood movies do not show any 'real' women on the screen, but only a stereotyped image of women which gives the spectators no easy opportunity for identification. In this first phase one assumed an unmediated relationship between cinema and society, where film was understood to form a reflection of reality. This relationship between reality and film was also considered reversible: by showing reality in a film, society could be changed. Thus, the liberating purpose of a feminist film practice can be easily deduced: women directors only have to break through the enchantment of false images by showing 'real' lives of 'real' women on the silver screen. Against the glamour of the female star created by men, such as Marilyn Monroe, women film-makers should show the realistic lives of ordinary women with their everyday problems.

The Color Purple is a good example of this kind of movie which is filmed from the perspective of the ordinary woman. This is of great importance for a female audience, even though the film does not break with the tradition of racist stereotypes in the usually lily-white Hollywood movie – where black women are stereotyped in minor roles as female servant (the 'mammy', like Hattie McDaniel in *Gone with the Wind*) or as sensual, exotic woman (often the Blues singer) (Alexander 1991). In *The Color Purple*, however, the main role is reserved for a black oppressed girl who, with the help of other black women, develops into an independent woman. This perhaps explains the contrast in its reception: the film has been received with much criticism in intellectual African-American circles (Wallace, 1990; hooks, 1990a), whereas non-professional black female spectators appear to experience *The Color Purple* rather positively and see Celie as a powerful heroine. As one black female spectator said of Celie, 'The lady was a strong lady, like I am. And she hung in there and she overcame' (Bobo, 1988: 102 and

93). In analogy to Culler, we can say that these spectators 'view-as-a-black-woman'.

Difference

Until now the call for equality and recognition can still be heard, in the sense that the female spectator wants to be able to identify with lifelike film heroines without having to be annoyed by sexist clichés. At a theoretical level, however, the perspective of equality in feminist film criticism was soon replaced with the French (post)structuralist way of thinking as it was introduced in the second half of the 1970s. The emphasis then came to lie more on difference than on equality between the sexes. Because the idea of sexual difference has dominated feminist film theory for a long time, I will discuss several related aspects from the perspective of difference. I will first look at the gaze in cinema and then at the female spectator and visual pleasure.

The gaze

Semiotics and psychoanalysis have provided a whole new impetus to a rapidly developing feminist film theory, which until well into the 1980s mainly restricted itself to the analysis of dominant Hollywood cinema. Marxist feminists shifted the attention to film production and to the importance of a film as a product which has to be sold ideologically and commercially. From a semiotic perspective, critics started to look at the crucial role of the film apparatus, such as camera work and editing. From a psychoanalytic perspective, film theorists started to introduce new concepts such as subjectivity, desire and visual pleasure. With these new theoretical approaches the project of feminist film theory changed fundamentally: the focus is no longer so much on the content of a film (what is the meaning of a film?), but on the process of signification (how does a film construct meanings?). In other words: a film is no longer seen as a reflection of a previously given meaning but as a construction of meaning.

Feminist film semioticians examine how sexual difference in a film produces meanings. Chapter 12, on semiotics, will deal more extensively with the impact of semiotics on women's studies; here I will discuss the semiotic analysis of Johnston (1973), which is concerned with the signification of 'woman' in classical cinema. She argues that the female character in cinema is a coded convention: a signifier. The signifier 'woman' only represents its ideological meaning for men. In cinema a woman signifies something in relation to men; in herself she signifies nothing(ness). According to Johnston women are in fact negatively signified as non-men: 'woman as woman' is absent from the film text. This ideological representation of 'Woman' is concealed by the realistic conventions of classical cinema. The film presents the constructed images of femininity as being self-evident and natural. For Johnston this process of signification is a masquerade which excludes and oppresses women in cinema.

The semiotic analysis of the image of woman in cinema still does not explain why women are made into objects nor does it explain cinema's fascination. In order to understand this further, feminist film critics have turned to psychoanalysis. In her influential and much-quoted article, Mulvey (1989/1975) develops a psychoanalytical approach to cinema. The fascination of cinema has to do with what Freud calls *der Schautrieb*; scopophilia, or the desire to look. Traditional cinema stimulates the desire to look by constructing structures of voyeurism and narcissism into the narrative and the image. Looking at a figure as an object produces voyeuristic pleasure, while narcissistic pleasure is produced by identification with the image.

Mulvey reveals how sexual difference functions to structure these two forms of visual pleasure in classical cinema. The traditional narrative structure establishes the omnipotence of the male main character, who actively carries both the look and the action. Narrative, camera work and editing make voyeuristic pleasure exclusively masculine; through the lens of the 'phallic' camera, the spectator in the theatre is sutured to the eyes of the male character in the film. This triple gaze – of spectator, camera and character – controls the female character and makes her into a spectacle; 'to connote to-be-looked-at-ness' (Mulvey, 1989/1975: 19).

Narcissistic pleasure can be understood with the concept of the mirror stage from Lacanian psychoanalysis. Just as a child forms her or his ego by identifying with the perfect mirror image, the spectator's derives pleasure from identification with the more than perfect image of the male film hero; the spectator is eager to identify with that 'more perfect, more complete and more powerful ideal ego' rather than with the distorted image of woman. The complex structure of cinematic ways of looking is usually referred to by the shorthand term 'the (male) gaze'.

As the story progresses in *The Color Purple* the camera perspective lies more frequently with Celie. She captures, as it were, the gaze. At the beginning we often see her through the eyes of the father and of Mr. ——; their male power is enhanced by filming from a relatively high camera angle, thus representing the women as small and defenceless and the men as larger than life. This can be seen, for example, in the scenes of Celie's labour and of the separation of the two sisters. In both cases camera position and movement, lighting and editing are rather rough and exaggerated, producing an eerie or threatening feeling in which the men dominate the screen and the women are reduced to helpless victims. By contrast, in the kissing scene between Celie and Shug cinematic techniques take a more subtle form.

In the corresponding scene in the novel Shug helps Celie to discover her sexuality. She asks her to look at herself 'down there' in a mirror. Celie finds her 'wet rose' very pretty and excitedly explores her naked body in the mirror. Of course, this cannot be shown as graphically as that in a popular film: showing the genital organs would border on pornography. In the film an interesting displacement has taken place. Shug tells Celie to look at herself in the mirror fully dressed up in Shug's red sequined gown. Celie is too shy to look at herself, casting her eyes down and covering her mouth. Shug gently takes away Celie's hand and dares her to laugh at her own reflection in the mirror. Tentatively, Celie starts to smile. Looking at themselves and each other in the mirror, both women open their lips to smile and laugh, finally bursting into a loud and liberating laughter 'because they are beautiful'. Timidly they start kissing each other. The scene ends with the camera discreetly turning away to tinkling chimes, suggesting that the erotic encounter between the women continues. The scene has thus been made perfectly respectable, but it has also lost most of its subversive power. Nevertheless, the displacement from one pair of lips to another, from orgasm to laughter, is quite suggestive. We here see the power of narcissistic identification with the mirror image.

Mulvey develops her analysis of classical cinema still further. From a psychoanalytical point of view, the image of 'woman' produces a problem, because her negative meaning (non-man) constantly reminds the male subject of her lack of a penis, ergo, of castration anxiety. A film can dissolve this threat in two ways. The first way is to link sadism to voyeurism. In that case, the female character is found guilty because of her 'lack' and must be either forgiven or punished. For the female character the film then classically ends in either marriage or death. The second way is the fetishisation of the female character. Fetishism is a psychic structure which simultaneously denies and acknowledges the missing penis by replacing it with a fetish. The fetish is thus a substitute for the absent penis. Thus, fetishisation of the female subject denies sexual difference in disavowing her difference from men. In Hollywood, fetishism takes the shape of the cult of the white female star. The gross exaggeration of femininity distracts attention away from her 'lack'. The threatening danger is converted into a satisfactory object with the help of physical, and fetishised, beauty.

This kind of fetishistic strategy is often seen in the representation of the sexually active female character, such as Shug Avery in *The Color Purple*. The way in which she is filmed in her sequined red dress during a performance at Harpo's place is a good example of the visual strategy of fetishisation; although she is often seen here from Celie's point of view. The scenes added in the film, in which Shug begs her father (a minister!) for forgiveness, are part of a narrative strategy which diminishes the threat of the sexually attractive woman by representing her as guilty. This question of guilt and paternal forgiveness is missing from the novel. Thus, Shug is tamed in the film; she is stripped of her sexual power and brought back into the patriarchal order.

The resisting spectator

Semiotic and psychoanalytical interpretations reveal how classical cinema constructs its meanings through particular representations of sexual difference. It seems that there is very little for the female spectator to enjoy at the cinema. In fact, early feminist film critics saw no other way for feminist film-makers than to disregard those traditional techniques of the cinematic apparatus and to develop the specific aesthetics of feminist experimental film, the 'counter-cinema'. A rather dogmatic view of feminist film practice emerged: experimental cinema was extolled while the more popular narrative women's cinema was maligned. This resulted in a paradox concerning the pleasure of the female spectator: the avant-garde film destroyed traditional visual pleasure along with the narrative structure, while women have always been denied that pleasure in classical cinema. Both theory and practice thus got caught in a polarisation between politics and pleasure.

E. Ann Kaplan (1983) was one of the first to attempt to bridge this opposition in defending the pleasure of the feminist popular film. She argues that the narrative film is much more heterogeneous and more complex than theory would allow for. Feminist cinema should not place itself outside dominant culture, but should instead use traditional filmic means for its own ends. For the time being, most feminist film critics remain distrustful of contemporary popular cinema, while the stream of feminist analyses of classical Hollywood cinema still increases. These readings offer an insight into the veiled ideology of popular cinema.

That insight enables the critical spectator to resist the manipulative power of films. An analysis of the camera work and editing in the film *The Color Purple* reveals the problematic effects of particular scenes

(Diawara, 1988). Take, for example, the shaving sequence. In this long sequence three unrelated scenes are edited parallel with each other: Celie whetting the knife to shave Mr. ——; Shug running through the fields to Celie's house; and a ritual ceremony in Africa. The three events are linked with each other by the sound track of drums and are cross-cut in increasing speed to the stirring rhythm of the African music. As Celie has just found and read Nettie's letters to her, which had been concealed by Mr. ——, the spectator understands that she wants to attack him with the razor. Her gestures are filmed in exactly the same way as the 'barbaric' ritual in Africa, thus suggesting that black people all around the world are linked by the same sort of primitivism. This impression is further strengthened by linking the events with Shug's intuition and fear; she appararently understands Celie's intentions from the rustling of the wind in the trees and runs to the house to stop Celie from cutting Mr. ——'s throat just in time. The film thus represents Africa as a source of evil, instead of emphasising the complex relationship between sexism and racism in the novel, as discussed in other chapters in this book.

Visual pleasure

When the pioneer period of feminist film criticism ended, film theory and film practice were diverging more and more. In breaking down narrative structures and visual pleasure, the artists of experimental women's cinema were creating a deconstructive practice. While feminist film-makers were in fact deconstructionists, theorists continued to focus single-mindedly on classical cinema from the perspective of sexual difference (Penley, 1989). Many feminist analyses of Hollywood movies may, however, also be seen as deconstruction; in feminist film theory the perspectives of difference and deconstruction increasingly run alongside each other.

In the 1980s the question of female subjectivity became increasingly urgent. Because subjectivity is intimately connected with desire, in cinema often represented by ways of looking, the question arizes whether the gaze is inherently male. Can women also have the gaze? How is the female character's desire represented? These questions gradually focused more on the visual pleasure of the female spectator.

The answers to these questions were, in the first instance, rather pessimistic. The standard scenario of classical cinema de-eroticises the female gaze. The female spectator over-identifies with a powerless female subject, whose subjectivity and desires are denied and destroyed over the course of the narrative (Doane, 1987). Therefore, the female spectator is better off if she identifies with the male hero and assumes his gaze (Mulvey, 1989/1975). Even when the new Woman's film from Hollywood offers the gaze to the female character, this does not mean that she also has the power to act on her desire, because a reversal of the gaze between the sexes does not change the underlying power structures (Kaplan, 1983). The difficulties in theorising the female spectator have led Jackie Stacey (1987) to exclaim that feminist film critics have written the darkest scenario possible for the female look as being male, masochist or marginal.

Here we see how much feminist film theories have been caught up in the straitjacket of sexual difference; visual pleasure is exclusively understood in terms of sexual difference. Gertrud Koch (1989) is one of the few feminists who at an early stage recognised that women could also enjoy the image of female beauty on the screen, that is, the vamp, an image exported from Europe into Hollywood cinema. The vamp possesses a free look and provides the female spectator with an image of autonomous femininity. Koch argues that for women, too, their mother functions as a love object in their early childhood and that cinema can appeal to this pleasurable experience. The sexual ambivalence of the vamp, of for example Greta Garbo and Marlene Dietrich (and Shug ...), allows for a homo-erotic pleasure which is not exclusively negotiated through the eyes of men. The vamp's ambiguity refers to the mother as love object and can hence be a source of visual pleasure for the female spectator. The loss of the image of the vamp in cinema means a great loss of possible identifications and visual pleasure for the female audience.

The desire to desire

In the 1980s feminists published many psychoanalytical and semiotic studies on cinema. In *Alice Doesn't*, Teresa de Lauretis (1984) emphasises that subjectivity is not a fixed entity but a process through which the subject re-establishes itself continually. She builds her argument upon a Freudian rereading of narratology, making 'desire' her most important theoretical concept. Telling stories is one of the ways of reproducing subjectivity in any given culture. Each story derives its structure from the subject's desire ('the hero'). Narrative structures are defined by an 'Oedipal' desire: the desire to know origin and end. Sexual desire is intimately bound up with the desire for knowledge, that is, the quest for truth. The desire to solve riddles is a male desire *par excellence*, because the female subject is herself the riddle. 'Woman' *is* the question ('what does woman want?') and can hence not ask the question nor make her desire intelligible.

According to de Lauretis, not only desire but the subject, too, is male by definition, because the obstacle to the realisation of desire is the feminine or because the object of desire is female. In distributing roles and differences, narrative distributes power and positions. Even if a female subject figures in a narrative she always serves male desire. If she survives at all, at the end of the story she appears to have been *his* promise and prize: the destiny of the female subject is to be given away in marriage and to attain motherhood. The (psychoanalytic) narrative of female subjectivity is so cruel as to raise the question of female desire. One of the functions of narrative, de Lauretis argues, is to 'seduce' women into femininity with or without their consent. The female subject is made to desire femininity. Here she comes back to Mulvey's observation on sadism as inherent to narrative. For de Lauretis, then, desire in narrative is intimately bound up with violence against women (see also Smelik, 1993).

According to de Lauretis's theory, traditional film narrative allots the female subject a poor life and an equally pathetic desire. She is in fact a non-subject. In many Woman's films we see that the female character develops from non-subject into a subject. Thus, Celie manages to withdraw herself from all violence inflicted upon her and establish her subjectivity against oppression. In the slow process of becoming an autonomous subject she explores her lesbian sexuality and she establishes her economic independence, although this is hardly emphasised in the film. The film *The Color Purple* represents the enormous change in Celie by one small semiotic sign: when Celie has left Mr. ——, the following shot shows a close-up of a red glove. As the image zooms out we see Celie walking in an elegant black dress with a hat and red gloves. The glove refers to a better social status and the colour red to sexuality and femininity. In a single glance we understand that Celie has established her subjectivity.

Is de Lauretis more optimistic about the other female subject, the female spectator? As yet, hardly. Contrary to earlier feminist film theorists she does not assume that identification is single or simple. In Freudian psychoanalysis, femininity and masculinity are identifications that the subject takes up in a changing relation to desire. She distinguishes two sorts of identification in classical cinema: a visual (the gaze or the image) and a narrative one (narrative movement and closure). Film can thus activate a double identification for the female spectator, which yields her an excess of pleasure. However, de Lauretis interprets this surplus negatively: according to her this is the way in which the female spectator is seduced into identifying with a film in which a female 'non-subject' figures.

In her book on the Hollywood Woman's film in the forties, Doane (1987) studies representations of the female subject in cinema from an orthodox psychoanalytic perspective. Analysing how this classical genre constructs the female gaze, Doane comes to the conclusion that female identification and subjectivity are negatively signified in emotional processes like masochism, paranoia, narcissism and hysteria. In spite of the focus that the Woman's film puts on a female main character, these processes confirm stereotypes about the female psyche. The emotional investments lead to over-identification, destroying the distance to the object of desire and turning the active desire of both the female character and the female spectator into the passive desire to be the desired object. 'The desire to be desired' seems to be, then, the only option for women. It is no wonder that the genre of the Woman's film is called a weepy or a tearjerker. My ever-wet handkerchief indicates that *The Color Purple* also belongs to this tradition, be it one with a happy end.

A new voice

However fascinating feminist film theories may be, they do tell a gloomy story. Therefore, the question of the visual pleasure of the female spectator has become increasingly urgent.

To this end film critics are turning to films made by women. In feminist experimental films, including those by Laura Mulvey, Yvonne Rainer and Chantal Akerman, de Lauretis (1987) recognises ambiguity, heterogeneity, contradiction and paradox as strategies to do justice to the multiplicity of female subjectivity, without emprisoning it once more in the dualistic opposition of sexual difference. Experimental cinematic means produce different subject positions for the spectator. This plural perspective makes it possible to portray differences among women and within women.

When difference is no longer reduced to sexual difference but is also understood as difference among women, representation of an active female desire becomes possible, even in Hollywood films. Jackie Stacey argues (1987) that films like *All About Eve* or *Desperately Seeking Susan* produce narrative desire by the difference between two women; by women wanting to become the idealised other. Many films by women deal with conflicts and mutual fascination between women. The friendship may take on a lesbian aspect, as in the case of Celie and Shug.

The desire of women for each other acquires a theoretical basis in the work of Kaja Silverman. In her critical rereadings of psychoanalysis in *The Acoustic Mirror* (1988), she shifts the focus from the gaze to the voice, which allows for an original perspective on the female subject, awarding a privileged position to the mother. The voice is both physical and discursive, and hence the mother plays a frequently misunderstood but important role in both the pre-Oedipal stage (voice as body) and Oedipal stage (voice as language). The entry into language means the end of the unity between mother and child. Silverman argues that the loss and separation entailed by the acquisition of language lead both the male and female child to desire the mother. The girl then directs her desire to the mother in what is called the negative Oedipus complex. It is important to realise this can only happen after the pre-Oedipal stage, because distance from the mother is necessary for her to become an erotic object for the daughter. It is only after the event of the castration crisis, that is, the dramatic onset of sexual difference, that the girl enters the positive Oedipus complex and learns to direct her desire to the father (see, for a fuller discussion of the Oedipus complex, chapter 13). For the rest of her life the female subject remains split between the desire for the mother and for the father.

In situating the girl's desire for the mother in the negative Oedipus complex, Silverman recuperates female desire for the mother as fully Oedipal, that is to say as being within the symbolic order, within language and signification. This means that the female subject can also represent her desires. A lovely example can be found in one of the first intimate moments between Celie and Shug in the film. While Celie washes and combs Shug's hair in the bath, Shug begins to hum. Later, Shug will turn this melody into the Blues 'Celie's song'. The way in which the women treat each other in the bath scene is reminiscent of a mother–child relationship. However, they can shift positions: Celie mothers Shug in the bath while Shug wraps Celie in 'the acoustic blanket' of her voice. Thus, their contact does not begin with the aloof and objectifying gaze, but with the physical closeness of touch and voice. This intimacy is the beginning of a friendship which later becomes an erotic relationship.

Re-visions

Towards the end of the 1970s there was considerable criticism of the exclusive hegemony of psychoanalysis and semiotics within Anglo-Saxon feminist film theory. One major point of criticism was the universal conception of the subject dictated by psychoanalysis: the tendency to essentialise and universalise categories of 'man' and 'woman' and 'masculinity' and 'femininity'. As long as the female subject cannot be conceived outside the straitjacket of sexual difference it remains impossible to theorise female desire or pleasure. This leads to the paradoxical situation that in theory both the female subject and the pleasure of the female spectator are negatively understood as absence or passivity, while the experience of women in cinema may actually refute this. Moreover, such an ahistorical approach denies not only the practice and context of cinema, it also neglects differences among women – of ethnicity, class, age and sexuality.

Over the last few years we have seen a number of shifts within feminist film theory. Persistent criticism of psychoanalytic theory has come from black feminism for its failure to deal with racial difference. Jane Gaines (1988) is one of the first feminist film critics to point to the erasure of race in theories that are based on the psychoanalytic concept of sexual difference. She argues for an inclusion of black feminist theory and of a historical approach into feminist film theory in order to understand how in cinema gender intersects with race and class.

White film critics have universalised their theories of representations of women, although black women have been excluded from those forms of representation. The signification of the black female as non-human makes black female sexuality the great unknown in white patriarchy, that which is 'unfathomed and uncodified' and yet 'worked over again and again in mainstream culture because of its apparent elusiveness' (Gaines, 1988: 26). The eruptive point of resistance presents black women's sexuality as an even greater threat to the male unconscious than the fear of white female sexuality.

The category of race also problematises the paradigm of the male gaze directed at the female image. The male gaze is not a universal given but negotiated by whiteness: the black man's sexual gaze is socially prohibited. Racial hierarchies in ways of looking have created visual taboos, the neglect of which reflect back on film theory. The racial structures of looking also have repercussions for structures of narrative. Gaines discusses the construction of the black man as rapist, while in times of slavery and long after, it was the white man who raped black women. The historical scenario of interracial rape explains much of the penalty of sexual looking by the black man, who was actually (rather than symbolically) castrated or lynched by white men.

Interventions, such as by Gaines, show that the category of race reveals the untenability of many one-sided beliefs within feminist film theory, and points to the necessity of contextualising and historicising sexual difference. Intersecting theories of sexual difference with those of differences of race and sexual preference, along with ethnicity and class, will eventually make other forms of representation thinkable. As the work of black feminist critics like bell hooks (1990b, 1992 and 1994a) and Michele Wallace (1990, 1993) shows, it will also engender a more diversified theory of female desires and subjectivities and of female spectatorship. For bell hooks, black female spectators do not necessarily identify with either the phallocentric gaze or white womanhood as lack, but they rather 'construct a theory of looking relations where cinematic visual delight is the pleasure of interrogation' (1992: 126). For hooks this is a radical departure from the 'totalizing agenda' of feminist film criticism, and the beginning of an 'oppositional' spectatorship for black women. From the experience of black women as resistant spectators, Michele Wallace also seeks to expand the notion of spectatorship not only as potentially bisexual but also [as] multiracial and multiethnic' (1993: 264).

The primacy of sexual difference has gradually been broken down. Lesbian feminists were among the first to raise objections to the heterosexual bias of feminist film theory. As we have seen, differences between two women enable a play of identification and desire that specifically addresses homosexual pleasures of female spectatorship. In her most recent work, de Lauretis (1991, 1994) explores the possibilities for theoretising the lesbian subject (see also chapter 10). She criticises both Stacey and Silverman for conceiving of desire between women as 'woman-identified female bonding' and failing to see it as sexual. To counter the impossibility of representing lesbian desire and lesbian subjectivity, conditions of representation in cinema have to be changed. Lesbian films that serve up positive images of lesbians in a conventional narrative keep the heterosexual structures intact, rendering lesbian desire invisible. Codes and conventions can be deconstructed by fantasy, dreams or hallucinations, a play of masquerade, or a play of visual images like a film within a film, a video screen or a camera. This creates a distance between reality and representation, and within this gap lesbian desire and subjectivity can be made visible.

Post-modernism

It seems then that the issue of 'difference' has forced feminist film theory to open up to theories and disciplines beyond the paradigms of semiotics and psychoanalysis.

The exclusive focus on classical Hollywood cinema is giving way to more studies on films by women. Here we see a historicising trend in which films are situated in their social context. Lucy Fischer (1989), Judith Mayne (1990) and Sandy Flitterman-Lewis (1990) place women's films in relation to film tradition. These studies shed a new light on the ways in which female film-makers use aesthetic conventions for different ends. For example, many feminist directors self-consciously play on the tradition that has made women into a visual object. In their films they thematise the screen by using mirrors, pictures, painting or video images within the cinematic screen.

The issues of the female spectator and her viewing pleasure continue to dominate most of the agenda of feminist film theory, even though some major shifts in theoretical paradigms occurred towards the end of the eighties. Two collections that are very much dedicated to the pleasures of the female audience, *The Female Gaze* (Gamman and Marshment, 1988) and *Female Spectators* (Pribram, 1988), are indicative of the turn away from psychoanalysis and a turn towards cultural studies. Both books contest the dominance of psychoanalysis in feminist film theory for the same reasons as the lesbian and black critics that I discussed above: the neglect of differences among women.

These criticisms bring the tension between politics and pleasure back into full swing. The neglect of the female spectator either as individual or as a social group has resulted in a feminist endorsement of alternative cinema and simultaneous dismissal of mainstream cinema. Both Gamman & Marshment and Pribram argue that such somewhat dogmatic views reinforce women's exclusion from cultural production and reception and are therefore politically unproductive. Instead, they are interested in how feminists may intervene in mainstream culture and emphasise women's presence in popular culture. It is then to issues surrounding the female audience as historical participants in popular culture that these books address themselves. In other words, they take film and television seriously as a source of pleasure for women. Jacqueline Bobo's article on the reception of *The Color Purple* among black female spectators is a good example of an ethnographic study which foregrounds the possible pleasures of popular culture.

In this turn to cultural studies, increasing importance is also being given to post-modern culture. Sometimes this interest is directed towards avant-garde film and video (Mellencamp, 1990), but more often film critics take popular culture as the object of study: science fiction, for example, (Penley et al., 1991) or the video clip (Kaplan, 1987). According to Kaplan, the video clip is an expression of post-modern culture full of contradictions and ambivalences, not least concerning sexuality. Madonna is a prime example of a pop star who exploits and subverts images of femininity in a staggering succession of masquerades. Post-modern pop stars produce a visual culture which throws set ideas about femininity, masculinity, blackness and whiteness into considerable confusion.

But what exactly is this post-modernism? Post-modernism can be understood as a historical condition: it is the complex and often contradictory culture of post-industrial society. Kaplan (1988) argues that two post-modern cultural practices coexist: a utopian post-modernism developed from feminist and post-structuralist theory; and a commercial or annexed post-modernism, closely linked to hi-tech capitalism. What both post-modern practices have in common is a tendency to transcend the Western tradition of binary thought. They also share the lost ideal of the unified subject. The deconstruction of oppositions, and the deconstruction of a universal subject, i.e. the white middle-class heterosexual male, together form the utopian aspect of post-modernism for feminist and anti-racist theory.

Feminist film theory has provided an insight into the way in which femininity and masculinity, whiteness and blackness are represented in film and other visual media. These insights may assist the female spectator in the interpretation of these representations. Thus, she can see how the subversive power of the novel *The Color Purple* melts away in the film in the teardrops of the happy end, in the smoothing over of lesbian love and in the trivialisation of Celie's economic independence. Insights from feminist film theory also show how traditional representations of femininity (may) change. The female spectator thus learns to look at new representations of femininity in cinema and on television in a critical manner, but with political involvement and with pleasure.

Looking, the gaze of the female spectator, is also central to feminist theatre studies. For the deconstruction of femininity on the stage we will now put the spotlight on Clytemnestra, Antigone, Dora, Cecilia and many others.

Literature for further study

Bad Object Choices (ed.) (1991) *How Do I Look? Queer Film and Video*. Theoretical and political reflections on lesbian and homosexual representation, with critical attention being paid to ethnicity.

Carson, Diane, Linda Dittmarr, and Janice R. Welsch (eds) (1994) *Multiple Voices in Feminist Film Criticism*. Anthology with focus on the practice of international feminist cinema, including black and 'third world' cinema. One part of the book is dedicated to thematic 'course files'.

Erens, Patricia (ed.) (1990) *Issues in Feminist Film Criticism*. Anthology of the most important articles by feminist film theorists. With many classics, including Johnston and Mulvey.

Haskell, Molly (1987 revised edition; original 1973) *From Reverence to Rape: The Treatment of Women in the Movies*. Easy, readable classic. Illustrates the concept of equality in feminist film criticism. Sociological approach to women in cinema with many sweeping statements.

hooks, bell (1990b) *Yearning*, (1992) *Black Looks*, and (1994a) *Outlaw Culture*. In short and readable essays the author discusses the representation of femininity and masculinity in relation to colour in cinema and popular culture.

Kaplan, E. Ann (1983) *Women and Film: Both Sides of the Camera*. Accessible work of reference. Clear explanation of semiotics and psychoanalysis. Discusses the representation of women in both classical Hollywood cinema and feminist cinema.

Kaplan, E. Ann (1987) *Rocking Around the Clock: Music Television, Postmodernism and Consumer Culture*. Good introduction to the post-modern phenomenon of the video clip. Deals with the way in which different genres establish or suvbert traditional representations of femininity and masculinity within the video clip.

Kuhn, Annette (1982) *Women's Pictures: Feminism and Cinema*. Like Kaplan (1983), a good introduction to feminist film theory. Clear explanation of semiotics, psychoanalysis and deconstruction. Examines Hollywood and feminist cinema.

Lauretis, Teresa de (1984) *Alice Doesn't: Feminism, Semiotics, Cinema*. A (difficult) work of reference, which lays a philosophical basis for feminist film theory.

Lauretis, Teresa de (1987) *Technologies of Gender: Essays on Theory, Film and Fiction*. Interdisciplinary study of feminist cultural criticism.

Silverman, Kaja (1988) *The Acoustic Mirror: The Female Voice in Psychoanalysis and Cinema*. Theoretical work of reference. Revision of psychoanalysis in relation to cinema, with special attention to the mother–daughter relationship.

Journals

The oldest and best-known feminist film journal is the German journal *Frauen und Film*. *Camera Obscura: A Journal of Feminism and Film Theory* features articles from semiotic and psychoanalytic perspectives, and also postmodernism and cultural studies. Feminist articles on cinema, video and television appear regularly in the film journals *Jump Cut*, *Wide Angle* and the authoritative *Screen*.

7
Women in the limelight: feminist theatre studies

MIEKE VAN SCHERMBEEK

Introduction

> Women have burnt like beacons in the works of all the poets from the beginning of time – Clytemnestra, Antigone, Cleopatra, Lady Macbeth, Phèdre, Cressida, Rosalind, Desdemona, the Duchess of Malfi, among the dramatists. ... Indeed, if woman had no existence save in the fiction written by men, one would imagine her a person of the utmost importance; very various; heroic and mean; splendid and sordid; infinitely beautiful and hideous in the extreme; as great as a man, some people think even greater. But this is woman in fiction. (Virginia Woolf, *A Room of One's Own*, 1945: 44–5)

The relatively new discipline of theatre studies was initially conceived of as a historical discipline. Within the dominant view of theatre studies as the history of drama, feminist critics have at first aimed at re-interpreting historical material from a woman's perspective. As well as reinterpretating historical sources and drama texts, feminist drama critics have developed a critique of the theoretical underpinnings of theatre studies.

Theatre is concerned with different types of text which can be an object of study, both individually and in relation to each other: printed texts, which can be read as literature; the text the director reads as a preparation for rehearsals; the text the actors use; the 'text' the audience receives when seeing the performance.

From the moment a director takes up her or his work, the printed text is transformed into a theatrical text, that is to say a different sign system is employed in order to stage the producton received by the audience. The final production is largely determined not only by the written text but also by the way in which the text is spoken and visualised. This visualisation comes about in a chosen space with the help of decor and setting, props, lights, make-up, costumes or masks, the actions performed by actors, gestures and facial expression. By including all these different sign systems, meanings can be suggested to the viewer. Each sign can be analysed with regard to the way in which it represents gender. Thus, at present feminist theatre studies has emerged as having two aims: on the one hand a study of the meanings that have been assigned to femininity in drama throughout the ages; on the other hand, a study of new signs and meanings of femininity in contemporary productions by women.

Just like feminist critique in other disciplines within the humanities, the development of feminist theatre studies can be outlined according to three lines of approach, from which the signs and meanings of femininity can be explored. The first framework is characterised by the struggle for equality between the sexes and here the focus lies on the various signs of the oppression of women in the world of theatre. The second framework is concerned with the difference between the sexes and with representing what is specifically female on the stage. In the third framework, feminists concentrate on the deconstructive analysis of the ways in which masculinity and femininity are represented on the stage.

In the light of equality

Feminist research within theatre studies is initially based on all kinds of historical material. From the outset, feminist theatre historians have concentrated on the representation of women in classic drama texts. Drama texts are taken to be a source of information about real life. The position of women in a particular historical period would be read from the drama texts. Thus the characterisation of figures such as Medea or Antigone and the description of their life circumstances is supposed to convey information about the prevailing conditions for powerful women in ancient Greece.

The work of male authors of all important periods – Aeschylus, Sophocles, Shakespeare, Calderon, Molière, Corneille, Ibsen, Strindberg and Brecht – has been analysed from a socio-economic point of view for data about the society in which they lived. These data were then compared with documents about laws, social practices and economic restrictions imposed on women. These sources revealed a privileging of public life. Accordingly data about private life remained relatively invisible. It is no coincidence that the private is mostly a female sphere whereas public life is dominated by men. Sue-Ellen Case relates this difference to the distinction between fact and fiction. The split between public and private is expressed by the split between the lives of 'real' women and the representation of 'woman' on the stage:

> As a result of the suppression of real women, the culture invented its own representation of the gender, and it was this fictional 'Woman' who appeared on the stage, in myths and in the plastic arts, representing the patriarchal values attached to the gender while suppressing the experiences, stories, feelings and fantasies of actual women. (Case, 1988: 6-7).

Throughout the ages female main characters have populated the stage as projections of a male fantasy. Many famous women's names – Clytemnestra, Electra, Iphigenia, Penthesilea, Andromache, Cleopatra, Lady Macbeth, Rosalind, Desdemona, the Duchess of Malfi, the Dame aux Camélias, Nora, Hedda Gabler, Miss Julie, Lulu, Salomé and Mother Courage – fill the pages of the great works of the history of drama. But, according to Case, these male-produced fictions have little or nothing to do with historical women.

The history of theatre provides a fascinating illustration of the discrepancy between fiction and reality with respect to the status and position of women. Until the seventeenth century women were banned from the stage and female characters were played by men. In the eyes of feminist theatre historians the classical theatrical convention, which excluded women from the possibility of giving form to their own fantasies, has made the world of the stage an accomplice to the oppression of women. Since her appearance on the stage the actress has had to fight her suspect reputation more than her male colleagues. Until the end of the nineteenth century the term 'actress' was more or less synonymous with whore. As a rule women were paid less and there were and are still too few roles for women, especially for older women.

This historical legacy causes feminist critics on the one hand to question the socio-economic, political and religious motivations for the exclusion of women, as well as the motivation for their return to the stage at the end of the sixteenth century. On the other hand they wonder about the implications of exclusion for the representation of femininity on the stage. Thus the effect of specific forms of classic drag, men playing women's roles, is an object of study. One such study examines the significance of classic drag for femininity in ancient Greece, the Shakespearean period and the contemporary post-modern stage (Herrmann, 1989).

The historical exclusion of women from the world of theatre can still be found in the relative absence of women in contemporary theatre production. The difficulty of creating theatrical productions of women and/or by women is not only restricted to the history of theatre. In the search for dramatic texts by female authors, only a few names and texts have survived history to the mid-twentieth century: the medieval nun Hrotsvitha von Gandersheim; a small group of female comedy writers from the English Restoration period, including the fairly well-known Aphra Behn; the seventeenth-century Spanish female writer Sor Juana Ines de la Cruz and the eighteenth-century American dramatist Mercy Warren.

Dutch feminist theatre critics have rediscovered a group of Dutch female dramatists who between 1900 and 1940 produced a large number of texts which were staged. These plays were written in the tradition of Ibsen's realism with a certain ambivalence concerning contemporary feminism. In the years around the turbulent fight for women's suffrage, women writers highlighted themes such as the dependency of married women before the law, the choice of a life as an unmarried working woman and the possibility of divorce. The happiness of the female main characters depends on their choice of the right partner. For well-to-do middle-class circles, marriage is the arena within which the fate of women is decided. Such sporadic research has as yet been able to make few changes to the dominant view of the canon of drama texts. Judith Graves Miller concludes with regard to France:

> Throughout the 'grand' theatrical tradition in France, the producing, writing, or originating voice of the text has primarily been male. Major women playwrights appeared only after World War II. And there has not yet been a re-evaluation of the canon which has discovered or recuperated lost women playwrights whose interest can be termed other than 'socio-historical.' (Graves Miller, 1989: 5)

This study of women writers of the past was temporarily buried under the torrent of contemporary theatre productions which occurred internationally since the 1970s. Not until the 1990s did interest in the cultural heritage left by women authors from the past revive.

In the period after 1968 political theatre emerged and flourished. Class struggle was the starting point, which resulted in spotlighting 'working people' in experimental theatre, so-called social-cultural theatre. Feminists promoted the discussion of the relationship between class struggle and women's struggles. In all possible areas of society which the 'engagé' socio-cultural theatre addressed, the central problem was whether class equality would automatically lead to social equality for women. The history of social struggle had already revealed that equal entitlement for women never came automatically. Socialist feminism has drawn its conclusions from this historical lesson and has developed its own political programme.

Women working within this socio-cultural theatre of the 1970s launched the 'anti-patriarchal' struggle in their politically oriented programmes. Feminist theatre activists sought to express feminist themes on the stage: abortion, rape, the inequality between men and women in the nuclear family. They took and adapted the forms of improvising on the basis of their own experience, not only from political theatre, but also from the practice of feminist consciousness-raising. They also shifted the location of the productions away from the stage into the streets, society and especially into women's centres, which were mushrooming at the time. Although women's productions were initially received with enthusiasm, at the beginning of the 1980s an increased resistance emerged against such relentless feminist realism and the consequent stereotypical and humourless image of woman as a victim. Therefore new feminist theatre groups unsevered the link between feminism and realism and looked for new theatrical forms which problematised solidarity by exploring the differences among women.

How would an equality-minded feminist theatre director adapt the novel *The Color Purple* by Alice Walker for the stage? The novel consists of a long series of events which cover almost the whole life of the main character. With regard to time alone it is impossible to maintain a similar sequence of events on the stage. Thus for an adaptation a selection of a small number of scenes has to be made, in which the great volume of information about the course of the life of the heroine, Celie, is condensed into single crucial moments. In the light of the pursuit of equality, feminist theatre criticism would probably lay the emphasis on the oppression of black women. Therefore the playwright would choose scenes such as the rape of Celie by her stepfather; her exploitation by her husband with the double burden of care for his children and work on the land, and the acquisition of an independent existence through sewing trousers. These text ingredients could easily acquire a Marxist tone, by which means Celie's individual struggle comes to stand for the collective struggle of the oppressed.

Because feminist theatre criticism from this pioneer phase considers the stage to be a reflection of a socio-historical reality, the adapted drama text would be given a realistic form using theatrical media. Different sign systems would be used to emphasise the socio-historical framework of the story. From this perspective, the feminist theatre director would explore how decor, lighting, costumes, actors' movements and phrasings could express the changes in the life of a black woman living in the South of the United States before and after World War II.

From the perspective of difference

The shift in perspective within feminist theory, from equality between men and women to a greater emphasis on and appreciation of the difference between the sexes, goes hand in hand with the shift in literary theory from author to text. Whereas in the first stage of the feminist history of theatre works of authors were read in the light of socio-economic data about life in their time, in the second stage the focus has been shifted to the different meanings of femininity in the text (the term 'text' refers to both the drama text and the whole of the semiotic signs of the performance).

Not only the traditional repertory theatre but also feminists in theatre attempt, through ever-changing interpretations, to give new meanings to heroines from tragedies, comedies and conventional drama. This confrontation with theatre leads feminist theatre critics to question the way in which traditional representations can provide examples of independent, intelligent and even heroic women. What strategies are indicated in the text or developed within the theatrical tradition in order to finally tame the shrew? What is changed in the meaning of a female figure when an actress appears in women's roles originally written to be played by men? Can new meanings and subversive intentions be created in these roles by the introduction of the female body and the female voice? (Showalter, 1985). Or are the Medeas and Antigones of the theatre of ancient Greece and the Rosalinds and Cleopatras of Shakespeare caricatures of femininity, and should they again be played by men in order to emphasise the fact that classical roles are a form of 'classic drag'? (Case, 1985).

New theoretical impulses from semiotics and psychoanalysis are giving rise to a growing dissatisfaction with traditional theatrical conventions. These theories enable feminist critics, such as Janelle Reinelt (1989), to conceptualise gender as a convention. Next to an analysis of theatrical conventions and representations of gender, the perspective of 'difference' encourages a discussion of the absence of the female voice and the female body in a male-dominated theatrical fiction. Feminist critics examine plays by contemporary women authors in which the absence of the female voice is problematised. In plays like *The Singular Life of Albert Nobbs* by Simone Benmussa and *India Song* by Marguerite Duras, the female main character appears on stage without speaking. She is talked about by off-stage voices, which give form to male desire (Diamond, 1985). This approach (the representation of the female as a construction of male fantasy) has the result that feminist theatre exists solely on the basis of negation.

Hélène Cixous achieved a breakthrough in the looming impasse for feminist theatre. In *The Laugh of the Medusa* she calls on women to write: 'woman must write woman' (1976: 877) as the ultimate possibility for change. For theatre, she is the most important example of *écriture féminine*. The feminine writing that Cixous advocates is not simple or straightforward but ambiguous and polyvocal. The language of women knows no formal boundaries: 'Her language does not contain, it carries; it does not hold hold back, it makes possible' (1976: 889).

This writing style can be found in Cixous's drama text *Portrait of Dora* (1983). As studied in more detail in Chapter 13 on psychoanalysis, this play is a feminist rereading of Freud's famous case study of Dora, as described in his *Fragment of an Analysis of a Case of Hysteria* (1905a). In her text Cixous interweaves two layers: the therapeutic discussions between Dora and Freud, and Dora's dreams, memories and fantasies. Cixous deconstructs the patriarchal discourse of psychoanalysis and gives the 'hysteric' her own female voice. *Portrait of Dora* is a good example of the way in which feminists approach sexual difference by representing the feminine positively.

The writing style of *écriture féminine* requires a completely different form on the stage from the usual realistic one. The theatrical media must be in harmony with the feminine style of the drama text. For feminist theatre critics this means that they must look for a theoretical set of instruments in order to be able to analyse the new forms of feminine imagination. Under the influence of semiotics, psychoanalysis and deconstruction, the focus is shifted to the structure of dramatic narratives. Feminist critics look for the effects of fragmentation and repetition on the representation of the feminine, and for theatrical means for giving expression to the ambiguity of the meaning of femininity on stage. This can take the form of doubling roles for example or of allowing a character to be played by two or more actresses. Thus the representation does justice to the complexity of the female character when compared with the unambiguous character fabricated by Freud.

Just as Cixous rewrote Freud's text, a feminist playwright could rewrite *The Color Purple* from the perspective of difference. She might select scenes from the novel in which femininity is given specific representation. The emphasis would then lie on moments in which women share experiences with each other and give expression to the physicality of those experiences: Celie, who with her own body protects her sister from abuse by her stepfather and husband; Sofia supporting her sisters and using her physical power to protect herself against the attempts to subject her of her man, Harpo; the erotic power of Shug's voice; Shug and Celie's discovery of sexual pleasure in her love for Shug. In such a performance the emphasis would lie on details, such as the women stitching together a quilt or Celie washing and combing Shug's hair. The decor is stripped of any form of realism in order to indicate with minimal means the limited space women are given to speak. All theatrical means are used to highlight language; the performance should enact the linguistic transition between the narrated events and the experiences performed in dialogue. Remembering Cixous's words, the actress should invest completely in her voice and 'it's with her body that she vitally supports the 'logic' of her speech. Her flesh speaks true' (1976: 881). It is the language that counts, the language of the exchange between women, the language of body and gesture (Wilson, 1989).

With an eye to deconstruction

The approaches of equality and difference developed within early feminist theatre studies were to be found throughout the 1980s in women's theatre. In theatre, feminists still reinterpret the myths and images of women, as in experimental representations of Medea or in reinterpretations of works by Strindberg, Lorca, Shakespeare and Chekhov. They also explore the representation of women's worlds through the works of female authors, such as Djuna Barnes, Jane Bowles, Katherine Mansfield, Dorothy Parker and Christa Wolf. Others have performed drama texts by writers like Yourcenar, Sarraute, Duras, Jelinek and Churchill.

This stream of feminist productions, often developed in close connection with theatre studies, requires a broader set of tools in methods and theories if they are to be analysd as new forms of female representation. The connection between language and body, as is assumed by the thinkers of *écriture féminine*, presupposes a particular conceptualisation of the female gender, a view which has been criticised for its essentialism. That is to say that difference-minded feminists could too easily overlook the economic and socio-historical conditions which determine the way in which men and women are written into cultural processes.

Studies of the socio-historical situation of the significance of sexual difference, or in other words, the deconstruction of sexual difference, heralds a third direction in feminist theatre studies. New studies involve analysing how femininity (and masculinity) are represented in theatre. These studies consult other disciplines: from anthropology and sociology the idea of 'gender' as a construction of sex is borrowed; narratology provides the tools for an analysis of the structure of dramatic narrative; for the analysis of the performance and of identification processes film theories are studied; post-structuralism offers deconstructive ways of reading.

Where formerly feminist criticism assumed that it knew what a woman is, yet rejected specific representations of women on stage, now the signifier 'woman' is questioned. 'At this point, the entire gender-category "woman" is under feminist semiotic deconstruction', writes Case (1988: 118).

The acquired theoretical baggage allows theatre critics to analyse how the codes in the main and additional text of a play represent particular conceptions of femininity. (The 'main text' is the dialogue between the characters; the 'additional text' is all the remaining text such as the title, scene classification, instructions about the characters, stage directions.) They analyse the theatrical conventions which give form to the stage codes in the acting style, costume, make-up, gestures and phrasings of the characters. These studies demonstrate that the distinction between male and female is defined not only by sex-specific codes, but also by codes of class, sexual preference, race and ethnicity. All these codes can conflict with each other in the construction of one character.

The analysis of the signifier 'woman' presupposes a reciprocal process of coding, that is, the production of meaning in the text and performance, and decoding, that is, the deciphering of codes by reading the text and watching the performance. Studies of the interaction between coding and decoding have brought about a shift of focus from the author or the text to reception by the reader or spectator. The idea behind this shift is that a text or performance has no meaning as long as it is not read or seen. Reception is considered to be a process in which meaning is gradually produced on the basis of an arrangement or rearrangement of the signs in the text or performance. These signs can guide reception.

In order to study these mechanisms in the text, feminist theatre critics have turned to narratology (Bal, 1985). For example, one can analyse a process of focalisation: how the text produces a vision *of* and a vision *on* the female character. One of the problems with this kind of analysis has to do with the difference between plays and novels. In novels, focalisation is presented to the reader by a narrator. Plays do not usually have a narrator, although the events and the characters are focalised to a certain extent. Focalisation is produced by an interplay between the different levels of narrativity, such as the additional text, the segmentation into scenes, and the information in dialogues and monologues by characters intended to inform not each other but the audience.

The spectator's reception is also guided by certain mechanisms in the performance. In order to analyse these, feminist theatre critics rely on film theories about 'the gaze', as explained in Chapter 6. On the stage, just as in films, different sign systems, such as lighting, foregrounding, the address of speeches, the looks and actions of characters, are embedded in order to control the gaze. But the most important instruments in the organisation of the gaze in cinema are technical film processes, such as camera work and editing, and these cannot be deployed on the stage. Although theatre and cinema are not completely comparable in this respect, it can generally be assumed that in theatre, just as in other media, the organisation of the gaze serves male pleasure; the representation of women is considered to be an image seen through the eyes of men. Whenever a female character makes her stage entrance she is observed by the audience as if seen through the eyes of the male protagonist. The combination of her presence, her costume and the lighting is designed with the aim of emphasising her as the object of his desire.

These kinds of theatrical codes and conventions contribute to a form of identification on the part of the spectator. The degree of identification also determines viewing pleasure. This information brings feminist film and theatre critics to the question of female pleasure. What pleasure does the female spectator experience in identifying with a passive object of male desire? Is identification gender-specific, that is to say, can women identify only with female characters or does their imagination allow them the freedom to change in identifications between male and female main characters? What does the possibility for changing identification depend on? These questions highlight the broad spectrum which the perspective of deconstruction has opened up for further research by feminist theatre studies.

Purple Blues

The Dutch-Surinamese writer Astrid Roemer has made an adaptation of *The Color Purple* with the title *Purple Blues*.[1] This drama text illustrates the multiplicity of codes by which femininity can be represented on stage. Roemer has written a one-act play in the form of a monologue around the female main character Celie, called Cecilia in this version.

Roemer has chosen the moment in the novel where Celie has returned to the house of her birth as the point-of-attack (the moment at which the dramatic action begins). This occurs towards the end of the story. Roemer has used this by representing the life history of the main character as being fragmented into scraps of memories which disturb the chronology of the story, alternated with reflections on the here and now of her life, and with work on the sewing machine. This fragmentation of her life story offers the possibility of representing the character from a constantly changing perspective. Thus it is impossible for the audience to construct an unambiguous image of Cecilia from the surplus of the information provided. This version incorporates different semiotic signs which give meaning to the female character. Signs of the socio-economic past are embodied in 'my sister in Africa', for black slaves in America a symbol of the return to the motherland; in the narrative about Sofia and the mayor's wife and her situation in prison and her period in service thereafter; and in the recurrent memories of the moment when Shug inspired her to start sewing trousers. Signs of her sexual preference recur repeatedly in Cecilia's expressions of love and jealousy for her lover Shug. Roemer introduces an ethnic dimension with reference to Surinamese customs, a contemporary touch in a performance for a Dutch audience.

Roemer allows Cecilia to describe herself in a recurring refrain: 'I have a house, I have a trade, I have a husband, I have a woman lover, I have a son, I have a daughter – and most of all you are there my sister.' This multi-layered representation of the female character undermines any unambiguous meanings which may be attached to the feminine. Cecilia acts both in the private and the public sphere; she takes up positions of both heterosexuality and homosexuality, of mother and sister.

One can highlight different aspects of feminist theatre studies in its many phases of development. In any case, the representation of women and of femininity on stage are in the limelight, but from different angles and perspectives. As we have seen, feminist theatre critics alternatively direct the spotlights on a reflection of historical reality, a representation of that which is absent and a deconstruction of the feminine.

Note

1. Astrid Roemer adapted *The Color Purple* at the request of the Dutch-Surinam actress Orsyla Meinzak. The première took place under the direction of Rufus Colllins at the Stagedoor Festival in 1985. This adaptation, *Purple Blues*, has not been published, but a handwritten version may be read in the library of the Netherlands Theatre Institute in Amsterdam. I thank Babs Boter for drawing my attention to her archival discovery.

Literature for further study

Case, Sue-Ellen (1988) *Feminism and Theatre*. This book provides an overview of developments in feminist theatre studies.

Case, Sue-Ellen (ed.) (1990) *Performing Feminisms: Feminist Critical Theory and Theatre*. This anthology contains a large number of articles from *Theatre Journal* about lesbian representation, class and ethnicity, and the construction of gender in the portrayal of female characters by men. The book contains, inter alia, the articles by Elin Diamond, 'Refusing the Romanticism of Identity: Narrative Interventions in Churchill, Benmussa, Duras' (1985) and Anne Herrmann, 'Travesty and Transgression: Transvestism in Shakespeare, Brecht and Churchill' (1989).

Dolan, Jill (1988) *The Feminist Spectator as Critic*. A lucid book about the way in which feminists look at theatre. Dolan examines questions about the canon, the male gaze and female aesthetics. She briefly discusses *Portrait of Dora* by Cixous.

Hart, Lynda (ed.) (1989) *Making a Spectacle: Feminist Essays on Contemporary Women's Theatre*. A useful collection of essays on contemporary feminist, mainly American, drama texts. Articles on metaphors, voyeurism, masquerade and the relationship between women and post-modernism in performance art.

Lauretis, Teresa de (1984) *Alice Doesn't: Feminism, Semiotics, Cinema*. The chapter 'Desire in Narrative' is of great importance for a feminist critique of narratology and psychoanalysis, as well as of the identification process of the female spectator.

Modern Drama (vol. 32, no. 1). A special issue on women in theatre. Includes articles by Janelle Reinelt, 'Feminist Theory and the Problem of Performance', and Judith Graves Miller, 'Contemporary Women's Voices in French Theater'.

Journals

Women and Performance, New York: Department of Performance Studies, New York University. This journal, which appears irregularly, has a specific focus on feminist studies of theatre and other types of performance.

8

How purple can purple be? Feminist art history

MIRIAM VAN RIJSINGEN

Introduction

The central question for the feminist art historian is the ways in which meanings are (re)produced in works of art and in art history. Or: how can a woman artist create new images of femininity out of existing forms of representation? And how can the feminist art historian write a different art history within the present paradigms?

Those critical questions of feminist art historians should break open the closeted world of art history in order to allow new art histories to emerge. Therefore it is better to speak of feminist interventions in art history than of a feminist art history. In the course of twenty years feminist art historians have written quite a few new 'stories'. Feminist artists and critics have become visible through happenings, exhibitions, documents and research. They have intervened successfully in many (but as yet not all) art history institutions. Research has shifted from the quest for forgotten women artists to feminist art criticism of the traditional object of art history, the artist and his work. The critical gaze has moved to the mechanisms operating in art history as an academic discipline.

Why are there no great women artists?

Linda Nochlin's article, 'Why Have There Been No Great Women Artists?' (1973) is considered to be the genesis of feminist art history. Nochlin was not the first to look at art from a political point of view, but she was really the first to pose a crucial academic question about art history which implies more than a search for forgotten women artists. She outlined three lines of study for a possible answer to her question of why there have been no great woman artists in history.

First, Nochlin proposes to promote studies of forgotten women artists on a large scale, so as to rehabilitate their work and rewrite art history accordingly. This kind of research has been going on for quite a while, but according to Nochlin is likely to come to a dead end because the reasons for the exclusion from the canon have been neglected. Therefore structural questions about the concepts of *art* and *history* are not being raised. She warns of the negative effect of research that has not been fundamentally thought through.

Second, studies are being made of the difference between women and men artists, women's and men's worlds. The articulation of the female experience is the most important paradigm in this kind of research. When Nochlin's article appeared, discussions concerning a specific female art and aesthetics were just beginning to get under way. On this point Nochlin is somewhat hesitant. Even though she agrees that the social situation and position of women differs from that of men, as do their experiences, she is wary of the danger of essentialism. When comparing artistic works by women through history, Nochlin sees no 'subtle essence of femininity'. She dismisses the assumption of a female essence in art as fundamentally ahistoric. In her view, femininity is an effect of socialisation. Consequently, Nochlin does notice differences in the choice of subject by male and female artists but that difference can and should be studied in its historical context. According to Nochlin there is a prevalent structural misconception about art:

> The problem lies not so much with the feminists' concept of what femininity in art is, but rather with a misconception of what art is: with the naïve idea that art is the direct, personal expression of individual emotional experience – a translation of personal life into visual terms. Yet art is almost never that; great art certainly never. The making of art involves a self-consistent language of form, more or less dependent upon, or free from, given temporally-defined conventions, schemata, or systems of notation, which have to be learned or worked out, through study, apprenticeship, or a long period of individual experimentation. (Nochlin, 1973: 5)

Nochlin cannot see the production of art and art history as anything other than a contextual process.

This takes her to the third line of research: the study of the conditions of the production of art. Art and the world of art have been dominated by white men – not only with regard to institutions (museums, art academies and universities), but most of all with regard to the concepts which operate in art and art historiography. She then points to the great role of the nineteenth-century concept of *genius* – the mysterious essence of the Great Artist. This concept, which has appeared in texts about art since the Romantic movement, distinguishes the creative artist from ordinary people. It marks him out as god-like or as a gifted visionary and places him above and beyond everyday life.

As if the genius were a truly autonomous subject on a solitary mountain top.

All descriptions of these mythical qualities of the artist as a genius refer exclusively to the middle-class, white, male subject. Within this view a woman cannot be a genius, nor anybody with a different ethnicity that white. Therefore, from this perspective there can be no great women artists nor can there be great black artists. It is important for feminists to analyse this context. As Nochlin puts it, they need to unmask and expose the romantic, elitist, individual-glorifying and monograph-producing structure of art history.

Forgotten women artists and the canon

The three lines of study which Nochlin had set out at an early stage developed further within feminist art history: the quest for women artists; the study of the feminine in art; and a critique of the discourse of art history as a discipline.

From the perspective of equality between men and women, a search has been initiated for forgotten and undervalued women artists in order to change the one-sided picture of the history of art. The motive behind this historical research is the idea that the work by women artists should be given just as much social and cultural recognition as that of men: Judith Leijster (1609–61) just as much as Frans Hals; Angelica Kauffmann (1741–1807) just as much as other members of the Royal Academy; and Suze Robertson (1855–1922) just as much as Vincent van Gogh. Making women artists and their work visible raises the question of how they should to be situated historically: within the canon or outside it as a separate women's history? The tendency has initially been to admit women artists and their work into standard history. This results in historical overviews like the book *Women Artists: Recognition and Reappraisal* by Peterson and Wilson (1976); in catalogues such as *Künstlerinnen der Russische Avantgarde* (Cologne, 1979) and monographs on the work of women artists like Paula Modersohn-Becker (Perry, 1979) and Käthe Kollwitz (Kearns, 1976).

More and more studies are appearing and exhibitions are being organised about and by women artists. This mostly stems from the dissatisfaction with the under-representation of female artists in large overview exhibitions and books. Women artists have been made visible, but mainly within feminist historian circles and for a mainly female public. However, the results of these empirical studies did not automatically bring about changes within the established history of art. Many of these studies failed to question their relation to canonised history.

Equality between female and male artists cannot be expected without contextualising gender and the mechanisms of exclusion from the canon.

This type of critical studies by women is beginning to take off. Feminist art historians are starting to analyse the stereotypical representation of women in art. For example, studies have appeared on the *femme fatale* in art and the objectivisation and fragmentation of the female body in twentieth-century art (Kingsbury, 1973; and Berger and Hammer Tugendhat, 1985). The critics conclude that these images have nothing to do with real women, but are fantasies of male artists.

Françoise d'Eaubonne (1977) attempts the beginning of an answer to the question of why the number of women artists in history is proportionally inverse to the number of representations of women. She contends that the category of gender is much more structural than class. Following Simone de Beauvoir, she stresses the process of the socialisation into femininity and the consequent powerlessness of women. This powerlessness extends not only to women artists as living beings but also to women in their function as symbols, as signs.

Renate Berger (1982) studies the opportunities for female artists in the socio-cultural field of the nineteenth century. Berger concludes that female artists are always considered as women first. Their gender determines the limits of their opportunities. Because of their gender women have to deal with the generally accepted antithesis of dilettantism and professionalism, and as women they 'naturally' belong to the former. On the one hand this is a result of the fact that women artists are given fewer opportunities for training than men. A crucial component of academic training, the life class with a nude model, was forbidden territory for women artists until the end of the nineteenth century.

The stereotypical images of the female nature restrict women artists' opportunities. In the nineteenth century the idea of specific male and female characteristics prevailed. One of those female characteristics was that women could display their creative activity only within the domestic sphere. Feminine craftwork was seen as a woman's natural aesthetic field and that marked her out by definition as a dilettante in the field of great art. Until the twentieth century these kinds of views about an active male and a passive female function dominated the field of art. It is remarkable, though, that just as women artists were becoming active such writings on the essential nature of femininity began to appear.

A critical rereading of the origins of art is an excellent way of coming to understand the mechanisms of exclusion, not as natural facts, but as constructions of a particular discourse. Studies like those by Berger and d'Eaubonne show how art historical discourse is constructed, especially in the nineteenth century, and how a feminist interpretation of historical sources can expose this discourse to be a hierarchical and dualistic construction of so-called facts. Thus art history 'facts' can be seen in a completely different light.

The feminine

As a result of the rediscovered work of women artists and alongside the attempts to admit art by women into the canon, studies are also being made of the specifically female in art.

Since the beginning of the 1970s, feminist artists have been organised in collectives and feminist critics have written articles about a new female – and feminist – aesthetic. In this respect the American text *From the Center* (1976) by Lucy Lippard is a reference book. She and others postulate the difference of female experience. This female experience brings new contents into art, such as a new view on the female body, on the household and on men. The female (body) is related to a different visual language: labyrinthine, flowing, round/spherical, chaotic. The choice of material and treatment is also different.

By illuminating particular forms of female craftwork and female techniques as forgotten, other, but no lesser, forms of art, feminist critics blur the hierarchy between 'high' and 'low' art. Quilting is a good example. Quilts are seen as art works which are unjustly banned from museums (Parker, 1984; Parker and Pollock, 1981).

Women also developed a democratic way of collaborating in projects, such as the *Woman-house* project of 1971, in which a group of women artists put together an 'environment' around everyday female experiences. The enormous production by women artists also has the function of breaking down old, stereotypical images of women and developing new images. Another well-known example is *The Dinner Party* (1979) by Judy Chicago, in which she has worked for years with a large group of people on a joint project to honour women from the past in a work of art in the form of a set dinner table. The plates are inspired by vaginal and clitoral forms.

In the 1970s the personal was political and thus personal accounts and diaries by women artists were published, of which the best-known is Judy Chicago's *Through the Flower* (1977). These give an insight into the struggle which women artists had to – and still have to – wage against the prejudices and power mechanisms of the art world and the forms of resistance which they could adopt.

The question of the feminine in art is primarily a polemic, that is, a discussion about the limits of art, the world of art and the academic world of art history. Exceptions apart, women art historians and artists who emphasise sexual difference aim at devising strategies to break open the bastion.

The discourse of the discipline

One of the aspects of Nochlin's question regards the discipline, namely how does art historiography define art and history? How does art history construct its subject and object, the artist and his work, as an autonomous subject and object? What are the conditions by which great art is defined and what is excluded?

The aim of these questions is to develop a gender-specific view on the history of art. Who can follow the requisite training; who visits exhibitions; who can move, look and speak most freely in the public sphere; who dominates the media, the market, the money; what is expected of whom; who takes care of what.

Many studies aim at the deconstruction of the relation between art, power and gender – a relation which has been brushed aside by traditional art history, because it is neutralised on the assumption of the autonomy of artistic subjectivity.

Feminist scholars like Lisa Tickner, Griselda Pollock and Sigrid Schade support a pluralistic approach to art and art history. They use theories and insights from other disciplines, such as semiotics and psychoanalysis, to analyse and counter the paradigms of art historical discourse, such as the concept of genius and the assumed autonomy of artist and work.

Tickner offers a lucid deconstruction of the development of present art history. She argues that some definitions of art, some stories, concepts and methods, are dominant in the history of art. Of the two great traditions – the empirical English and the more philosophical German – the former has had the upper hand. According to Tickner this is what we now call 'bourgeois' or 'modernist' art history, with its emphasis on style, attribution, dating, authenticity and rarity. The artist is the most important point of reference of the work. Both the artist and the viewer are seen separately from economic, social and sexual relations. Formalism thus predominates. In fact this trend follows on seamlessly from the old concept of genius; within formalism the idea of the individual artist–hero is also dominant. Formalism supports the idea that art is an individual expression; the work of art is seen as objective and universal. The intrinsic universal value of the work of art renders it an autonomous work which transcends the social reality in which it is produced and received (Tickner, 1988: 94).

The modernist perspective is considered to be the most important tradition of Western culture in the twentieth century. It is the most influential representation of art practices. Modernism gives priority to some art practices, like the avant-garde, while it marginalises others as irrelevant. Such analyses of the paradigms of modernist art history have consequences for the conceptual bases of feminist art history. How can they shift and change these paradigms in such a way that femininity is no longer marked out as a natural, absolute and excluded deviation from the norm, but as a positive difference? This complex project starts from the premise that the social order is based on gender, that art historical discourse constructs masculinity and femininity in specific ways and that the subject unconsciously reproduces the effects of this.

The three fields in which femininity can be studied are the experience of women as artist and viewer; the position of the feminine in art historical discourse; and the construction of female subjectivity in works of art. These three aspects can be found in the work of the contemporary artist Mary Kelly. Women produce art from an ambiguous position because they are always part of a social and cultural system which marginalizes them as 'the other', as difference. Women artists who create work in such a symbolic system simultaneously both belong and are marginal to that system. As a woman she functions as an object, as a sign, but as a woman artist she assumes a position of a subject with agency. In her work Kelly problematises this ambiguous position of women in the symbolic system.

She looks for the way in which women can transform meanings by using the means of that very system. Kelly's projects deconstruct the production and reproduction of the feminine in a patriarchal society. Crucial to her work is a moment in a woman's life in which a particular experience cannot be completely controlled and objectivised by patriarchal discourse. In her project *Interim* women aging is the central theme and in *Post Partum Document* childbirth. Kelly collects fragments from different discourses, such as psychoanalysis, works of art, photographs, interviews, diaries and artefacts. She unites these fragments in a Brechtian montage of objects, texts and images. Her works read as a multi-layered process in which conventional meanings are displaced through fragmentation, combination and association. This activates the viewer to reflection: it is the viewer who has to give meaning to the work.

Kelly represents any expectation of a harmonious and unambiguous subject as a fantasy, a construction. That which is hidden under conventional meanings of motherhood and wisdom becomes visible by means of montage and association: fears and desires associated with childbirth and ageing. Kelly's work confronts the viewer with the way in which masculinity, femininity and sexuality are consciously and unconsciously reproduced.

Mary Kelly can be called a theoretically inspired, post-modern woman artist, but her work is also a form of feminist art historical research. She establishes a female position in the symbolic order by means of an exploration of shifts in meaning, peculiarities and symptoms. As a feminist art historian she plays with the laws and rules of art historical discourse. She studies the way in which femininity is visually and discursively constructed, which assumptions form the basis of those constructions and how she can displace them.

Similarly, as an art historian, I read *The Color Purple* as a text in which colour and material bring about a shift from conventional Western meanings to other possible meanings. Just where the discursive explicitly evokes the visual, the text transgresses the borders between word and image. The intersection between the discursive and the visual in this text illustrates how and where the restrictions of the symbolic order can be transcended. In a brief analysis of the function of colour and material in the text of *The Color Purple* I will illustrate how a feminist art historian can read this text as a quilt, one in which a pattern is woven that expresses Alice Walker's ideas of identity. In this way, with conventional meanings, a specific and different story about female subjectivity is told.

Colour and fabrics

> Somethin purple, maybe little red in it too … I say blue. (20)

When Celie is allowed to select fabrics for herself for the first time, it is a special and festive occasion for her. It is as if she is 'tasting' these colours when talking about them. In the novel *The Color Purple* colours and fabrics are the raw materials with which Celie and the other women produce their liberation and identity, as it were, and that not only because Celie attains her economic independence by making clothes out of these fabrics.

The quilts form an important, and at a particular moment even a crucial, sign for Nettie's recollection of Celie. Quilts are made of old scraps of materials sewn according to a determined pattern of colours and fabrics. Each quilt is therefore different and signifies a particular moment in a woman's identity. In the quilt personal memories are preserved, representing history in a particular pattern. Thus Nettie reminds the sick Corinne of Celie's history through a quilt:

> Do you remember buying this cloth? I asked, pointing to a flowered square.

> And what about this checkered bird? She traced the patterns with her finger, and slowly her eyes filled with tears. (159)

By means of this keepsake Celie has a right to exist and is indisputably the mother of the children adopted by Corinne.

In *The Color Purple* much value is attached to the tactile and visual quality of the fabrics. The fabrics are touched: they are soft and supple, they give warmth. And they are looked at: they are a pleasure to the eye. Fur, silk and satin are fabrics which express Western luxury. They are the fabrics of the successful Shug and the English ladies. However, the Olinkas wear cottons, which seem to belong to an African climate. Cotton is pleasant to wear and can be nicely printed. These visual and tactile properties of textiles are not only functional or pleasurable; they can also acquire a subversive power. For example, in the text it is argued that, given the visual characteristics of lamb's wool, the Western portrayal of Jesus as a white man does not agree with the text of the Bible: his hair was woolly like the kinked hair of blacks. The familiar story of the white Jesus is undermined by reference to a visual feature. The biblical text evokes conflicting meanings and Celie is inclined to believe in the visual information.

Furthermore, in this novel colours function to disturb established structures. Colour has meanings, though it can do without form and therefore colour is not tied down to conventions of form. Colours are thus very suitable for expressing the complexity of identity. In the novel, white and black do not occupy a hierarchical position in relation to each other. White and black do not refer to the traditional sequence of difference: white–black, clothed–naked, faith–disbelief, civilised–primitive. In this text, in fact, the word black rarely occurs. The minister Samuel, a black man, is dressed in 'black', and black is the colour of the small Bible he carries around with him. In this way black appears to be the colour of the Word, of faith. Black also implicitly signifies 'not-naked', because white stands for naked: 'Black people cannot be naked because they cannot be White' (232). In the Olinka burial ritual, white robes are worn and faces are painted in white. Here, in contrast to Western conventions, white is associated with death and mourning. In some places in *The Color Purple* black refers to a conventionally white position (that of the Word of God) and white to a conventionally black position (the primitive status of the nudity).

Samuel distinguishes himself as a black American from the Olinkas who are called blue-black: 'blacker than black – blue-black' (119). The African Olinkas usually wear blue robes. This blue is called indigo, a colour prepared from sub-tropical raw materials. This blue seems in fact to refer to African origins. Yellow, on the other hand, refers to mixed race, as shown by one of Squeak's songs: 'They call me yellow/ Like yellow be my name' (85). As a term of abuse yellow refers to an American rather than an African identity, and thus to a dual position, belonging to neither the white nor the black community.

Red, the colour of passion, belongs primarily to Shug. It evokes passion and lust. But red is also attached to Sofia, and here the colour obtains an added value of power:

> One leg be purple, one leg be red. I dream Sofia wearing these pants one day was jumping over the moon. (184)

Purple – the colour in the title – has many references in the book and is therefore the most productive colour. Its conventional significance has a strongly Christian connotation; purple refers to the human confession of guilt for the death of Jesus. In Walker's text the colour purple refers on the contrary to a pantheistic vision of God. According to Shug, God is omnipresent, in trees, in people, in a field of purple flowers. In her vision God is not about guilt and penance but about pleasure and enjoyment:

> I believe God is everything, say Shug. Everything that is or ever was or ever will be. And when you feel that, and be happy to feel that, you've found it. ... Listen, God love everything you love – and a mess of stuff you don't.
>
> But more than anything else, God love admiration.
>
> You saying God vain? I ast.
>
> Naw, she say. Not vain, just wanting to share a good thing. I think it pisses God off if you walk by the color purple in a field somewhere and don't notice it. (167)

But how purple can purple be? As well as this subversive image of God (Shug also knows for certain that God loves sex very much), in Walker's text purple is the colour mixed from blue and red: 'Then finally one day I made the perfect pair of pants. For my sugar, naturally. They soft dark blue jersey with teeny patches of red' (180).

In *The Color Purple* colour is a metaphor for identity. Just as colours are mixed from other colours, so identity is also mixed. In this way the triangle blue–red–purple represents the process of forming identity, by combining lust and power (red), Africa (blue) and religion (purple).

We will remain on non-discursive grounds. Having explored the meanings of colour and fabrics for a female identity, the following chapter explores the possibilities for a feminist study of sound, rhythm and voice in relation to femininity.

Literature for further study

Barta, Ilsebil, Zita Breu and Daniela Hammer-Tugendhat (eds) (1987) *Frauen. Bilder. Männer. Mythen. Kunsthistorische Beiträge*. German anthology of varied studies as to subject and method. For a deconstructivist article, see Schade-Tholen, 'Der Mythos des "Ganzen Körpers"'.

Berger, Renate (1982) *Malerinnen auf dem Weg ins 20. Jahrhundert: Kunstgeschichte als Sozialgeschichte*. This German book gives a lucid view of the position of women artists in the nineteenth century. Many kinds of sources are critically reread in relation to a couple of case studies.

Betterton, Rosemary (1987) *Looking On: Images of Femininity in the Visual Arts and Media*. Good examples of studies in which an analysis of the gaze is made productive for art history. See especially the article 'How Do Women Look? The Female Nude in the Work of Suzanne Valadon'.

Broude, Norma and Mary D. Garrard (1994) *The Power of Feminist Art*. Collection of essays by many of the artists, critics, and art historians who participated in the Feminist Art movement of the 1970s in the United States of America. The book writes the history of that movement, chronicles the multiple forms of feminist art and examines both the backlash against 1970s feminism and the continuing impact on subsequent generations of feminist artists. Includes many reproductions of art works.

Lindner, Ines, Sigrid Schade, Silke Wenk and Gabriele Werner (eds) (1989) *Blick-Wechsel: Konstruktionen von Männlichkeit und Weiblichkeit in Kunst und Kunstgeschichte*. A number of themes are studied in this German collection, such as identification, the art business as women's work, the question of 'male' and 'female' art and the representation of power, violence and sexuality.

Lippard, Lucy (1976) *From the Center: Feminist Essays on Women's Art*. Collection in which Lippard, a leading art critic, investigates American art criticism and attempts to define 'feminist art'. As well as general essays this book contains monographs, fiction and description of a number of feminist art projects.

Nochlin, Linda (1973) 'Why Have There Been No Great Women Artists?' The first feminist article with a fundamental critique of art history. Nochlin opts for a social history from the perspective of *gender*. She later develops this, with more examples, in her article 'Women, Art and Power', included in N. Bryson et al. (eds) (1991) *Visual Theory: Painting and Interpretation*.

Parker, Rozsika, and Griselda Pollock (1987) *Framing Feminism: Art and the Women's Movement 1970-1985*. Good overview collection of reprinted and new articles about recent work by women artists, including Mary Kelly. In 1987 Parker and Pollock edited the classic *Old Mistresses: Women, Art and Ideology*.

Pollock, Griselda (1988) *Vision and Difference: Femininity, Feminism and the Histories of Art*. Pollock explores the possible relations between feminist and Marxist interventions and art history. She also incorporates a semiotic and psychoanalytical approach to feminist art history. She discusses art from the Impressionists via the Pre-Raphaelites to the 1970s.

Robinson, Hilary (ed.) (1987) *Visibly Female: Feminism and Art Today*. Includes the article 'Feminist Art and Avant-Gardism' by A. Partington, which enters a debate with a number of articles from *Framing Feminism*. Also contains articles on black women artists.

Tickner, Lisa (1988) 'Feminism, Art History, and Sexual Difference'. Outstanding introduction to the feminist problematic in art history. With many references to authors and with examples from art history, Tickner outlines a possible set of theoretical instruments. Includes bibliographical references in the notes.

Journals

Women's Art Journal (four issues a year). Laverrock (Philadelphia, US): Women's Art Incorporated.

Art history journals in which feminist contributions are regularly published

October, Cambridge, Mass., and London: MIT Press.

Kritische Berichte: Zeitschrift für Kunst und Kunstwissenschaften, Marburg (Germany): Jonas Verlag für Kunst und Literatur (feminist guest editors one issue a year).

History Workshop: A Journal of Socialist and Feminist Historians. Oxford: Oxford University Press.

9
Theme and variations: feminist musicology

JOKE DAME

Introduction

In the spring of 1991 the American musicologist Susan McClary published her book *Feminine Endings: Music, Gender, and Sexuality*. In the introduction the author writes:

> This is a collection of essays written between 1987 and 1989. Together they set out the beginnings of a feminist criticism of music. (31)

At first sight this may seem a presumptuous remark. After all there have been books about women and music for much longer: at least since the beginning of the 1980s. However, McClary is right. The majority of these early publications contained only biographical information about the composers, their primary motive being to dispel the invisibility of women in music. Other publications are related to the position of women in musical life; as a rule they were devoted to an analysis of the reasons why so few women were and are active in classical music. As a result there was little or hardly any feminist discussion of the medium of classical music itself, that is, a feminist critique of music.

Nevertheless, almost as soon as McClary's book appeared it became clear that her study did not stand alone. In the spring and summer of 1991 several conferences about feminist musicology took place, successively in Utrecht (as part of a much larger women's music festival), in Minneapolis and in London. For these three conferences, each in their own way, the theme 'Musicology and Feminist Theory' served as a starting point. Especially during the conference in Minneapolis, a large number of feminist musicologists, usually in isolated positions at various American universities, appeared to be involved in musicological studies on the basis of recent feminist theories, such as had been developed in other academic disciplines, especially at departments of women's studies.

Equality: the concern for women composers

Under the influence of equality feminism, women musicologists have focused primarily on the (re)-discovery of forgotten, or unknown, women composers and their compositions, and on publishing the scores of music composed by women. As a compensation and a form of justice, from the beginning of the 1980s, a stream of anthologies, monographs and bibliographic editions was published, sometimes including recordings of compositions by women, usually performed by women. Feminist musicologists argue that the absence of women in the reference books of music history does not arise from the actual absence of women from the history of music itself, but from sheer neglect.

> 'Do look after my music!' These words, uttered by the composer Irene Wienawska Poldowski shortly before she died in 1932, capture the spirit and intent of this book. We are 'looking after' women's music – and women musicians themselves – by remembering them through the methods historians apply in their attempts to objectify the past. (Bowers and Tick, 1986: 3)

It is in fact thanks to feminist musicologists who aim to bring about equality between male and female composers that works by important women composers of all centuries have been rediscovered and made accessible to those who want to perform or listen to them. Interesting personalities like the twelfth-century abbess Hildegard von Bingen; the medieval female troubadours and trouvères from France; the seventeenth-century Italian polyphonists Francesca Caccini and Barbara Strozzi; the German Romantics Clara Schumann, Fanny Mendelssohn and Alma Mahler-Werfel; the British Ethel Smyth around the turn of the century; the twentieth-century Dutch Henriëtte Bosmans and the American Ruth Crawford Sieger: these are but a few of the by now familiar names which have found their way into recent music history books (see Weisweiller, 1981; Neuls-Bates, 1982; Bowers and Tick, 1986; Briscoe, 1987). Still, new studies of women composers are anthologised and published for a wider audience.

As well as making women composers and their work visible, studies are being made of the status of women in music. The social position of performing women artists, women music teachers and patronesses were studied (see for example the works of the German musicologist Eva Rieger from the beginning of the 1980s and also Citron, 1990, and Pendle, 1991). These studies analyse the reasons why women are not at all, or hardly represented, in the written history of music and the musical canon. These well-known feminist questions concern women in general and their participation in social life in particular. For musicologists this also raises the depressing questions: can women really compose? Is it actually true that women cannot compose masterpieces? Can women be conductors? Until now much of feminist musicology has been implicitly or explicitly marked by a defensive attitude against such tendentious questions. Feminists of this trend tend to see their emancipatory activities exclusively as a form of compensation, that is to say as a temporary evil, which is necessary for as long as the invisibility of women lasts. In this respect Marcia Citron's attitude is exemplary when she states that the final goal of feminist musicologists may not be separatism, but integration into the mainstream of the Western history of music (Citron, 1990: 104). This recalls a sentence in the introduction to the proceedings of *The Seventh International Congress on Women in Music: Beyond Biography* (Utrecht, 1991):

> We hope that the lectures, the concerts ... exhibitions and the information centre will bring us closer to the day when a congress like this will no longer be necessary.

Difference: the female voice

The strategy of equality-minded feminists is one of emancipation and integration. Thus, they fail to recognise the specificity of the 'embodied' female subject. This is the point of criticism for feminists who work from the perspective of sexual difference. They argue that emancipation involves no more than adapting as quickly as possible to the norms and values of a male-dominated society, and therefore also to its views of the musical tradition and the history of music. Therefore, for them emancipation is not enough. It does not suffice to add a higher percentage of works by women to the musical canon – just as it is also meaningless to allow more women to participate in musical life – unless their contribution in fact makes some difference. What is at stake is to study what is specific to compositions by women and how their body of work can be distinguished from that of men.

However, this question runs feminist musicology into difficulties. It may well be that individual feminist musicologists get sick and tired of the classical scheme of oppression in which the names of Hildegard, Francesca, Fanny, Alma, Ethel and Henriëtte must be quoted constantly in support of the idea that women are capable of success if only given the opportunity. Yet, they are embarrassed by the call for specific female traditions and a specific female aesthetics which are central to the feminist concept of difference. In contrast to feminist academics in other art disciplines, feminist musicologists cannot immediately imagine what a – metaphorically intended – 'female voice' could mean. No wonder, then, that the answer remains vague and scanty in the few articles that tackle the question of a female aesthetics in music. In this respect the question marks in the title of Eva Rieger's article 'Weibliches Musikschaffen – weibliche Ästhetik?' ('Female Compositions – Female Aesthetics?', Rieger, 1984) and of her 1991 lecture at Utrecht, 'Is There a Female Aesthetics?' are telling.

In my opinion, three interlinked causes are to blame for the impasse which struck feminist musicology in this phase of women's studies. The first is related to the nature of the medium of music itself, in combination with the approach of early feminist art criticism. This criticism – think of feminist literary theory – developed in the first instance as resistance against sexism on the level of *content*. Equality feminism is concerned with the impossibility as a woman of identifying with the female characters described or represented by men, whereas difference feminism is concerned with the presentation of positive images of femininity. However, this referential route makes no sense in music, for music has no content, except for music linked to text and even then it lies exclusively in the text, not in the sound. Thus, according to accepted wisdom, opera *texts* can indeed be studied for sexism and misogyny (see Clément, 1988), but not opera *music*. (This view would however prove to be untenable in the third phase of feminist musicology). In this way feminist musicologists have long been hampered by the thought that musicology simply cannot develop a feminist critique, because the object of research has no referential content.

The second reason for women's studies and musicology being temporarily at odds is the following. Unlike feminist literary critics who can discuss a school like *écriture féminine*, feminist musicologists feel disadvantaged, because no *écriture féminine musicale* has emerged in classical music practice. That is to say, in this second phase of feminist musicology there is no feminist movement of theoreticians and composers claiming specific developments in music on these or comparable terms.

The third cause is related to the fact that music proves to be resistant to any form of interpretation, whether feminist-oriented or referential. Semiotics, just like psychoanalysis, has a difficult entry into music. Moreover – as Susan McClary has shown – there is a taboo on questions concerning meanings in music. Musicologists are encouraged to do formal analysis and empirical research, while questions which refer to meaning and interpretation should be avoided as much as possible (McClary, 1991: 4).

The interdisciplinary fields of ethno-musicology and the study of popular music can be mentioned as exceptions to this impasse in feminist musicology (Koskoff, 1987; Jones in Pendle, 1991). In music of non-Western cultures and in folk songs, female traditions can be easily identified, although the distinction here becomes somewhat tautological. The strict social separation between men and women in some cultures results in male and female traditions. In ethno-musicological studies this distinction has usually been understood as a 'natural' fact, and has rarely been problematised. As L. JaFran Jones writes in her article 'Women in Non-Western Music':

> There are, indeed, differences virtually everywhere between men's music and women's music. There are repertoires, instruments, and musical contexts exclusive to one gender and forbidden to the other. ... Each culture defines 'men' and 'women' and prescribes the behavior (including musical behavior) appropriate to each. (Jones in Pendle, 1991: 317)

Studies of popular music have mainly been initiated by sociology. They have led to descriptions of female traditions in Blues and jazz music and also in girls' vocal groups in American popular music of the 1960s. In this field of research the emphasis obviously lies more on the role and function of music in social life than on the music itself.

Deconstructive listening

Whereas equality-minded feminism offers insufficient guarantees for the development of a specific female subject, the theory of difference implies the risk of essentialism: of fixed, inescapable positions for men and women, based on the idea that biological differences determine the essential and unchanging distinction between male and female subjects. But what feminist escape is then possible? Cannot sexual difference be in any way a useful category, but without a hierarchical relation between the poles of this opposition? Feminists who have been inspired by deconstructivism maintain that this is indeed possible, but not after they have subjected 'masculinity' and 'femininity' to a process of de-construction. 'Difference' here no longer means '*different from* but different *so as to* bring about alternative values', in the words of Rosi Braidotti (1994: 239). In this way sexual difference represents alternative forms of positively valued otherness instead of the traditionally negative notion of difference.

Feminist musicologists defy the taboo on the question of meanings with the publication of semiotic studies of several hidden and explicit representations of women and the feminine in the medium of music. This also applies to so-called absolute music: music without a text and (apparently) without a story. American feminist musicologists ought to be mentioned first (McClary, 1991; Solie, 1992), but connections are also being made with this trend in women's studies elsewhere (see the special issue 'Women and Music' of the British journal *Women: A Cultural Review*; and Dame, 1992a/b and 1994a/b).

An example from McClary's book can illustrate this third phase in musicology. In the chapter 'Constructions of Gender in Monteverdi's Dramatic Music' McClary describes how in early seventeenth-century opera, alongside representations of power relations, a gendered semiotics is brought about. She studies the artistic codes with which the composer Claudio Monteverdi makes a musical distinction between male and female characters, a distinction which, in brief, comes down to translating stereotypical male and female features into musical characteristics. Tonal independence and determination (male) are contrasted with tonal dependence and ambivalence (female), assertive melodic phrases with hesitant melodics, rhythmic activity with rhythmic passivity. McClary gives a surprising reading of Monteverdi's most famous opera, *Orfeo*, by arguing that the role of Orfeo is based on an 'error': namely, that the character of Orfeo makes use of a rhetoric which in later operas is performed exclusively by female characters – the rhetoric of seduction and lamentation. This makes him into a feminine hero, an 'erroneous' representation of gender which probably contributed to the lukewarm reception of *Orfeo* by its seventeenth-century audience.

These three positions in the development of feminist musicology can be described differently, that is as analogous to developments in literary studies where the emphasis moves from author to text and from text to reader. Within a framework of equality, the emphasis lies on women composers through the centuries – their existence is unveiled from the history which buried them. Within a framework of difference, the emphasis lies on compositions by women, in a search for specific female traditions in music. Within a framework of deconstruction, the emphasis moves onto perception, to the listener, who – on the basis of post-structuralist and recent semiotic insights – is no longer considered neutral but gendered and as such increasingly treated as the determining factor in the production of meaning. Just as feminist literary critics resist dominant literary conventions by rereading and reappraising the literary canon, so do feminist musicologists resist accepted views of music, by deconstructive listening and reassessing the musical canon.

Miss Celie's song

How can a musicologist approach Alice Walker's *The Color Purple*? A book is not a musical composition – even when music plays a large role in it – and for musicologists the film would at best be of interest for those studying film music. Nevertheless there are possible entries into the text where each of the three types of feminist musicologists would be able to formulate their own questions. As an example I will confine myself to a single extract of the text:

> All three of us go down to Harpo's. Mr. —— and me sit at the same table. Mr. —— drink whiskey. I have a cold drink.
>
> First Shug sing a song by somebody name Bessie Smith. She say Bessie somebody she know. Old friend. It call A Good Man Is Hard to Find. She look over at Mr. —— a little when she sing that. I look over at him too. For such a little man he all puff up. Look like all he can do to stay in his chair. I look at Shug and I feel my heart begin to cramp. It hurt me so, I cover it with my hand. ...
>
> My head droop so it near bout in my glass.
>
> Then I hear my name.
>
> Shug saying Celie. Miss Celie. And I look up where she at.
>
> She say my name again. She say this song I'm bout to sing is call Miss Celie's song. Cause she scratched it out of my head when I was sick. (64–5)

A feminist musicologist working on the basis of the theory of equality would underline the name *Bessie Smith;* and in doing this she (or he) would immediately step out of the fictional world. Such a musicologist might study the life of 'the Empress of the Blues', write her biography and then put together a discography of her recordings. It is also possible that this musicologist would study the position of Bessie Smith as a woman – or of women in general – in the world of Blues.

A feminist musicologist working from the perspective of difference would underline *Bessie somebody she know. Old friend.* This lays the emphasis on the model function which Bessie Smith fulfils for Shug Avery in Walker's book, and also for other women Blues and jazz singers, including Billie Holiday, Mahalia Jackson, Dinah Washington, Odetta and Janis Joplin. The charting of the tradition of female singers could end by mentioning Janis Joplin's tribute to Bessie Smith when she put a commemorative stone on her unmarked grave. On this stone it says: 'The greatest blues singer in the world will never stop singing' (see also Michael J. Budds in Pendle, 1991).

The feminist musicologist who supports a deconstructivist perspective follows a different line of approach. She (or he) would study Bessie Smith's interpretation of the *song* mentioned, 'A Good Man Is Hard to Find', and study the *timbre*, the type of voice, the voice tones that the singer successively employs in her performance. These methods are comparable to those of musicologist John Shepherd who, in his article 'Music and Male Hegemony' (1987), links the concepts of masculinity and femininity with voice characteristics in music. Shepherd distinguishes a number of gender-specific vocal timbres in various kinds of popular music, which determine the meaning of the song. He argues that a male or female singer often applies differing voice tones in a song and thus conveys meanings that are parallel with or in contrast to those of the text:

> In 'A Good Man is Hard to Find', for example, Bessie Smith frequently begins a vocal phrase with a growl of 'sexual' aggressiveness appropriated from the traditional 'macho' timbre, then moves to her standard, hard, 'woman-as-sex-object' timbre for the majority of the phrase, and then lets the phrase fall away with a hint of the softer 'woman-as-nurturer' timbre. Such changes in voice tone imply a dialogue with the unseen male-as-voyeur, initial aggressiveness and closure moving to openness of personal encounter. (Shepherd 1987: 171).

Shepherd's descriptions of the different timbres is exemplary of the ways in which the gender of the listener is a determining factor in the process of signification in the extract quoted above. This is no neutral listener but a (traditional) male subject – a subject who, when contrasted with a woman and her active sexuality, is unable to acknowledge her own sexual identity, to see her as a subject. He successively attributes to Bessie Smith's voice the qualities of 'sexual' aggression, self-appropriation of the traditionally 'macho' timbre, of 'woman-as-sex-object' – object of male desire – and of the 'nurturing woman', 'offering herself as a source of emotional nourishment'. Shepherd thus reduces her first to a derivative of man and then to a function for man. These meanings are predictably linked with dominant and stereotypical views of femininity, formulated from the male subject position.

Nevertheless Shepherd's approach to a *song*, through the timbre of the singer's voice, is interesting enough to inspire feminist studies. For example, we could examine the way in which (that is to say with what kind of voice and timbre) Shug Avery sings 'Celie's song'. Unlike the book, the film allows us to hear the song 'in reality'. It is true that we look at the film from Celie's point of view, yet we actually hear Shug Avery sing. As it is unmediated by words, contrary to the book, we are immediately seduced by Shug Avery's singing and form our own opinion of her voice. At least so it seems – because what we hear is thoroughly mediated. What we hear is director Steven Spielberg's rendition of this scene from the book. What did Spielberg imagine? We see and hear Shug Avery while she sings her first song (for that matter not 'A Good Man Is Hard to Find', the song specified in the book). The male section of the audience reacts to the physical and sexual connotations of the timbre of her voice (which Shepherd would describe as 'sexually aggressive' and as a copy of the 'macho' timbre). Shug obviously enjoys manipulating the audience with her voice. When she announces the second song – Miss Celie's song – the atmosphere changes. The audience becomes quiet and disappears into the background. Shug inserts four different timbres in succession into this song. She begins by humming while she is at a distance from Celie. Approaching Celie her timbre becomes semi-ironic, semi-intimate: 'Sister, we're two of a kind –' Here the emphasis lies strongly on the text. It is as though she is addressing Celie: 'I'm something, I hope you think you're something too.' The third timbre is warm and inviting – 'trust me' – but is quickly taken over by the reintroduction of the second 'ironic/intimate' timbre: 'remember your name'. In the film, the emphasis on text and the content of the words gives Miss Celie's song the character of a political feminist pamphlet. The intimacy is one of 'sisters' sharing each other's fate, encouraging and supporting each other in the struggle. Then Shug ends with the physical/sexual timbre of her first song: 'For honey, the Shug is feeling fine –' The male members of the audience respond immediately as though they were Pavlov's dogs. With this fourth timbre Shug is no longer addressing Celie, but the audience. It is no longer a matter of intimacy between Shug and Celie.

How does the scene in the film relate to the scene in the book at this point? The book says:

> First she hum it a little, like she do at home. Then she sing the words. It all about some no count man doing her wrong, again. But I don't listen to that part. (65)

Unlike what we see in the scene in the film, what matters to Celie is neither the words nor the text. What primarily matters to her is the sounds – the non-discursive aspect of singing. The humming (a sound in which the body audibly resonates) is more important, and this humming – together with the reference to 'home' – provides intimacy, in which the pub scene so alien to Celie fades into the background. Shug's song is thus a subtle, but open and very personal overture, to which Celie responds shyly. She acknowledges the value of Shug's song when she says:

> I look at her and I hum along a little with the tune. First time somebody made something and name it after me. (65)

In the autumn of 1991 a review of McClary's *Feminine Endings* by the American musicologist Elizabeth Wood was published in *The*

Women's Review of Books 8/12. Wood begins her criticism with the following quotation:

> Listening to you sing, folks git to thinking bout a good screw.
> Aw, Miss Shug, say Mary Agnes, changing color.
> Shug say, What, too shamefaced to put singing and dancing and fucking together? She laugh. That's the reason they call what us sing the devil's music. Devils love to fuck.

Wood comments that McClary, who gives her book the subtitle *Music, Gender, and Sexuality*, which is provocative in the traditional world of music, would agree with Shug without a blush. According to McClary, music arouses unambiguous desire and, conversely, music is shot through with notions of sexuality and gender. The taboo on attributing meaning to music is thus broken down. With a hell of a bang.

Literature for further study

Bowers, Jane, and Judith Tick (eds) (1986) *Women Making Music: The Western Art Tradition 1150–1950*. One of the first anthologies with reference to women and music, consisting of biographies of composers and performing women artists as well as analyses of compositions by women, ranging from the early Middle Ages to the twentieth century. Contributions from specialist musicologists, including Marcia Citron, Anthony Newcomb and Ellen Rosand.

Brett, Philip, Gary Thomas and Elizabeth Wood (1993) *Queering the Pitch: The New Lesbian and Gay Musicology*. Collection of essays which illluminates the lesbian and homosexual point of view on traditional musicological subjects. Contributions by Suzanne Cusick, Joke Dame and Susan McClary.

Citron, Marcia J. (1993) *Gender and the Musical Canon*. Citron addresses the question of why music composed by women plays such a marginal role in the standard 'classical' repertory of music. She examines the notion of 'canon', its place in cultural discourse, the process of canon formation, and the role of academic musicology in that process. The chapter on reception and response connects musicology and recent reader response theories in literary theory.

Clément, Catherine (1988 [1979]) *Opera, or the Undoing of Women*. With a foreword by Susan McClary. Textual analysis of over thirty famous operas, which shows how nineteenth-century opera in particular perpetuates the traditional fate of female heroines in literature (death or subjection in marriage).

Koskoff, Ellen (ed.) (1987) *Women and Music in Cross-cultural Perspective*. In fifteen essays, preceded by a lucid introduction, the role of women in musical performances from very diverse cultures is described. The contributions refer to Eastern Europe, North Africa, Asia, South-East Asia, North and South

America. There are two central questions. First, in what way does gender ideology influence a particular culture and the consequent behaviour of the different sexes, ideas about music and musical performance? Second, how does music function in society in such a way that inter-sexual relationships are reflected and/or influenced?

McClary, Susan (1991) *Feminine Endings: Music, Gender, and Sexuality*. This first feminist music *criticism* consists of an introduction and six essays, divided into two groups according to musical subject. The first three examine the meaning of gender in compositions from the standard repertoire of Western classical music (Monteverdi, Bizet, Tchaikowsky, Donizetti, Strauss). In the last three McClary focuses on the work of contemporary women composers and musicians (including Laurie Anderson and Madonna) who explicitly problematise their sexual identity in their music.

Neuls-Bates, Carol (ed.) (1982) *Women in Music: An Anthology of Source Readings from the Middle Ages to the Present*. A chronological selection gathered from different sources about the works of women in Western art music. Sources used are letters, diaries, autobiographies, reviews, poems and passages from novels, travel writing and interviews.

Pendle, Karin (ed.) (1991) *Women and Music: A History*. An overview of women's activities in music as performing artists, composers, teachers and patronesses, from ancient Greece until today. The emphasis lies on art music from Europe and the United States. There are also chapters about women in pop music, jazz and non-Western music. The book ends with an essay on feminist music aesthetics.

Rieger, Eva (1981) *Frau, Musik und Männerherrschaft*. Comprehensive research into many aspects which have contributed to the invisibility of women in music, on the themes: women in music training (from the Middle Ages until now); music as support for gender; creative women in collision with husbands and music (Clara Schumann, Cosima Wagner, Alma Mahler); professional performance in music; and (briefly) the question of a specific female aesthetics.

Solie, Ruth A. (ed.) (1993) *Musicology and Difference: Gender and Sexuality in Music Scholarship*. Examining Western and non-Western music, composers from Francesca Caccini to Charles Ives, and musical communities from twelfth-century monasteries to contemporary opera queens, the contributors explore questions of gender and sexuality from a wide range of viewpoints. Some take for granted the usefulness of categories of difference; some contest their value; and some investigate their historical force.

Part Two

In the first part of this book each chapter gave an introductory overview of feminist cultural studies within a specific field. In addition to offering a great deal of information the texts have probably also raised some questions. As well as finding answers to questions academic studies should indeed also have the function of asking the right questions. We hope, therefore, that readers will be stimulated to conduct further research into feminist cultural studies. The second part of the book provides more theoretical background for further study. Most of the chapters in Part One contained references to lesbian studies, black studies, semiotics and psychoanalysis as political and theoretical guides for feminist cultural studies. In chapters 10–13 these fields of study are examined in more depth from a feminist perspective. Part Two begins with a discussion of lesbian sexuality in the field of culture.

10

Heterosexual screening: lesbian studies

RENÉE C. HOOGLAND

Prologue

Is Alice Walker's *The Color Purple* (1982) a feminist novel, a black novel, or a lesbian one? Does its critical and commercial success represent a landmark in the traditions of feminist, African-American or lesbian fiction? Or, to frame the question slightly differently, can Walker's novel be justifiably 'claimed' by feminist, black or lesbian literary critics? To pose these questions in this way is to underline their unanswerability. This does not mean that these are merely silly, even irrelevant questions. For what they point up is that the question of meaning is never a simple one, and that different readers bring different histories and experiences to texts, which in turn will generate different answers. But as questions of definition, they also alert us to a problematic inherent in the topic of this chapter, lesbian sexuality in the context of cultural studies.

The ensemble of critical theories and practices subsumed under the phrase 'lesbian cultural studies' has only recently begun to be recognised as such. One reason for its late emergence on the academic scene is precisely the question of definition. What are the concerns of the lesbian critic? Does she focus on lesbian sexuality as a theme in literary and other cultural texts? Or is it possible to speak of lesbian cultural studies as a particular way of reading, or even a theoretical perspective? In the past two decades, lesbian scholarship has evolved into a distinct mode of practice and theory in which lesbianism functions as an interpretative framework that encompasses more than questions of (lesbian) sexuality *per se*. To illustrate what this may entail, I will conclude this chapter with a rereading of *The Color Purple* from a lesbian perspective. First, I will sketch the developments that have led to the establishment of lesbian cultural studies as such.

Lesbian feminism or does sexuality equal gender?

In the late 1960s, when the phrase 'women's liberation' was rapidly gaining currency in Eurowestern societies, the word lesbian acquired newly political significance. From a merely stigmatising label, it was transformed into a term of self-identification and henceforth became a banner for social organisation and radical action. Lesbianism was immediately closely associated with feminism, if only because the existence of lesbians proved that Women's Lib was not just a utopian fantasy: lesbians had, after all, long been living their lives in a way that became central to the early feminist dream, i.e., in financial, emotional, and sexual independence from men. The responsibilities such independence entailed did not mean that lesbians shared the same privileges as men. Lesbians and feminists initially found common cause in the struggle for the equal civil rights that were denied to both.

Dominant media, however, depicted feminists as a bunch of man-hating, bra-burning lesbians, too ugly and frustrated to gain – or, indeed, deserve (the love of) men. The threat of lesbianism, consisting in precisely this sexual and social autonomy, was thus effectively used as a weapon against the unfeminine ideas and disruptive politics of the Women's Liberation Movement (WLM). Many feminists feared, therefore, that the association would prove counter-productive to their fight for social reform, and insisted that the lesbian input of the movement was both publicly and privately played down. Betty Friedan, founder of the American-based National Organization of Women (NOW), rejected the 'insult' of lesbianism on national television. Denounced as the 'lavender menace' that would harm the feminist cause, NOW's lesbian members were subsequently systematically expelled.

Refusing to be silenced or sent away, some lesbians formed their own feminist groups. In 1970, one of these, calling themselves Radicalesbians, showed up at a major feminist conference, wearing Lavender Menace tee-shirts. They took over the platform to present a political manifesto entitled 'The Woman Identified Woman' (Koedt, Levine and Rapone, 1973). The Radicalesbians' demands did not focus on equal civil rights for women. Their aim was a total commitment of women to women, a complete disengagement from and rejection of men and male institutions. This they saw as the only viable way to end patriarchal power. Lesbianism was upheld as the ultimate mode of feminism, and the 'woman-identified woman' was proclaimed to be the prototypical feminist revolutionary. In its insistence on female independence, their widely distributed manifesto would set the agenda of the WLM as a whole for many years to come. But the NOW/Lavender

Menace controversy (Gever and Magnan, 1991/1986) was representative of attitudes towards lesbianism prevailing within many branches of the WLM, also outside the US. Relations between lesbianism and feminism were explosive from the start and have since remained tense (Abbott and Love, 1973/1972; Myron and Bunch, 1975; Snitow et al., 1984).

Around the same time that lesbians were becoming aware of their oppression as women, gay men began openly to resist their oppression as homosexuals. Fighting back when the police once again raided a gay bar in New York, they started in 1969 what has become known as the Stonewall rebellion, after the name of the bar in question. This led to the foundation of the gay liberation movement, which operated in close alliance with other radical social movements.

Many lesbians became involved in both women's and gay liberation. In the forefront of the WLM's revolutionary campaigns, they were, however, held back from bringing up the issue of sexuality, and in particular the right to define one's own (deviant) sexuality as a central concern of feminism. The 'lavender menace' continued to be an 'embarrassing' challenge that heterosexual feminists preferred to relegate to the non-political sphere of one's 'private life'. Within the gay movement, lesbians did not fare much better. Joining the fight against queer-bashing and police harassment, they were to find that the more subtle forms of lesbian oppression, associated with their less obvious presence within the gay movement and in society at large, failed to penetrate the thinly disguised partition of misogyny prevailing in both. Where the 'equal rights' demanded by the new social movements unfolded along the discrete lines of gender and (homo)sexuality, those of lesbians were 'equalised' and thus neutralised by both: with all minority subjects proclaimed equal, some proved to be more equal than others.

Just as lesbian concerns were eclipsed within feminist and gay liberation, so did the insistence on gender- and homosexual (in)equality obscure the specificity of lesbian sexuality in the critical discourses that, in the course of the 1970s, developed out of these respective counter-cultural movements. A thorough awareness of different forms of difference, and especially of the distinct nature of lesbian sexuality in relation to both heterosexual gender- and homosexual differences, therefore lies at the heart of the lesbian critical project.

From platform to classroom or from equality to difference

Whereas most lesbians were also feminists, lesbianism tended to fall by the wayside in mainstream feminist practice as it had in literary history generally. In the first feminist anthologies, lesbian texts hardly made any appearance at all. If they did, it was usually as a separate category, considered relevant and of 'special interest' only to similarly inclined sisters (Wiesen Cook, 1992/1979). The need arose for the demarcation of a specifically lesbian cultural tradition. By giving voice to 'neglected' lesbian writers, past and present, and by foregrounding their sexual – as distinct from gendered – otherness, lesbian critics began to expand the limitations of general as well as feminist literary scholarship.

Continuing the (pre-movement) work of pioneer-bibliographer Jeanette Forster (1985/1956), efforts were made to rediscover a 'lost' tradition of lesbian writing (Rule 1975; Grier 1981). Marginalised and 'unclassifiable' figures such as Gertrude Stein and Ivy Compton-Burnett were taken out of the critical closet and brought back into the limelight. Others, like Elizabeth Bowen and Willa Cather, whose work had never before been read as such, were squarely placed within a lesbian tradition. A striking case of lesbian rediscovery is Virginia Woolf. Rescued by feminists from her token position as 'honorary man' among male modernists, Woolf was equally allotted a central place in a tradition of 'Sapphic modernism'. Rereading her work against the background of the author's autobiography, and in relation to her neglected, fanciful study of androgyny, *Orlando* (1928) – which was in fact a lengthy 'love-letter' to Vita Sackville-West, with whom Woolf was having a passionate affair at the time – lesbian critics disclosed an outspoken lesbian subtext underlying Woolf's writings, including her celebrated novels *Mrs Dalloway* (1925) and *To the Lighthouse* (1927), and the famous feminist lecture series *A Room of One's Own* (1929).

The historiographic undertaking immediately ran into a problem that proved the lesbian project to be actually quite different from that of mainstream feminism: lesbianism in texts, unlike female authorship, or 'images of women', turned out to be a quality not so easily determined, especially since the designation 'the love that dare not speak its name' had, in most cases, to be taken quite literally. Even in Radclyffe Hall's *The Well of Loneliness* (1928), often considered the first lesbian novel proper, the word 'lesbian' does not once appear on the page. Hall's reluctance to utter the 'forbidden' word, incidentally, did not prevent defenders of the contemporary moral order bringing the author to trial on charges of 'obscenity'.

Censorship laws and fear of social disapprobation had forced many lesbian writers to deal with their scandalous subject in masked or coded terms. Tracing such inscriptions back as far as the Greek poet Sappho on the isle of Lesbos, lesbian scholars began to chart the intertextual relations among a wide range of texts, to identify the privileged signifiers and contextual realms that had allowed artists to articulate their 'unspeakable' desires in veiled, yet overdetermined terms (Marks, 1979; Benstock, 1990). One of the central images through which lesbian sexuality had traditionally been spoken in both male- and female-authored texts was the eighteenth-century concept of 'romantic friendship,' i.e., lifelong affectionate bonds between 'kindred spirits' that often co-existed with one or the other's 'companionate' (heterosexual) marriage (Faderman, 1985/1981). In the nineteenth and twentieth centuries, such highly charged female intimacies gave rise to an expanding series of boarding-school stories. Situated in an all-female community, a secluded domain out of the 'real world' (of gendered heterosexuality), the adolescent characters are usually shown to have passionate (and hopeless) 'crushes' on an admired teacher or, alternatively, to indulge in 'unnatural practices' with one another. Films like *Mädchen in Uniform* (1931), and its 1958 sanitised re-make (starring Romy Schneider and Lilli Palmer), as well as novels such as Colette's *Claudine* sequence (1900–1903), Rosemary Manning's *The Chinese Garden* (1962), Violette Leduc's *Thérèse et Isabelle* (1966) and Elizabeth Jolley's *Foxybaby* (1985), all productively exploit the setting of the girls' school to explore female same-sex desire. Harking back to Sappho's *gynecaeum*, the boarding school constitutes one of the most widespread topoi of lesbian sexuality in Eurowestern culture.

Another, related set of 'telling' lesbian images concerns the 'unequal couple'. Here an obvious, sometimes exaggerated inequality (usually in age, but also in terms of power, wealth, knowledge) serves as a sign of illicit desire between two female characters. Often a tutor–pupil relationship, the younger woman's desire for an enigmatic older Lady was, during the earlier decades of this century, described in fairly undisguised terms, as in Bowen's *The Hotel* (1927). The repressive post-war moral climate necessitated a more deceptive language to express such sentiments: significant forms of dress (navy blue suit and pumps versus crew cut and open-necked sports shirt), and sustained patterns of imagery serve to mark the difference of lesbian desire in texts like May Sarton's *The Small Room* (1961) and Sylvia Plath's *The Bell Jar* (1963). This model extends into contemporary novels such as Harriett Gilbert's *The Riding Mistress* (1983) and Donna Deitch's popular film *Desert Hearts* (1985), adapted from the novel *Desert of the Heart* (1964) by Jane Rule. To some extent, such textual masquerades were the correlate of a deviant lifestyle that had always been forced into concealment. But practices of narrative encoding and linguistic masking have not remained merely an unfortunate result of repression and denial: lesbian writers still frequently make tactical use of 'lesbian masquerades', so that disguise and mystification have historically developed into intrinsic aspects of lesbian culture (Pattynama, 1990). A recent example is Jeanette Winterson's *Written on the Body* (1992), where the sex of the self-conscious protagonist/narrator remains a secret to the end.

Whilst giving rise to a distinct tradition in (sub)cultural production, the lack of explicitness surrounding the lesbian's 'unspeakable' desire pinpoints a problem that has beset lesbian cultural studies from the beginning, and that is, once again, the problem of definition. For what makes a text into a lesbian one? Does the author have to be a lesbian to make it so? And what if the author is 'known' to be one, but does not explicitly deal with the issue in her work? Does that still qualify as 'lesbian'? Is there such a thing as lesbian writing, even a lesbian aesthetic, as distinct from a female or feminist one? And finally, what is the role of the reader/critic? To what extent does s/he determine what counts as lesbian? Can any text be read from a lesbian perspective, and does this mean that any reader can (learn to) read 'as a lesbian' – including (heterosexual) men?

No final answers can, then as now, be given to any of these questions. Lesbian critics have nonetheless mapped out a field of lesbian art and literature which proved much larger and more varied than had been expected (Rule, 1975; Stimpson, 1985/1981). Some use a literal definition, such as Catherine Stimpson, who reserves the term 'lesbian' for a 'woman who finds other women erotically attractive and gratifying' (1985/1981). This literalness allows us to distinguish the lesbian's specific physical presence in the (textual) world from affectionate female bonding, surfacing in the model of 'romantic friendship'. Analyses of narrative patterns in openly lesbian texts – the protagonist's eventual, 'inevitable' death (often suicide), in contrast to the heroine's escape from confiningly lesbophobic surroundings – allow a further distinction between so-called 'narratives of damnation' (e.g. Hall's *The Well of Loneliness*, or Djuna Barnes' *Nightwood* [1928]), as opposed to 'narratives of reversal' (e.g. Rita Mae Brown's *Rubyfruit Jungle* [1973] and Jeanette Winterson's *Oranges Are Not the Only Fruit* [1986]), whose heroines break free from their repressive home grounds to venture into the world as lesbians. But, as the African-American critic Barbara Smith argues, lesbianism in literature need not be confined to explicitly sexual relations (1985). Toni Morrison's widely acclaimed novel *Sula* (1973) can also be read as a lesbian text, in that it centres on the female characters' (implicit) desire for each other, and because the novel as a whole represents an incisive critique of heterosexual social structures. Rather than undermining the lesbian project, such diverging definitions have, in effect, opened up a much larger textual realm for critical investigation than otherwise would have been possible. They have simultaneously widened the theoretical range of lesbian cultural studies.

Just as lesbian sexuality has traditionally been obscured within Euro-western culture as a whole, so was the lesbian voice insistently muted within both dominant and non-dominant critical discourses. Obliged to read between the lines of feminist and gay male theory (just as they had always already been doing with regard to cultural production generally), lesbian scholars exploited the blind spots and internal contradictions in these reverse-discourses to give voice to their own critical and theoretical concerns. Well-practised in marking out a space for themselves within a socio-discursive domain of either hetero- or homosexual indifference, lesbians have, by necessity, become very skilful in (re-)constructing their own 'different' meanings and identities. In fact, they might well be argued to have been practising deconstruction (Munt, 1992), long before the critical community came under the sway of this major theoretical trend of the 1980s.

Are women (really) lesbians or are lesbians not women?

Early lesbian theory emphasises the interconnectedness of the terms 'lesbian' and 'woman'. A groundbreaking essay exploring the links between gender and sexuality is 'Compulsory Heterosexuality and Lesbian Existence' (1984) by the poet/critic Adrienne Rich. Rich offers a radical vision on the personal and political meanings of gender in a social analysis that centres on institutionalised heterosexuality. At the heart of women's oppression, she suggests, lies the system of compulsory heterosexuality, defined as a closely knit set of socio-sexual practices formalised in/by marriage. It is the practice of heterosexuality which not only keeps straight women in thrall to men and male institutions, but also serves to divide women from one another. Presupposing the existence of original bonds between mothers and daughters, Rich launches her famous notion of the 'lesbian continuum'. Encompassing all modes of female same-sex loyalties, the 'lesbian continuum' represents a global network of female bonding that must be restored before all women (heterosexual, bisexual and lesbian), united on the basis of gender, can be liberated.

Rich's argument shows that heterosexuality is not a biological given but, instead, a complex set of ideologically imposed practices. At the (unquestioned) centre of social reality, the heterosexual institution succeeds in passing itself off as 'natural' or 'self-evident', and *in precisely this way* exerts its constraining power on all levels of experience, private as well as public. This insight at once critically undermines the primacy of gender in socio-cultural relations and calls into question the emphasis on sexual difference in mainstream feminist theory. If institutionalised heterosexuality is central to the maintenance of established gender relations, it follows that the category 'lesbian' does not merely refer to 'women who love women'. Lesbianism, falling outside the terms of the founding social contract (which is heterosexuality), represents a socio-cultural slot of radical difference in relation to the sex/gender system as a whole (Rubin, 1975; 1993). Rich's analysis of female oppression brings forcefully to light the fact that normative (hetero)sexual arrangements are the precondition, if not the very foundation, of the 'natural' distinctions between the sexes.

The phrase 'lesbian continuum' was picked up by mainstream feminism not to show that 'all women are (really) lesbians', but rather to give further strength to the argument that lesbians are not 'really' all that different from female heterosexuals, in that both are first and foremost oppressed as *women*. Despite such mainstream (mis)appropriation, the 'lesbian continuum' opened up a discursive space for lesbianism as a mode of subjectivity, as a particular position within heteropatriarchal social relations. No longer restricted to privately performed sexual practices, the category 'lesbian' came to designate a specific way of 'being in, with and against the world' (Stimpson, 1990). The idea of socio-sexual positioning was further explored by both Anglo-American and French lesbian feminists who contended that the lesbian's 'ex-centric' (rather than marginal) position represents a privileged site from which to launch a critique of heteropatriarchy.

French feminist Monique Wittig proposes the category 'lesbian' as a revolutionary signifier within a materialist analysis of heteropatriarchal culture (1992). Eurowestern society, Wittig argues, consists of a complex system of socio-symbolic power relations in which the heterosexual relationship functions at once as foundational centre and as a 'natural' core that lies beyond the realm of critical analysis. Whereas science and knowledge are commonly recognised as cultural constructs that play a determining role in the material exercise of power, the knowledge of sex paradoxically continues to succeed in resisting examination, in escaping the terms of social critique. That this should be so is not because sexuality as such is 'outside' culture or, indeed, 'natural'. The ostensible elusiveness of sexual power/knowledge issues from the pervasive operations of what Wittig designates 'the straight mind', i.e., the conglomerate of (unconsciously) acquired ideas, values and conceptual structures that assumes heterosexuality to be the only natural form of sexual behaviour and emotional expression. The 'straight mind' functions as one of the founding perceptual screens through which we learn not only to recognise ourselves but also to project onto a screen of otherness the less valuable or unwanted aspects of/in ourselves. Institutionalised heterosexuality forms one of the mainstays of the phallogocentric symbolic order.

If sexuality is not a 'natural' given but, instead, produced by a psycho-cultural script that is both taught and learnt, the refusal to play one's preappointed role in the heterosexual scenario is not just a radical political gesture. As a way of 'being in, with and against the world', lesbian self-identification entails a specific way of orienting oneself with regard to a world that does not recognise such an identity. Socio-sexual positioning, however, inevitably informs the way each of us, in our own ways, looks at and attributes meaning to ourselves and our surroundings. What is more, our sexual orientations also, though largely unconsciously, determine the ways in which we pay attention to the people and things we wish to come to know, or understand. And, no less importantly, to what we do not wish to know or understand: to that which is of no particular interest to us, we tend not to pay too much attention. Any reader with no particular interest in lesbian sexuality, can – without perhaps even being aware of it – simply overlook the critical significance of lesbian meanings in a given text. This, as I will show shortly, is precisely the case in most critical readings, feminist or otherwise, of *The Color Purple*.

Queer perspectives on gender (de)construction

Lesbian debates in the 1980s increasingly focused on the relations between sexuality, subjectivity, language, and processes of signification themselves. Inspired by French feminist thought and by neo-Freudian and Lacanian psychoanalytic theory, Anglo-American critics redefined the stylistic experiments of early twentieth-century writers like H.D. (Hilda Doolittle), Djuna Barnes, Gertrude Stein, and Virginia Woolf, as textually encoded inscriptions of lesbian desire (Marcus, 1987; Benstock, 1990). Disruptive narrative practices, e.g., the transgression of generic boundaries, a deliberate mixing of styles, and overall linguistic excess, were additionally re-employed to create a 'new' language in which the unsaid – or, rather, the 'unsayable' – could finally be articulated (Daly, 1978; Wittig and Zeig, 1979).

Alongside further theoretical sophistication, the 1980s also saw a rapid diversification of lesbian cultural production. Growing numbers of 'serious' literary and autobiographical texts began to appear, e.g. Audre Lorde's *Zami: A New Spelling of My Name* (1982), Cherríe Moraga's *Loving in the War Years* (1982), Sarah Schulman's *Girls,*

Visions, and Everything (1986), and Margaret Erhart's *Unusual Company* (1987). Lesbian film production was on the increase; Lea Pool's *Anne Trister* (1986), Patricia Rozema's *I've Heard the Mermaids Singing* (1987), and the above-mentioned *Desert Hearts* made their way to mainstream cinema screens. A distinctly lesbian tradition in popular fictional genres demarcated itself. Barbara Wilson's *Murder in the Collective* (1984), Mary Wings's *She Came Too Late* (1987) and Claire McNab's *Lessons in Murder* (1988), among others, gave birth to the lesbian sleuth. Science fiction and romance novels (S. Miller Gearhart's *The Wanderground* (1980), Joanna Russ's *The Female Man* (1985), Katherine V. Forrest's *Daughters of a Coral Dawn* (1984)) combined elements of popular genres to (re-)construct various lesbian utopias. Theoretically more refined tools were further developed to analyse the intertextual relations among dominant and lesbian (sub)cultural forms of artistic production.

From the mid-1980s onwards, mainstream feminism began to take into account the interactive operations of 'racial'/ethnic and gender differentiation. Questions of sexuality at the same time curiously faded into the background. By the end of the decade, the figure of the lesbian drops out of mainstream debates altogether. Lesbian critics henceforth begin to disentangle themselves from the feminist mainstream, and to widen their perspective to encompass a more broadly defined interdisciplinary field. What assumptions underlie the contemporary lesbian theorist's focus on the connection between sexuality and textuality?

Cultural texts – or public fantasies – partly serve to (re)inscribe the rules and norms that fix us in our socially sanctioned (hetero)sexual positions. Novels, films, paintings, and music do not, however, address us on the level of consciousness only: they also speak to our imaginations. In the realm of fantasy, boundaries are not fixed: in our imaginations, the borderlines between the 'normal' and the 'abnormal' are continuously in motion. By addressing us on the level of our private fantasies, 'outrageous' sexual images or subversive narratives of desire may thus critically affect the ways in which we (have learned to) give meaningful shape to our selves. To be more specific: in Eurowestern societies nobody is taught to become a lesbian. On the contrary, from commercials, magazines, billboards, popular cinema, soap operas, to life insurance policies, adoption laws, and the daily paper, we get the pervasive impression that the only way to enjoy life (cigarettes, clothes, food, soft drinks, health, babies), to be happy – or, simply, *to be* – is to be heterosexual. Representations of alternative ways of being, living, loving and enjoying oneself not-being-heterosexual may inspire us to shift away from our 'normal' slots in the cultural realm and take up positions that we have been taught to reject as 'taboo'. The interactive operations between public and private fantasies may thus enable us to rethink our identities, and to change our perspective on the world in which we find ourselves. Critical investigations of such fictional texts as either implicitly or explicitly speaking to the lesbian reader's (private) imagination are one way of making their often hidden subversive meanings available to a larger reading public.

Appropriations of psychoanalytic theory have furthermore created a space for lesbian sexuality no longer defined in terms of sexual practices only. By exploiting the gaps and contradictions in such 'master-texts' as Freudian and Lacanian psychoanalysis, lesbian artists and theorists have sought to disengage their 'perverse desire' – i.e., 'deviant' only in the (non-pathological) sense that it is not directed at heterosexual reproduction – from its restricted niche in dominant realms of thought. In a special mode of deconstructive practice, in which radical revisions of 'scientific' ideas are linked up with close cultural analyses, they have established a discursive space in which the lesbian figure no longer figures in either desexualised or derivative terms. Neither man *manquée* nor perennial adolescent, the lesbian has been reconstructed as an autonomous subject who takes up a significant socio-sexual position in dominant (hetero)sexual scenarios (Roof, 1991; Hoogland, 1994; Butler, 1994; de Lauretis, 1994).

Shifts in theoretical perspectives have entailed new terms of designation. Recent forms of collaboration between lesbian and gay male theorists have resulted in a first institutionalisation of Gay and Lesbian Studies at several North American and West European universities. The outbreak of the AIDS crisis, which reunited gays and lesbians on the political platform as well as in the (sub)cultural sphere, occasioned the emergence of what is currently gaining recognition as Queer Theory/Practice (de Lauretis, 1991). Such efforts at theorising sexuality in cultural praxis across the lines of gender have neither prevented nor reduced the need for the sustained development of lesbian cultural studies as a distinct field of critical inquiry. The specificity of the lesbian critical project, indeed, its radical potential, resides in its ability to question both the hetero/homo-distinction and the gender divide which not only underpin Eurowestern culture as a whole but also cut across mainstream feminist and gay (male) thought. Lesbian cultural analyses hence often centre on the interactive operations of these distinct axes of exclusion. To illustrate what this may entail, I will now return to *The Color Purple*.

The lavender menace and the colour purple

It was no accident that Betty Friedan called the lesbian membership she feared would 'discredit' the National Organization of Women the 'lavender menace'. The colours violet and lavender have a history of association with lesbianism that goes as far back as 600 BC, to the poet Sappho and her female lovers, who reputedly wore violet tiaras in their hair. By choosing *The Color Purple* as a title for her novel, Alice Walker unmistakably places the issue of lesbian sexuality at the focus of her narrative, and at the centre of Celie's epistolary coming-into-being, without actually uttering the 'forbidden' word. This returns me to the questions I began with. Is *The Color Purple* a lesbian novel? Does it belong to a lesbian cultural tradition? And how would a contemporary lesbian critic go about answering such questions?

Thematically, in terms of characterisation and as far as narrative development is concerned, I would say, yes, *The Color Purple* is definitely a lesbian novel. Celie's struggle against patriarchal power, her gradual acquisition of a position of sexual autonomy, and her eventual socio-economic independence, all form clearly recognisable aspects, or stages, in an established tradition of lesbian stories of development or *Bildungsromane* (Zimmerman, 1983). That Celie's story is outspokenly lesbian, and not just any woman's coming-to-consciousness, is underlined by the precise nature of the dynamic force that causes its (and her) development: her discovery of her *lesbian* sexuality.

The Color Purple's plot is not triggered off by Celie's discovery of her sexuality regardless of its orientation, as many feminists have argued. The moment of narrative combustion, the protagonist's moment of 'awakening', is emphatically rendered as a non-normatively 'female', i.e., a *lesbian* moment of self-discovery. In the letters that make up the first half of the text, the force of Celie's same-sex desire for Shug is frequently, explicitly remarked upon. The overtly physical nature of their relationship highlights the experience of lesbian sex at the core of the heroine's burgeoning subjectivity. This is underscored by the interconnected meanings of the novel's title. The colour purple literally refers to a field of flowers that comes to symbolise the protagonist's rejection of God as a white male authority and his transformation into a non-Christian, depersonalised spiritual force. On a metaphorical level, however, the colour purple, with its long-standing tradition of associations, signifies sex between Celie and Shug, and lesbianism generally. It is thus suggested that it is only as a lesbian, in her emotional, intellectual *and* sexual independence from men, that Celie can become an autonomous subject, the author of her own perceptions, and, ultimately, of her own discourse.

Explicit recognition of the narrative focus on Celie's 'deviant' sexuality may, at least partly, solve one of the problems critics have been struggling with: the novel's relative neglect of questions of 'race' – in other words, the fact that all the 'bad guys' are black men, whose significance, just like that of their female counterparts, is confined to the black community, and not taken out into the wider context provided by the racist society of the American South (hooks, 1990a). Seen from a lesbian perspective, this is not necessarily a political flaw, but rather an indication that 'race' does not stand, or at least not exclusively, at the novel's centre.

A lesbian approach also helps to explain a further, otherwise unresolvable, problem, one with which feminist critics in particular have had difficulties: Celie's 'inexplicable' mildness towards Mr. —— at the end of the story. Only if we acknowledge the structural importance of the fact that it is Shug, another woman, who constitutes the object of Celie's desires, and who, in course of time, becomes the 'significant other' to the heroine's self, are we able to see that the latter's relations with Mr. ——, and men generally, are of a nature best described in terms of complete *in*difference. Celie's subjectivity does not depend on her relations with men or, more generally, on her assuming her place in male-defined institutions. On the contrary, her budding sense of identity and emergence as a subjective agent are precisely enabled by her rejection of the role prescribed to her in the patriarchal script of gendered heterosexuality. Since she does not rely on a male/other to differentiate herself, the protagonist has, in the end, nothing to lose or to gain from being 'nice' to Mr. ——. Outside the socio-symbolic ring in which the battle between the sexes is traditionally most savagely fought out, the domain of (hetero)sexuality, Celie occupies an ex-centric position in the sex/gender system from which she can afford to be generously indifferent to members of the opposite sex.

Despite such evidence to the contrary, I would still hesitate to call *The Color Purple* a lesbian text. My reluctance to do so stems from the manner in which the lesbian subject is dealt with, especially in the latter half of the novel. bell hooks has pointed out that one of the problematic aspects of *The Color Purple* is its fundamental de-politicisation of lesbianism. Gainsaying the undeniable homophobia pervading Eurowestern social reality and, even more palpably, the black community, Celie and Shug can openly carry on having a sexual relationship without causing so much as a ripple within the heterosexual order: 'Homophobia does not exist in the novel' (hooks, 1990a). This is not only quite odd in a narrative which, notwithstanding its sometimes surreal atmosphere, deliberately inscribes itself in the tradition of social realism. It also implies that Celie's deviant desires remain an ultimately private affair. Unlike her entrepreneurial activities, and her eventual role as a house- and landowner, the heroine's sexuality does not obtain in a social context. Since there is no public reality in which Celie can express her desires, they carry no meaning outside her relationship with Shug.

Its reduction to a matter of private preference implies that Celie's sexuality has no significance beyond the walls of the bedroom in which she and Shug perform their perverse practices. Hence, once Shug returns to the normal order of (unhappy) heterosexuality, Celie does not merely stop having sex, she stops being a sexual subject altogether. Lacking any collective sense of lesbian identity, Shug's betrayal means the end of the lesbian performance as a whole. The residues of the heroine's de-sexualised self become subsequently inscribed in the 'masculine' accoutrements belonging to the stereotypical 'mythic mannish lesbian' (Newton, 1989). Celie may in the end be wearing the pants around the house; that is indeed the only remaining marker of her subversive sexuality. The text succeeds in conclusively neutralising her 'abnormal' desire by eventually implying its integration into love of kin, in particular for her sister Nettie. The potentially disruptive force of the heroine's sexual self is thus contained within the traditional family structure – however strangely assorted a group the members of Celie's 'family' in the novel's closing section may be.

Celie's is not, however, the only character to be effectively robbed of its radical edge. Shug too is unmistakably stripped of the autonomous sexual power that has defined her character from the start. When she leaves Celie for a man half her age, it is not because she is hankering after a new sexual adventure. On the contrary, prior to this final venture into the heterosexual market, the formerly so glamorous, autonomous Shug is recurrently portrayed as a fat, ageing woman, fearful of losing her looks, and therewith the only means she has to wield power (over men). Given the matter-of-fact, even dispassionate tone of voice in which this erotic disempowerment is depicted, it comes as no surprise that, after a brief fling with the young musician, Shug fails to hold his sexual attention, and instead of playing his lover, ends up performing as his substitute mother.

Shug's heterosexualisation strikes me as an uncalled-for turn of events within the narrative context as a whole. What I find disturbing about the character's demeaning restoration to the heterosexual order, however, is the fact that it is presented, without a trace of narrative critique, as the inevitable conclusion to a – perhaps unusually active – career of (hetero)-sexual womanhood. In other words, what is essentially a thorough devaluation of her character is uncritically held up as the female subject's ineluctable fate in the 'natural' order of things, an oppressive socio-symbolic order the novel itself in the end takes great pains to restore.

Celie's desexualisation and Shug's socio-sexual disempowerment jointly constitute a narrative divestiture of lesbian agency which coincides, if it has not actually been brought about by, the breaking off of their sexual relations. Taken together, the respective situations in which we leave the two characters, plus the fact that the novel nonetheless ends on a happy note of harmony, considerably undermine *The Color Purple*'s subversive potential as a feminist, as an African-American but also as a lesbian text. Some critics have rejected Walker's bestseller for its lack of realism, its unconvincing happy ending, for being more of a romantic fairy tale than a critical piece of realist fiction. As a lesbian reader, I am perhaps primarily disappointed with the novel for precisely *not* being that: a romantic fairy tale. Fairy tales have of old offered both readers and writers opportunities to range freely the never-never land of their wildest fantasies. *The Color Purple* precludes such possibilities. In my imaginary, ideal lesbian fairy tale, the fantastic, alluring, and unregenerately lesbian lovers would not be stripped of their life-giving force so as to be brought back into a very real, heterosexual order: they would, quite extraordinarily, end up living happily ever after. But that, of course, is another story.

Literature for further study

Abelove, Barale and David M. Halperin (1993) *The Lesbian and Gay Studies Reader.* A bulky collection of critical and theoretical essays (26 out of 42 female-authored) presenting a wide range of scholarly disciplines. Includes an extensive list of suggestions for further reading.

Frye, Marilyn (1983) *The Politics of Reality: Essays in Feminist Theory.* Highly accessible anthology of essays that explores the nature and effects of lesbian sexuality in heteropatriarchal society and in relation to feminism from a philosophical perspective. Very useful as a theoretical introduction to the field.

Fuss, Diana (ed.) (1991) *Inside/Out: Lesbian Theories, Gay Theories.* Mixed collection of essays seeking to cross the gender gap in various disciplines of gay and lesbian studies (pedagogy, musicology, sociology, film theory, literary criticism), though the majority deal with gay issues.

Griffin, Gabriele (1993) *Heavenly Love? Lesbian Images in Twentieth-century Women's Writing.* Griffin offers an even-handed yet critical assessment of the representation of lesbianism in Anglo-American literature. Contains a bibliography of fictional as well as theoretical and critical works.

Hamer, Diane and Belinda Budge (eds) (1994) *The Good, the Bad and the*

Gorgeous: Popular Culture's Romance with Lesbianism. One of several volumes to deal with the sudden appearance of 'the lesbian' on the popular cultural scene. Short and accessible pieces focus on subjects as diverse as Madonna, popular and country music, crime fiction, Martina Navratilova, prime-time television, and various Hollywood film genres.

Lauretis, Teresa de (1994) *The Practice of Love: Lesbian Sexuality and Perverse Desire.* Theoretical exploration of lesbian sexuality from a psychoanalytic perspective. While using a variety of primary texts as a starting point, and drawing connections between such public fantasies as films, plays and novels and the private fantasies that are played out on the level of the unconscious, de Lauretis attempts to arrive at the heart of the lesbian's 'perverse desire'.

Lorde, Audre (1984) *Sister Outsider: Essays and Speeches by Audre Lorde.* This book, by one of the most influential black lesbian writers/activists, contains fifteen relatively short and highly accessible pieces that powerfully bring to the fore the complicating operations of sexuality, gender, 'race' and class in the context of post-war America and the early days of (lesbian) feminism.

Munt, Sally (ed.) (1992) *New Lesbian Criticism: Literary and Cultural Readings.* Representative collection of essays in contemporary lesbian studies covering a broad range of cultural production (literature, film, television, popular fiction, and pornography).

Roof, Judith (1991) *A Lure of Knowledge: Lesbian Sexuality and Theory.* Theoretical study of lesbian sexuality as a 'problem of knowledge' in the context of various discourses that lie at the basis of current Western culture, e.g. feminist theory, psychoanalysis, film, and literature. Requires some familiarity with post-structuralist and deconstructive thought, but is stylishly written and provides lucid insights into the complexities of the subject.

Zimmerman, Bonnie (1990) *The Safe Sea of Women: Lesbian Fiction 1969–1989.* This book presents an illuminating critical history of twenty years of lesbian fiction, set against the background of lesbian feminism and its various aftermaths. Contains select bibliogaphy of primary and secondary sources.

11

Strangers and double self-consciousness: feminism and black studies

PAMELA PATTYNAMA

Introduction

> Dear God,
>
> ~~I am~~ I have always been a good girl. Maybe you can give me a sign letting me know what is happening to me. (3)

These are the opening lines of *The Color Purple* by Alice Walker, an African-American epistolary novel which has become a bestseller in the United States and Europe. *The Color Purple* shares with us the life of Celie, a black, exploited and poor woman, who is practically illiterate and, moreover, a practising lesbian. Celie is in complete contrast to the figure considered in Western culture as the centre of power and position: the white, heterosexual man. Moreover, the ingredients of *The Color Purple*, black culture, racial discrimination, poverty, male terror and incest, raw and realistic as they are, do not belong among the favourite themes of the Western canon.

You would expect that readers would rapidly dismiss such a 'realistic-black' text as food for anthropologists and sociologists; because it is too trivial, too limited and too strange for literary pleasure and recognition.

However, *The Color Purple* is a bestseller. It has won various prestigious prizes and has been adopted into the American canon. The film version by the famous (white) director Steven Spielberg has drawn full houses. How can this be? How has this 'limited' novel with its 'strange' themes become a bestseller? There is no simple answer to these questions. In this chapter I will show that the triumph of *The Color Purple* is by no means a purely literary question, but that, just as with every process of signification, political and economic power interests, social developments and processes of identification have played a role. Therefore I will examine the historical and cultural context of the text rather than the novel itself.

White superiority

A feminist female colleague, someone who is used to problematising matters which are self-evident, once said to me: 'What are you called again, a difficult name, oh, yes –', and my non-European surname was confused with the first name of a female academic who does not look like me, who carries out research in a completely different field, but who, like me, is non-white. I saw this incident as a form of 'everyday racism' (Essed, 1991). Not so much because my colleague forgot my 'difficult' name, but because I had evidently been left lying around piled up in a 'non-white' memory compartment, nameless and stripped of any individuality.

With this personal experience I want to emphasise that racism and ethnocentrism are two-sided phenomena. On the one hand they are embedded in the foundations of the society in which we live. On the other hand these always involve questions of power with regard to individual subjects, personal commitment and personal experiences. The confusion of name and person shocked me personally, and I blamed my colleague even though I am convinced that this incident was the result of unaware, internalised racism. Racism and ethnocentrism are not characteristics of 'nigger haters' or neo-fascists; they are social structures which are fundamentally embedded. Anyone growing up in the West consciously or unconsciously breathes racism. Whites are not aware that they must make a conscious effort to drive out this internalised racism. What happened to me is futile in comparison with the racist lynch mobs of the southern United States or with ethnic cleansing in former Yugoslavia. Yet these kinds of experiences with the gaze of the other, making race or ethnicity in the West an essential part of oneself, are constitutive of subjectivity, identity and self-consciousness. Western history has been permeated from way back by a 'white' ideology, in which people of white colour determine the absolute norm and anything else is considered inferior. According to this 'white supremacy' (hooks, 1989), an external sign – 'whiteness' of the skin – indicates superiority, power and a high degree of civilisation. A coloured skin (black, brown, yellow, red) or non-Aryan racial features are perceived unfavourably because they are seen as indicating inferiority, primitivity and a low level of development. These literally dark signs form the counterpoint, the reverse side of the lily-white culture.

One of the foundational discourses of Western culture which underlie the rigid and hierarchical way of thinking in terms of white and black is the Christian doctrine. In our so-called atheist times individual existence is determined by the Christian ideology of good on the one hand and bad on the other. In the cultural unconscious of the West, 'white' still holds the radiant and shining connotation of the Good God and 'black' almost always symbolises the threatening, demonic and ugly Evil. In reality *myths* form the basis of the far-reaching meanings attached to differences in colour. bell hooks deconstructs the white = good myth in her essay 'Homeplace: A Site of Resistance'. As a little black girl she was confronted in white neighbourhoods with 'that terrifying whiteness – those white faces on the porches staring us down with hate' (1990b: 41). In this experience hooks shows that, from the perspective of blacks, white radiates no goodness and calm, but on the contrary embodies a threat. Every black American child has imprinted upon her/himself the knowledge that white means danger, which is regarded as essential for survival. The fear and the threat that black arouses in whites does not appear to be inherent in black, but is a question of perspective and mythical power.

Every culture, including that of the West, is built on myths. These myths, also called ideology, are perpetuated through a process of internalisation. Individuals appropriate the prevailing ideas in such an unconscious way that they think that these are natural and 'really true'. Myths are in fact subjective, psychological structures. However, they cannot be separated from economic power and group interests. This connection between economic and psychic structures is unmistakable in the Western history of colonisation: whoever colonises and oppresses the other can only do so by attributing him/herself superior power out of megalomania. The idea of white superiority is therefore a necessary condition for colonialist exploitation. Colonisation, as an example of internalised ideology, shows that so-called natural racial and ethnic differences are the consequence not of nature or of divine creation, but of *views* of race and ethnicity which arise from a rigid system of meanings dominated by profit and power. Paradoxically enough, not only whites but blacks as well internalise the dominant views on white supremacy. In *The Color Purple* we find an example of this 'strange' internalisation in the difference between Celie's view of God and that of Shug. The naive Celie writes letters to God, the only one who would be able to hear her. She imagines him as a friendly, white, bearded man with blue eyes. Shug, the woman of the world, dismisses this mythical God as a product of the 'white folks' white bible':

> How come he look just like them, then? she say. Only bigger? And a heap more hair. How come the bible just like everything else they make, all about them doing one thing and another, and all the colored folks doing is gitting cursed? [166]

Shug shows Celie that her God is an internalised idea that serves white supremacy. Celie's God also actually supports the projection of divinity by men onto themselves:

> Man corrupt everything say Shug. He on your box of grits, in your head, and all over the radio. He try to make you think he everywhere. Soon as you think he everywhere, you think he is God. But he ain't. (168)

Shug's view refers to the universal effect of ideology which insidiously nestles in the mind, even in the minds of those for whom the dominant idea is a disastrous loss of self-worth and self-consciousness. What I refer to by 'black' in this chapter is therefore not a skin colour, but a condition. Black indicates that whoever occupies the black position in the Western black–white dichotomy stands outside the centre of power, is objectified by, and therefore always subjected to white norms and values. Black subjectivity is strange, not because black is strange *by nature*, but because black and ethnic implies deviation from what is considered normal, good and reassuring in a white culture. Each individual who is oppressed on the basis of race or ethnicity is confronted with oversimplified stereotypes which are printed onto the whole group. Whoever is not white and living in a completely white context will always have to struggle to escape stereotypes in order to achieve self-definition. This process of identity makes the black experience an ambiguous, simultaneously self-conscious and alienating experience. Looking at oneself through the eyes of the other means that the self-image is also formed through the image that the other has imposed. It is, among other things, these strange-dual experiences which black texts express.

Literature is one of the discourses which, in addition to old values and ideas, also supplies constitutive elements for self-perception and identity. Black texts which originate in a white context reveal both the continuation of traditional notions and the search for identity. Globally one can distinguish three ideas which recur time and again in black textuality. Firstly, experience plays a role in black texts, in the sense both of individual perception and of collective experience. The individual emotions expressed in black texts are thus not irrevocably connected, but are still bound to a collective group which, because of race or ethnicity, is considered as intrusive or strange by those around them. Experience is the textual inscription of this strange-dual consciousness. The search for a separate identity, or the desire for self-definition, is the second distinguishing characteristic of black and ethnic texts.

A third idea played out through black textuality/subjectivity is the specific national history. In connection with the experience of being strange, this history is active in the whole process of identification and self-definition. Thus the history of slavery has a different influence on the consciousness of self from the immigration history of the Chinese, for whom ancient China disappeared under a communist regime; similarly, the forced 'repatriation' of Indonesians to the Netherlands, a country they have never known, affects subjectivity in a different way than does the experience of a Moroccan child taken by her father to a rich Western European country where he has been tolerated as a foreign labourer. The identity crisis resulting from guilt felt by Jews who survived World War II is a completely different crisis from that of second-generation immigrants from the West and East Indies. Every ethnic group brings along its own history, stories and metaphors. These ideas of history, (collective) experience and the search for identity are revealed in both ethnic studies and black fiction.

Until now I have mainly considered the place and meaning of black textuality and subjectivity in a white context. In order to analyse the effect of gender on black experience, I will elaborate the development of a specific literary feminist group, black women writers in the United States. I have chosen this group because African-Americans have made themselves seen and heard most successfully in the West as a social group with a distinct black signature.

Black feminism

When describing black textuality one should not uphold the traditional dividing lines between theory, autobiography and fiction. Genre boundaries cannot be clearly drawn because black texts poignantly foreground the fact that (collective) experience and identity are embedded in fictional stories, which in return refer to social and political developments. For the history of black feminism, the three theoretical approaches of equality, difference and deconstruction cannot be separated from social history and the process of becoming subjects in black fiction.

In order to further describe the history of black feminism, I will primarily start from fictional stories written by black women. The autobiographical *I Know Why The Caged Bird Sings* (1970) by Maya Angelou and *The Bluest Eye* (1970) by Toni Morrison have been considered the starting point of black female writing. Both I-novels give a picture of the lives of young black girls, growing up in a world of white power, shattered black communities, indifference, incest and rape.

Although black women, unlike black men, have received attention from literary circles only since the early 1970s, their texts did not suddenly appear from nowhere in American literature, though it may seem so from the point of view of the dominant canon. Moreover, the frequently held idea that black feminism is a contemporary sub-division of white feminism is misguided. The social and literary history of black women stretches back to the seventeenth century, when Africans were carried away from their land as slaves and set to work in the southern parts of the United States as the property of white plantation owners. For centuries American slavery systematically stripped away any racial pride and personal autonomy among blacks. Slaves even had no control over their body, the primary sign of Self: men worked for their white masters purely as a mechanised work force and women were raped and robbed of their children. Only when slavery was abolished in 1865 did black Americans acquire self-determination over their experiences, but history continues in racist language, expressions and attitudes. The literature of African-Americans is therefore marked by desperation, stigmatisation and ghettoisation, the immediate consequences of slavery and xenophobia.

Oral and autobiographical traditions are characteristic of African-American texts. During slavery oral story-telling was one of the few available forms of communication and the autobiographical form was first a necessity and then an instrument in the search for a separate voice. The earliest forms of black literature are the surviving *slave narratives* told by slaves and ex-slaves themselves. The authenticity of these stories was often disputed (Cudjoe, 1990). People could apparently not imagine that a black voice had its own story to tell. Later, around the turn of the century, the idea of emancipation emerged, which initially produced a plea for an improvement in the lot of blacks. Frances E.W. Harper, for example, with her *Iola Leroy, or Shadows Uplifted* (1892), focused on a white audience: 'her story's mission would not be in vain if it awakens in the hearts of our countrymen a stronger sense of justice and a more Christian-like humanity' (Sato, 1972: 67). That Harper did not address herself or the black community, but a white audience, is a sign of the times. The uniquely black self-consciousness as we now know it only developed later. Harper wants to refute the stereotypical images which whites hold of blacks: her characters have to demonstrate that blacks are basically equal to whites. The heroine therefore appears to be a black prototype of the ideal which white women hold most respectable: the nice, pure, decent, gentle and dependent 'lady'.

At the time of the Harlem Renaissance, a black cultural movement at the beginning of the twentieth century, women writers fought consciously against the negative images which the white public nourished about blacks. Black women, just like white women, were seen only as part of a collectivity rather than as individuals. For them this process of signification, however, follows a more complex pattern because the gaze of the other carries not only a sexist but also a racist dimension. An important first condition in the black search for a separate voice and identity is therefore the struggle against stereotypes and reductive images.

The women writers of the Harlem Renaissance focused primarily on the problematic of race. Like Harper, they addressed a white audience; but they explicitly addressed women, believing that femininity was a universal quality. If there were no racism, they argued, blacks would be exactly like whites. The fact that the concepts of femininity and masculinity are also problematic is left unsaid. Nevertheless Barbara Christian (1985), in her historiography of black fiction, shows that the lines along which race and sex are organised also intersect in these early novels. The attempts of the women writers of the Harlem Renaissance to raise race in the minds of whites involve not only the white-washing of their black heroines but also their feminisation. According to the yardsticks of the time, the images which are forced onto black women are negative because being the opposite of white femininity, they are 'masculine'. In order to emphasise that black women are not male *bitches* but 'real' women, the women writers present their black characters in the prescribed model of femininity. At the same time, the black women do not come across in the novels as behaving in a manner that conforms to the *white* model. Their behaviour is more suited to the experience of black women and shows features of obstinacy and independence. This unbalanced construction of character thus betrays the inner tensions between constructions of white and black femininity and the related tensions between masculinity and femininity.

The most famous woman writer of the Harlem Renaissance is undoubtedly the essayist, folklorist, anthropologist and novelist Zora Neale Hurston. Hurston's work differs in several respects from the conventional black novels of her time. She does not plead for the equality of blacks and whites but brings instead this black difference to the fore. In her texts the female self is foregrounded. Her most famous novel, *Their Eyes Were Watching God* (1937), for instance, is structured around the self-consciousness and development of the heroine, Janie Crawford. Hurston's use of language as a means of exploring black femininity is interesting and innovative. She first elevates the black American speech of the southern states – the vernacular of poor, illiterate blacks – to the status of a literary language. The radical effect of Hurston's work on the African-American tradition was not recognised until much later. In *In Search of Our Mothers' Gardens* Alice Walker, who supports the idea of a specific and distinct literary tradition of black women, refers to Hurston as the great predecessor. Hurston's influence on *The Color Purple* can be clearly discerned in linguistic style and motifs.

Apart from Zora Neale Hurston, black women writers gave a white identity to their black characters up until the 1950s. Only Gwendolyn Brooks, in *Maud Martha* (1953), paints a black, realistic and yet positive portrait. This novel inaugurates a phase in which black consciousness-raising begins to replace the white ideal of the refined lady. The great turnaround actually took place during the 1960s. Then blacks organised themselves, peacefully at first, in the Civil Rights Movement, under the leadership of Martin Luther King Jr, in which many women were active. Later the much more militant Muslim Black Power and Black Panther movements started up. These two demanded more than just equal rights as American citizens. They turned away from the available white norms and values and aimed for a separate nationalist black state within America. In the Black Arts Movement this aggressive attitude was expressed in a black aesthetics, approaching art from a black perspective, giving it a social function and addressing exclusively a black audience (Neal, 1975).

The black revolution in the 1960s had the positive effect that blacks began to consider their 'blackness' as a distinct category, both for the perception of Self and for group identity. Its negative aspects were the idealisation of unity, particularly between black men and women, the denial of sexism and the superior attitude of men with regard to women. Black Power was a men's movement, and women were told by the leader Stokely Carmichael that the only position they could obtain within it was the horizontal one. Also, through impulses from the white feminist movement, black women began to recognise that their experiences were affected by the connotations of race and, to an equal extent, of gender.

In this context Barbara Smith's pioneering 'Toward a Black Feminist Criticism' (1977) paved the way for a black feminist theory. Smith approached black feminism in its complexity of race, gender and psycho-sexuality. She introduced black feminism as a racial experience different from white feminism; as sexual difference from men, and, moreover, she pays attention to lesbian difference. She stresses that black women are part of a different literary tradition. The quest for a black female identity and own voice cannot be separated from the social and political questions surrounding race and sexuality. Thus, in Smith's theory we again see the central notions of experience, history and identity. Apart from critiquing sexism in its own ranks, African-American feminist criticism also focuses explicitly on the tendency of white feminists to consider their experiences and struggles as universal women's problems which apply to every woman. White experiences (however much related to women) are just as selective and collective as those of men. Stereotypes such as the 'southern belle', 'angel in the house', 'middle-class housewife' which white feminist resist are, for example, of a wholly different nature from those which burden black women. The processing of these developments can be read in recent literature by African-American women. The tumult of the 1960s resulted on the one hand in a shift of focus: from now on the black community is the audience. On the other hand the community itself is criticised whenever internalised racist and sexist tendencies remain unreflected. In the 1980s the range and the complexity of black femininity were revealed in the representation – remarkable, for the puritanical American public – of lesbian sexuality. The anthology *This Bridge Called my Back: Writings by Radical Women of Color* (Moraga and Anzaldúa, 1981) and work by Audre Lorde, especially her autobiographical *Zami: A New Spelling of My Name* (1982), present the interconnection of (lesbian) sexuality, social context, autobiography, theory and fiction. Loyalty between women and their mutual friendships were always motifs in black female writing. The subsequent questioning of the naturalness of heterosexuality in black and ethnic communities is an important step in the unravelling of social constructions.

Also, because blacks recognise a past of dispossession and denial, the search for a voice of their own always involves establishing a specific (literary) tradition. This means that as well as the continuing attempts at cultural analysis through deconstruction of language, critical attention would also be focused on representation and the construction of characters.

An example of such an analysis is Barbara Johnson's 'Metaphor, Metonymy and Voice in *Their Eyes Were Watching God*' (1984). In this essay Johnson deconstructs the traditional hierarchies of both theory versus fiction and of white versus black. By using Zora Neale Hurston's fictional text (black, female) as an authority which undermines the existing theory (white, female), she follows a plural strategy. She adds something new to the routine debate among Western cultural theoreticians by foregrounding the *difference* of black female textuality. At the same time her analysis is a tribute and contribution to the literary tradition of black women.

This tradition of black women makes women's central position visible not only in African-American history but also in the social and political developments of the United States. The metaphors, themes and narrative strategies in the work of Toni Morrison, Alice Walker, Gloria Naylor, Ntozake Shange, Paule Marshall and Audre Lorde, for example, originate from the strange-dual consciousness of black women. Their novels are political signals, fictional (auto)biographies which are at the same time history and utopia. The black heroines who populate the texts are complex and rebellious. They bear the traces of branded words, stereotypical images, white and black myths. They stand at a crossroads where the Western writing tradition and black oral traditions mix and where lines of gender, race, class and sexuality affect each other. These searching, dual-conscious, black heroines give unparalleled shape to the pluriform, mixed, multicultural nature of current Western societies.

Double strategy

After this exploration of the position of black textuality and subjectivity in a white context, I return to the question with which I began: how has *The Color Purple*, this 'limited' novel with its 'strange' themes, become a bestseller? A consideration of the context in which the novel is written and read leads me to the effect of the gaze of the other on black subjectivity; I think that the answer to my question lies in the black, strange consciousness. Walker plays in such a creative and ambiguous way with this consciousness that the text addresses different groups of readers. Taking inspiration from bell hooks's analysis (1990a), I shall explain what I mean.

I have already briefly mentioned above that the novel, with its use of the black vernacular, has adopted oral traditions. Moreover, the autobiographical convention is incorporated into the text. Through the structure of letters, the narrative perspective is anchored in an 'I-narrator'. A third African-American tradition, the African theme, is contained in Nettie's missionary work. The consistent focus on a black, female, realistic course of life places the novel alongside the work of Hurston, Brooks, Angelou, Morrison and Lorde. *The Color Purple* thus addresses explicitly a black audience, also because the action takes place entirely within the black community and culture. In this view, *The Color Purple* unmistakably conforms with the literary tradition of black women.

And yet the text is not exclusively understandable to a black (female) audience (see the next chapter for a white reading of *The Color Purple*). The concession to the white audience lies not in the interweaving of typical 'white' motifs or themes, but in the way in which the text is narrated. *The Color Purple* has adopted traditional Western conventions in its narrative structure. For example, we get to know Celie and the characters around her through the language with which they address God or each other. This vernacular actually reaches us in written language, in letters. The epistolary novel is a well-known eighteenth-century European genre. Because black orality so explicitly acquires the epistolary letter form, the novel in fact depends on a white convention.

In *The Color Purple* sexuality is represented in a candid way and leaves little to the imagination. That is progressive, but at the same time the reader is forced into the uncomfortable position of voyeur; bell hooks even suggests that there are pornographic conventions at work in *The Color Purple*. Another convention by which the reader is drawn into the novel is that of the fairy tale. There is a happy ending and ample use of sentiment. Like the ugly duckling, Celie turns out at the end of the novel to be a happy woman with her own business and property, surrounded by friends and family. The 'bad guy' Mr. —— has repented his ways and, on the basis of their mutual love for Shug, he and Celie can be reconciled. Celie has not really changed through a personal, psychological reversal or catharsis, nor by giving herself a place in the social order: all activities come from above and from outside. In fact she is, and remains, from the first sentences of the text ('~~I am~~ I have always been a good girl. Maybe you can give me a sign letting me know what is happening to me'), the innocent and, in some ways, good victim. Does this representation not draw on the white romantic image of the good, innocent child?

The most effective convention with which *The Color Purple* addresses a traditional white audience, however, is the portrayal of sexuality as romantic heterosexuality. That may sound strange, perhaps, given that the text so clearly portrays a lesbian romance. But how lesbian is this representation? In itself the representation of lesbian sexuality in our compulsory heterosexual culture is revolutionary (Rich, 1986). Ultimately meanings are reproduced by the way in which images are narrated. It is true that the lesbian romance between Shug and Celie is not represented as free of tension, yet it is idyllic. Neither Shug and Celie, nor the members of their family, have trouble with the phenomenon still generally considered threatening and unnatural. Which is all the more striking because black lesbians often bear witness to the aggressive homophobia and macho sexism among blacks. I believe that, in view of the rest of the realistic, safe black content of *The Color Purple*, this idyllic description of lesbian love is a concession to white, romantic and thus heterosexual conventions rather than a revolutionary, utopian representation.

The Color Purple is not threatening, strange or disturbing for whites.

Black men rather than white ideology are shown as a source of evil. The deliberately inward-directed focus of the text has the possibly undesired result that white readers are not encouraged to question their own racist assumptions. The crude representation of the few whites in the text, supported by the distance created by the fairy-tale tone, may give rise to aversion rather than identification on the part of white readers. The effect of the absorption of traditional white conventions is, therefore, one of familiarity. *The Color Purple* offers the white reader enough recognition, enough excitement and just enough strangeness for reading pleasure. Above I praised Walker's creative abilities, her capacity to use black strange self-consciousness to further the black cause in such a way that both whites and blacks are addressed. Although this strategy is admirable, the question still arises whether *The Color Purple* has been awarded so much praise because of its comfortable, conventional narrative method and traditional representation.

In short, no unequivocal judgement can be made of *The Color Purple*. As a contribution to black culture the novel is on the one hand revolutionary and socially critical, but on the other hand the text does not encourage the reader to any self-reflection. *The Color Purple* contains an ambivalent and contradictory tension which I can only ascribe to the double strategy of those who in the West have been met over the ages as the 'stranger' and the 'other'. The novel thus shows precisely the strategic power and the instability of the strange-dual self-consciousness of blacks.

Literature for further study

Christian, Barbara (1985) *Black Feminist Criticism: Perspectives on Black Women Writers*. Collection of old and new essays which focus on the representation and development of character in African-American novels. Also discusses lesbian desire.

Collins, Patricia Hill (1990) *The Social Construction of Black Feminist Thought: Knowledge, Consciousness, and the Politics of Empowerment*. Collins analyses the relation of knowledge and power from the perspective of the experience and ideas of African-American women.

Gates, Henry Louis Jr (ed.) (1990) *Reading Black, Reading Feminist: A Critical Anthology*. Inspiring and informative reader containing a large number of articles about the construction of a tradition, the deconstruction of myths and black feminist reading.

hooks, bell (1981) *Ain't I a Woman: Black Women and Feminism*. (1984) *From Margin to Center*. (1989) *Talking Back: Thinking Feminist, Thinking Black*. (1990b) *Yearning: Race, Gender and Cultural Politics*. (1992) *Black Looks:*

Race and Representation. (1994a) *Outlaw Culture: Resisting Representations.* bell hooks's work is characterised by short, critical and readable essays in which oppression in all its forms is the central subject. She challenges her readers to let go of more or less rigid ideas about race, sexuality and class and always illustrates her theoretical reflections with practical examples.

Kristeva, Julia (1991) *Strangers to Ourselves.* Psychoanalyst and linguist Julia Kristeva shows that the xenophobia always directed at others in the West is in fact a projection of the elusive stranger within ourselves.

Moraga, Cherrie, and Gloria Anzaldúa (eds) (1981) *This Bridge Called my Back: Writings by Radical Women of Color.* Important landmark of its time, containing many short, varied, often autobiographical pieces from both a lesbian and a heterosexual perspective, by women of different ethnicities.

Pryse, Marjorie, and Hortense J. Spiller (eds) (1985) *Conjuring: Black Women, Fiction and Literary Tradition.* Collection of essays by different authors making the literary tradition of African-American women visible. Focuses mainly on autobiography, (oral) story-telling and self-definition.

Said, Edward W. (1978) *Orientalism.* By 'orientalism' Said understands not the study of the East but the ways in which the West has represented the East. This representation is an expropriation and appropriation and thus says more about Western exercise of power than about the East itself.

Spivak, Gayatri Chakravorty (1987) *In Other Worlds: Essays in Cultural Politics.* In these varied pieces, in rather complicated language, Spivak primarily addresses the academic elite. She argues, inter alia, for using literature (classes) as ideological criticism and for racism, like sexism, to be recognised as Western phenomena. According to her, critical self-consciousness among academics is of the greatest importance for the deconstruction of power structures.

Tate, Claudia (ed.) (1983) *Black Women Writers at Work.* Interviews with Maya Angelou, Toni Cade Bambara, Gwendolyn Brooks, Alexis DeVeaux, Nikki Giovanni, Kritin Hunter, Gayl Jones, Audre Lorde, Toni Morrison, Sonia Sanchez, Ntozake Shange, Alice Walker, Margaret Walker and Sherley Anne Williams.

12

The colour of the sign: feminist semiotics

LIESBETH BROUWER

A semiotic experience on a Brazilian beach

The swimming suits Brazilian women wear are too revealing. They consist of an upper part with two small triangular pieces of cloth over the nipples, and a lower part which is hardly more than a string around the waist and a string with another small triangular cloth over the crotch; 'dental floss' in slang. Not only young girls wear such suits, older women also turn up in them. I found out that my perception of beach life in Brazil was culturally biased when a woman friend of mine dressed in the typical Northern European way. She took off the upper part of her bikini and wore what I thought was just a very decent pair of shorts. The nearly naked women and men who found themselves at some distance from us watched what we were doing, discussing it amongst themselves, nudging each other and judging this costume unacceptable. My friend's bare breasts were the source of great commotion, from which I inferred that the Brazilian women on the beach must have considered themselves to be properly dressed. We were the laughing stock of the beach, outsiders and foreigners. Naked they amused themselves with our nakedness.

Now who were more naked, the Brazilian women or we? If we ask this of a semiotician s/he will not give a straight answer. Views on nudity and clothing, s/he is likely to say, precede our perception; conventions and expectations about the world immediately master what enters our senses and determine its meaning. Events such as the one on the Brazilian beach make us realise that even seeing is not a simple thing. We can therefore ask the question whether we really see what we see. My experience with swimming suits in Brazil can rightfully be called a semiotic experience; it illustrates the semiotic axiom that perceptions are always mediated. This alienating event neatly introduces my discussion of feminist semiotics and *The Color Purple*.

Semiotics: an introduction

Some literary critics have placed the novel in a black literary tradition. This suggests that the novel is special in a particular way and that it matters that it is written by a black woman. The designation 'black literature' is provocative for me, a white reader. Would I, as a white person, be able to understand the novel? The label 'black' means that my own identity is at stake: my skin colour is addressed – I am not just I, I am a white I. Reading the novel, however, I did not have the feeling that I had read a work that differed greatly from 'white' literature. It would have been easy to ignore the label 'black literature' altogether, but then I would have done exactly the same as traditional literary criticism has so often done with the notion of 'women's literature'. Even though one might adhere to the idea that there is only one literature, this does not mean that there is only one literary tradition. Is ignoring the possible otherness of the novel not a missed chance? The novel may gain in richness of meaning if I permit it to address my colour.

This chapter deals with the question of the relevance of categories like 'black', 'white', 'female' or 'male' in semiotics. My discussion is prefaced by an introduction to feminist semiotics. I will indicate in what way labels like 'women's literature' or 'black literature' can be (made) meaningful. My position is that, next to a political meaning, they have a hypothetical value as literary historical concepts. If white or black acquires more than a historical and political meaning, and if it is assumed that they are based on essential differences, then the terms will function as exclusion mechanisms, ruling out the possibility of cross-coloured communication.

The Brazilian example emphasises that experiences and perceptions are not as direct and authentic as they appear. Semiotics takes into account the fact that every perception is mediated and that so-called authentic experiences are authentic only in as far as they have not yet been put in words. We may call this insight into the ever-occurring mediation the 'semiotic turn', a turn to semiotics, the study of signs. Charles Sanders Peirce (1839–1914) and Ferdinand de Saussure (1857–1913) were the founders of semiotics. Their work has influenced academics and theoreticians from different disciplines. The work of Saussure has been of great importance for the development of structuralist linguistics, semiotics and anthropology. Peirce's work has influenced such diverse fields of study as computer science and theology, logic and literary theory.

The reflection on women's and men's place in society and culture has also benefited from the semiotic turn. Questions about the nature of women and men are replaced by questions about frameworks of interpretation which determine how we experience femininity and masculinity. Initially there was some resistance within women's studies to this semiotic turn, because it involved a philosophical questioning of the category of 'woman', which was thought to hinder the struggle for the rights of women. However, this resistance was short-lived for the simple reason that the assumption of a different relationship between men and women implies that femininity and masculinity are not fixed and static entities. Moreover, the view that femininity and masculinity are produced in material and discursive practices in ever-changing forms is a more interesting starting-point for studying the complex relation between the sexes than the previous idea of this relation as one of oppression or exclusion.

Woman is a signifier – this is how we can sum up the discovery of a decade ago. Femininity and masculinity are constructed through narratives and discourses: for example, literary texts, pop songs, the Bible, medical and psychological reference works. This insight meant that feminists could stop questioning the nature of and truth about femininity and masculinity. At the very most they could say that the signifiers man, woman, femininity, masculinity will always remain. We do not know of a culture in which the distinction between femininity and masculinity is not meaningful, but the distinction can acquire different meanings because its meaning is not fixed. What it means to be a woman, or what it means to be a man, is highly contingent upon the culture and time in which the lives are lived. But also in our own life, in our own environment, being a woman sometimes means nothing, and sometimes means a great deal. For example, you have the right to vote, whether you are a woman or a man; but not so long ago being a woman or being a man had absolute meaning for the right to vote. On the other hand being a woman still means a great deal in heterosexual relationships, or in fashion.

Feminist semiotics aims at describing how our conceptions of femininity, masculinity and ourselves as sexed subjects are constructed and maintained; how they change; how they lead to problems; how they are constantly debated; and how they are connected to material practices, that is to say to the ways in which labour, production and reproduction are organised. Feminist semiotics is self-conscious and reflexive. It takes into account that the knowledge it produces is part of signifying practices, and that as such it also contributes to the signification of sexual difference. Feminist semiotics not only undermines theories that pretend to pronounce the ultimate truth about feminine and masculine identity, it questions the notion of the self-evident subject. As such it partakes in the adventure of de-centring the subject.

On the whole, feminist semiotics occupies a distinct place within semiotics. It is pragmatic and expansive; it looks primarily at how signs are used and how they function. As such, feminist semiotics is a branch of cultural semiotics. Various semioticians have argued that cultural semiotics is not a clearly defined field of study and that it is far too broad in scope, hence the term 'expansive'. Expansive semiotics is primarily associated with the work of the French-Bulgarian semiotician and psychoanalyst Julia Kristeva. This form of semiotics does not restrict itself to the study of the nature of the sign, but it encompasses the whole process of signification, or semiosis. Semiosis implies the production as well as the reception of signs. The feminist variant of this branch of semiotics concentrates on the role gender plays in the process of signification.

It should be understood that the construction of gender is usually a side-effect of discourse. This implies that attention is not only paid to discourses that explicitly address femininity and masculinity. On the contrary, representations of sexual difference are often incidental to discourses which are not explicitly about femininity and masculinity. Take, for example, the news media. It has been shown repeatedly that the press treats women politicians differently from their male colleagues. This is usually not the result of a conscious strategy but the reflection of differences which are perceived as self-evident. Since, as I have indicated above, feminist semiotics involves the whole process of signification, the way in which women and men produce and interpret signs can also be an object of study. Although after the semiotic turn gender is looked upon as a semiotic construction, it does not mean that semioticians do not take sexual difference seriously. Differences have been historically constructed, they have been institutionalised, and they are incorporated by individuals as real. The interesting point of feminist semiotics is that in looking at the reality of gender divisions as a semiotic phenomenon, the constitutive role of concepts, ideas and images about men and women is also taken into account.

Julia Kristeva's work has not been the only influence on feminist semiotics; other thinkers whose works have proved to be of great importance for theories on sexual difference must also be mentioned. First of all there is the work of the French psychoanalyst Jacques Lacan. Influenced by Saussure, he made psychoanalysis semiotic. Language is constitutive of human subjectivity, says Lacan; we do not express ourselves in language, language expresses us. When we learn to speak, we learn to subject ourselves to the order of language.

Louis Althusser, in his works, studies the consequences of the semiotic turn for Marxist theory. Marxism, as a theory of political praxis, was dominated by the opposition between ideology and truth, between false and true consciousness. Althusser states that one cannot escape ideology ('ideology is eternal'); he defines social reality as a struggle in and about ideology and he discards the idea of a true consciousness as an illusion.

The semiotic turn was also established in historiography. Michel Foucault, in his history of sexuality, started from the assumption that sexuality and sexual practices, are socially and historically constructed, and are far less spontaneous, far less 'physical' than we have been taught to think.

Finally, I want to mention the work of Jacques Derrida, which received much acclaim within feminist semiotics in recent years. Derrida claims to be taking Saussure's discovery to its extreme consequences. Derrida coined the expression 'there is nothing outside the text'. His philosophical project, deconstructivism, problematises the rhetorical peculiarity of language – as if language refers to a reality outside itself. The method developed by Derrida shows how individual texts (philosophical, scientific, literary) produce the illusion of conformity with reality. Derrida deployed his deconstructive reading strategies primarily against the founding philosophies of the Western world, the master discourses that created the illusion of 'presence', of a world of things and concepts that should form the ground of human language.

In contrast to expansive semiotics, micro-semiotics is concerned with the conditions which 'something' must fulfil in order to qualify as a sign. Though this is hardly a priority for feminist semiotics, it has an implicit understanding that in principle everything can become a sign. It sees the role of the subject in signification as fundamental; the subject is a subject by virtue of the fact that it signifies, that it makes and undoes signs. According to feminist semiotics, signs only exist when they are perceived. To put it simply: a red traffic-light is no sign if no one perceives it as such, or, to put it differently, if no one ascribes a sign function to the object. In short, one needs a framework of interpretation for something to become a sign. More precisely: frameworks of interpretation produce signs. This does not mean that, in the act of perception, a framework of interpretation comes first; different processes of interpretation go on at the same time. Objects can set the semiotic process in motion; but the object can lead to all kinds of meanings, depending on which framework of interpretation is activated. On the other hand, different frameworks of interpretation can be activated as well, so that the 'thing' acquires different and sometimes conflicting meanings. A sound can also be an object. Our linguistic competence enables us to perceive one sound as a word, a sign, while others remain just noise. Through our social and cultural competence – our knowledge of the world – we make and undo signs and fit them into our world.

Peirce has systematised the movements we can recognise in signification. We will not examine his system in detail here, but refer the reader to the introductions to Peirce's work mentioned in the bibliography. It is important to realise that a material object becomes a sign on the basis of *similarity*. An object becomes a sign on the basis of a perceived resemblance; in short, a ground is necessary in order to make a sign from an object, whether a thing, an image, or a sound.

Peirce distinguished three types of similarity, the *iconic*, the *indexical* and the *symbolic*. An iconic relationship consists of specific congruences of object and sign: a photograph of a woman resembles the woman herself because of similarities of form; a mountain can resemble a woman's breast, a tower a penis. Indexical similarities indicate contiguity. For example, when we see stiletto heels under a table in a movie, we understand not only that a living being is around but also that it is a woman. Finally, a symbolic relationship exists by virtue of agreements and conventions: a pink triangle refers to involvement in gay rights; a flag indicates a nation or a state. Derrida and Pierce are agreed upon signs; there is nothing about the flag or the pink triangle, in shape or form, to make one think of that to which they refer (homosexuality, the state). For that matter neither the pink triangle nor the flag – although we have almost forgotten the genesis of this latter symbol – are arbitrary conventions. In World War II in Nazi concentration camps homosexuals were forced to wear a pink triangle. The pink triangle identified homosexuals and distinguished them from other prisoners, especially the Jews, who were forced to wear a yellow star. In the 1970s the gay movement adopted this symbol so as to compare themselves to the persecuted homosexuals of World War II (icon), to express the historical fate of homosexuals (index) and to make it into a symbol of self- consciousness and resistance (symbol).

To a certain extent making signs of the world around us is an individual matter. Some persons will see things (make signs) where others notice nothing. The power to discern, which is the power to make and undo signs, depends on knowledge, sensibility and experience. We should be aware that interpreting the world is a complex thing, because we are somehow all the time busy generating meaning by a constant process of comparing and finding similarities. Semiotics aims at systematizing this complex process.

In spite of the fact that feminist semiotics is limited to that part of semiosis in which sexual difference is at stake, it still covers a wide field. Its focus on the ways in which gender is signified blurs the conventional boundaries between genres and discourses, for example between literary, scientific, and everyday discourses. Therefore, feminist semioticians are sometimes reproached for neglecting the specificity of the various genres and discourses and are accused of lumping all texts together. This accusation makes some sense: making gender a useful category of analysis has had the effect of upsetting conventional boundaries between formerly strictly seperated discursive domains.

The feminist semiotic approach to literary texts can roughly be divided in two. Literature is either considered as a discourse that, just like other types of discourse, engenders sexual difference, or it is considered as a domain which has a value in itself. I propose to call the first approach 'cultural semiotics' and the second 'literary semiotics'.

For cultural semiotics the aesthetic aspects of literary works (by women) are not so much at stake. It sees literature simply as an influential discursive field. Cultural semiotics studies what is characterised as female and male at a given historical moment in a certain discourse, which is then related to the social scope for action and experience granted to women and men in that period. In this perspective literature forms an interesting field of research, because it represents social and individual relationships in forceful ways: relationships among people and between people and the complex world around them. Obviously literature is not unique in this; religion, philosophy, art and popular culture also fulfil these functions. We can find examples of a cultural semiotics approach in the work of Julia Kristeva, Mieke Bal, Nancy Armstrong, Kaja Silverman, Teresa de Lauretis and many others.

In literary semiotics the aesthetic aspects of literary works are far more central. An important question here is whether gender can be a meaningful category in aesthetics. Is gender of any importance in relation to art and literature? For many non-feminist literary critics the category of gender meant a denial of the universal character of 'true Art'. To speak about gender in relation to literature conflicts with artistic ideals, in which a work of art is something spiritual and purely mental. This is perhaps one of the most deeply rooted representations in Western culture: the sexlessness of the spirit which is a symbol of purity and transcendence. It goes without saying that such a context does not facilitate references to gender. After all, if we see the spirit as sexless it does not matter whether a man or a woman has made a particular work of art. However, studies of the reception of literary works by women have demonstrated that they get a different treatment from men in literary criticism. The expectations which literary critics and scholars bring to a literary work are definitely guided by the gender of the author. Keeping in mind the fundamental principle of semiotics, we understand that these expectations – which form a framework for interpretation – could very well determine how the work is read and valued.

But even aesthetics gave in. Although the ideal of a universal art is not discarded art historians and literary theorists now acknowledge the immanent bias of the idea of the Great Tradition. This gave room to comparative studies of women's literature. Interesting parallels have been found in works by women writers which were not perceived in general literary histories (Showalter, 1977; Meijer, 1988). By the way, here we recognise our semiotic assumptions in practice: a new framework of interpretation produces signs and reads new, unsuspected meanings in 'old' texts.

The meaning of Alice Walker's novel also changes, depending on the perspective we choose. In the following pages I will give guidelines first for a cultural semiotic and then for a literary semiotic reading of the text. The cultural semiotic analysis focuses on the symbolic aspects of the novel; that is to say we concentrate on the representation of gender in the novel. A literary semiotic reading of the novel is much more open. We allow the novel to activate frameworks of interpretation that we could not have imagined beforehand. In such a reading it remains to be seen whether gender becomes an issue at all. In my literary semiotic reading I will take up the challenge which I feel is implied in the label '*black* literature': what does reading as a white woman mean?

The Color Purple in cultural and literary semiotics

A cultural semiotic reading of *The Color Purple* implies that we attribute symbolic meaning to the narrated story; we ask the question how the novel contributes to our knowledge of the world, and in particular to our knowledge about the attitudes and behaviour of men and women. In other words, which views of femininity and masculinity are represented in *The Color Purple*? We consider Celie's life as *pars pro toto*; it stands for the lives of (black) women. The way in which the story is narrated also becomes part of a cultural semiotic analysis.

The novel begins with a loss of identity – '~~I am~~ I have always been a good girl. Maybe you can give me a sign letting me know what is happening to me' (3) – and ends with a rebirth – 'Matter of fact, I think this the youngest us ever felt' (244). There is a clear reason for the main character's loss of identity: she, Celie, has been raped by her stepfather. This rape announces more misery and suffering to come; when her stepfather has had enough of her Celie is married off to a man who abuses her in all kinds of ways. She has no answer to what is done to her, apart from accepting her fate – 'Bible say, Honor father and mother' and 'But he my husband' (39). However, Celie's admiration for Shug Avery, aroused by a picture, indicates that her feelings are not yet numbed. When her husband, Mr. ——, brings her into contact with Shug the story changes its course. Gradually Celie discovers her own body, her own feelings, her own value. She and Shug enter into a relationship and Celie leaves her husband. Mr. ——'s frustrations about the course his life has taken leads him to hide from Celie the letters her sister Nettie has written to her. Celie is so furious when she discovers this, that she becomes paralysed and feels pressed to murder Mr. ——. She does not do this however and instead overcomes her rage by making a quilt. The final test of strength for Celie is that she has to cope with Shug's erotic adventure with a younger man. When she has also managed this she can finally accept life and even reconcile herself with Mr. ——. She succeeds in life's main goal as expressed by Shug: 'I think it pisses God off if you walk by the color purple in a field somewhere and don't notice it' (167).

The novel can be summarised even more briefly if we follow the development of Celie's image of God. The God to whom she writes letters conforms to the image of a severe, old, white man. Halfway through Celie's story she rejects God, but in the end she finds the divine in everything: in the trees, the mountains, in the colour purple of the fields, in the growing cobs of corn, in the other. Her last letter is addressed to 'Dear God. Dear stars, dear trees, dear sky, dear peoples. Dear Everything. Dear God' (242). From being a woman who lives under the lash of an oppressive and moralistic Christianity, Celie develops into a woman who shares her pleasure, love and joy with God. Parallel to this development, Celie's relation to men also changes. Originally she obeys the men who are placed above her: her father and her husband. Then she rejects them and in the end she is able to relate to them on an equal footing. Reversing the hierarchy is clearly a taboo in the novel. God is definitely not a She; men and women ultimately have the same vocation in life, that is, to sort out their existence on earth (239). There may be a difference in the social position of men and women but with regard to the fundamental matters of life there is no difference: femininity and masculinity are only veils over a hidden true humanity.

This summary does not do justice to the symbolic meaning of *The Color Purple*. We have not yet discussed the epigraph with which Walker begins her novel nor have we paid attention to the words of thanks with which she ends it, and to the alternation of the two sociolects she uses in the novel, the one of Nettie and the one of Celie. The epigraph – which reads 'To the Spirit:/ Without whose assistance/ Neither this book/ Nor I/ Would have been written' – and the words of thanks – 'I thank everybody in this book for coming. A.W., author and medium' – form an ambiguous comment on the narrated story. An ambiguity that concerns the status of the narrated story: is what is told imagined or is it real? The quotes make an unequivocal answer to this question impossible. Walker begins her novel with a dedication to the Spirit, 'Without whose assistance /Neither this book /Nor I /Would have been written'. She concludes her novel with words of thanks to 'everyone for coming' and signs as 'author and medium'. In *The Color Purple* the relationship between story and reality is complex. On the one hand Alice Walker's mediation suggests that 'everyone' was there before the book was written; on the other hand there is the author who created 'all of them'. On a higher plane, there is the Spirit – *conditio sine qua non* for both the author and her novel. Thus, Walker suggests that she belongs to a process of signification or to a Scripture which predates her. The story which she relates exists by virtue of what is written and is not simply the upshot of a black community which really exists. The black community becomes transformed into literature (Scripture, Spirit) and is thus signified.

The Color Purple belongs to that type of novels which we enjoy reading in our culture. It is expressive, forceful, vital, and optimistic, in spite of the terror that rages against the protagonist. As such the novel confirms the (Christian and modernist) ideal of the possibility of transcending suffering; it establishes the value of life in spite of all terrors. And above all the novel confirms the promise of a fulfilled life, for which self-consciousness and physical integrity are the conditions. The representation of gender relations in *The Color Purple* conforms to the ideal of emancipation and as such it is in keeping with the modernist attitude I just touched on. With the help of the women around her, Celie liberates herself from the misconceptions in her community regarding relationships between men and women, and she is thus in a position to fence off further aggression. Walker's message is that self-consciousness is the best weapon against the aggression of others as well as against one's own aggression.

Literary theoreticians are usually not inclined to pay much attention to the message or moral and political idea of a work of art. It does play an important role in cultural semiotics on the other hand. We do however not look at the message to embrace it, or to reject it, but we want to find out how the message is structured, what its roots are and how it relates to other social, political and philosophical discourses. That is why I called the message of *The Color Purple* modernist. In our times modernist messages have become conventional; they correspond to the spontaneous ideas many of us have about life and about social relations. Because of this conventional message *The Color Purple* offers (too) little resistance to easy appropriation. It is true that all understanding implies appropriation, but some novels impede appropriation and compel the reader to form a new framework of interpretation. In my view *The Color Purple* does not do this. In its complicated simplicity *The Color Purple* is the perfect emancipation novel. But it is also a novel which inscribes women in a familiar tale: it reproduces the modernist and liberal-democratic ideology which defines a task for women and men alike, that is, to strive for a fulfilled life.

Reading *The Color Purple* as a white woman: guidelines to a literary semiotics

As I indicated in the introduction to this chapter, I can only touch on a literary semiotic reading of *The Color Purple*. I decided to concentrate on one aspect: the label 'black literature'. It provides me with a framework for interpretation which makes me feel somewhat uncomfortable because it forces me to examine myself; it addresses my identity and I want my identity to be self-evident, although I know, theoretically, that it is not. The label 'black literature' thus has an alienating effect. (By the way a semiotician should always try to get alienated, because it makes her or him aware of the peculiarities of a text that would otherwise go by unnoticed.) White semioticians – like white people generally – are usually not so happy when their skin colour is a cause of alienation. White people prefer to think that their skin colour means nothing. But black people tell them what a difference the colour of one's skin can make (see also chapter 11). Therefore it seems to me that it is important to take up the challenge that is implied by this label and consider black and white as meaningful categories. I try to read *The Color Purple* as a person who is aware of her colour, to see whether I make other signs, whether I see things I would not have noticed when not challenged to do so. The scope of this chapter does not permit me to be exhaustive. I can just touch upon some aspects of reading as a white person, and invite the reader to carefully look at her or his own reading strategies.

Obviously the function that white people have in the novel is important for this kind of semiotic reading. It startled me to realise that

I do not consider Miss Eleanor a typical white woman; on the contrary, for me she is exceptional. I refuse to see Miss Eleanor as a symbolic sign; at the very most I want to see her as an iconic or indexical sign. That is to say: 'Miss Eleanor looks like white women in the south of the United States in the 1930s' (iconic) or 'white women in a racist society are like this' (indexical). Possibly this is one of the strategies which a white reader uses so as not to be manoeuvred into the position of a racist. Also, it is quite possible that for a black reader Miss Eleanor does have the typical features of a white woman, so that Miss Eleanor then becomes a symbolic sign.

I also find it difficult to consider the iconic merits of the 'black vernacular' that Alice Walker uses in Celie's letters. Her language is of course not as familiar to me as it is to women living in or coming from the countryside in the southern part of the United States, so that I cannot fully experience its beauty, musicality and richness. To me Walker's use of the black vernacular signifies once again that *The Color Purple* fits in the tradition of realist emancipation novels. In the class society that *The Color Purple* addresses and criticises, the use of language is read as a social sign. The use of black literature in the domain of literature is in itself an emancipatory act and as such it has symbolic meaning.

In my analysis of *The Color Purple* I have paid little attention to the fact that Nettie's letters are written in standard American English. I find this however meaningful. Nettie's letters are written from Africa, another world; but a world which for black people is probably teeming with symbolical meaning. Nettie's letters are written by a woman who has a view of the world that was formed by middle-class values; Nettie has had a 'proper' education, and therefore writes standard American English. In this sense, although her letters are from Africa, they are more common than Celie's letters – at least to a reader who is used to literature. Celie's letters seem to be more natural, more spontaneous, more 'wild', so to speak. It is my impression that, by putting the two worlds alongside each other, Alice Walker subtly comments on the romantic desire to found one's identity across generations, across great distances, in an imaginary original community. A desire which from the nineteenth century onwards plays a considerable role in Western political thought and activist movements.

What struck me most in *The Color Purple* was Mr. ——'s development. I know of no white novel in which a character who is responsible for the sorrow of the protagonist is given such a loving treatment as Mr. —— receives in Walker's novel. He is allowed inner growth and change without an excessive sense of guilt. In fiction it is almost a standard law that the reform of the villain requires punishment; it is administered to him either from outside or through inner feelings of almost unbearable guilt. Celie is improbably tolerant towards Mr. ——, their relationship even develops into companionship without mutual reproaches. Although the novel is about good and evil, it is not about crime and punishment. Precisely this aspect of *The Color Purple* has also been considered as unique by a black literary critic (Barbara Smith, 1990: 235). Therefore I would be leaping to conclusions if I were to consider the absence of punishment or of the paralysing sense of guilt as typical of the black literary tradition – much as I, as a white reader, would perhaps have liked that. The most common explanation for Celie's leniency towards Mr. —— is the idea of relationships between black men and women in a racist society such as the United States being more complex than the relationship between men and women among 'whites'. In this view, though black men exercise patriarchal power over their women, they, like black women, belong to the powerless and oppressed in a wider racist society, which would bring about more solidarity between them. The absence of punishment would then be a sign for the complex gender relations among black Americans.

This explanation is, however, only partly satisfactory, because it passes over the fact that in *The Color Purple* gender is ultimately meaningless. Together, Celie and Mr. —— discover what life is about: every person – of whatever gender or status – should come to terms with life, should learn to love and to forgive and should learn to appreciate the beauty of nature. As a white woman reader I am inclined to read 'every person' as 'irrespective of colour'. Significantly, this is not suggested anywhere. The greatest power of the novel is perhaps that whites do not join in at all and are thus marginalised. White people apparently know even less about life than black people do.

What then is the meaning of the label 'black literature' for a novel like *The Color Purple*, when its message is so similar to much of white realist literature? In the introduction to this article I suggested that the term 'black literature' has primarily political significance; whether it also has literary historical significance remains to be seen. By this I mean that influences, material, themes, plots, narrative means, etcetera, in black literature form a pattern that would justify the notion of a separate literary tradition. The political significance of the term 'black literature' is of course not to be underestimated. Such a term brings about an active reception of literary works which might otherwise be forgotten. Moreover such differentiation is also emancipatory. By creating a literature of one's own, a group provides itself with a desired object: to have a literature of one's own means to count, to matter, to exist. In conclusion, for me the label 'black literature' has the same minimal meaning as the label 'women's literature'. They are names for the desire within a certain group to decide for themselves what is important without being weighed down by the burden of tradition.

Literature for further study

Armstrong, Nancy (1987) *Desire and Domestic Fiction: A Political History of the Novel.* This cultural semiotic study relates the English romantic tradition of the eighteenth century, the rules of behaviour for young members of the well-to-do bourgeoisie and the emergence of the modern citizen in rise of capitalism.

Coward, Rosalind, and John Ellis (1977) *Language and Materialism: Developments in Semiology and the Theory of the Subject.* This anthology provides a good introduction to the work of Ferdinand de Saussure and Jacques Lacan.

Culler, Jonathan (1981) *The Pursuit of Signs: Semiotics, Literature, Deconstruction.* In this study Culler shows the possibilities of semiotics for literary theories.

Eco, Umberto (1976) *A Theory of Semiotics.* Eco belongs to the school within semiotics in which the structure of the sign is central; his work is less 'expansive' than that of Silverman, Kristeva, Coward and Ellis.

Kristeva, Julia (1987) *Tales of Love.* Semiotic analyses of stories about love in our culture (theology, philosophy, literature and psychoanalysis) are related to our contemporary conception of love.

Sebeok, Thomas A. (1986) *Contributions to the Doctrine of Signs.* This book discusses the theory and history of semiotics.

Silverman, Kaja (1983) *The Subject of Semiotics.* Silverman discusses the problematic place of the subject in semiotics. She introduces psychoanalysis for a further semiotic understanding of the subject.

Journals

SIGNS. Journal of Women in Culture and Society.

13

In the footsteps of Anna and Dora: feminism and psychoanalysis

ROSI BRAIDOTTI

Introduction

Although it was Sigmund Freud who formalised psychoanalytic theory, it is generally known that women have historically played a crucial role in its origins (Sayers, 1991). On the one hand feminist studies have illuminated the creative role played by women in psychoanalytic practice; on the other hand, they have criticised psychoanalytic theory from within.

In this chapter I will explore the importance of psychoanalysis for feminist cultural studies, by discussing the cases of Anna O. and Dora. In the first section, after a short introduction to Freud and psychoanalysis in general, I will focus on the possibilities offered by psychoanalysis for an understanding of the process of interpretation, with special reference to the case of Anna O. In the second part I will discuss the ways in which female subjectivity and sexuality are represented within psychoanalysis, with reference to the case of Dora and *écriture féminine*. This discussion includes a critique of the Oedipus complex and of its many feminist revisions. The overall aim of this chapter is to offer an insight into the relationship between feminist theory, cultural studies and psychoanalysis.

Psychoanalysis as practice and theory

The case study of Anna O. was published by Freud, together with Josef Breuer, in 1895 in *Studies on Hysteria*. The term 'hysteria' stems from *hustera*, the Greek word for 'womb'. Since time immemorial this word has been used to indicate the physical and mental disturbances of women. At the end of the nineteenth century, under the influence of traditional morality, sexuality was primarily defined in biological terms. Socially as well as medically, female hysterics were treated as deviant and abnormal. They were subjected to theories of hereditary degeneration and 'therapies' in the form of physical and mental punishment.

Freud displayed deep respect and sympathy for the suffering of his female patients and although he may come across to the present-day reader as paternalistic, in his time Freud's practice was revolutionary. He analysed hysteria as a neurosis which arises from unconscious sexual desires and he hoped to cure his patients of hysterical symptoms by making these desires conscious. Two important innovative ideas are central to Freud's new perspective: first, that sexuality can be a source of somatic illness for both sexes at all ages, including children; and second, that sexuality is linked to unconscious processes.

This had enormous implications for concepts of subjectivity. After Freud, sexuality was no longer seen as natural, but as a social construction. The psychoanalytical theory of the unconscious denaturalises sexuality and as such it contributes to a critique of the essentialist view of human nature. Whereas since Descartes the individual had been conceived as autonomous, rational and 'masterful', Freud emphasised the structuring role played by the unconscious. The psychoanalytic concept of the 'subject', in opposition to the humanist term 'individual', does not collapse subjectivity with the conscious self.

For Freud subjectivity is a laborious and endless process, in which the subject is torn back and forth between desires and drives on the one hand and cultural and social demands on the other. The Freudian three-fold division of the psyche reflects the fragmentation of the subject into dynamic components: the unconscious (id), the conscious personality (ego) and the cultural and symbolic image of the self (super-ego). This split subject is not the king of creation, as the Jewish-Christian tradition would have us believe, but the product of particular historical circumstances.

At first, psychoanalysis was received negatively by medical and psychiatric specialists, on account of its ideas about sexuality and subjectivity. Freud was repeatedly accused of advocating pan-sexual perversion. In the anti-Semitic climate of the period, the fact that Freud and his early supporters were of Jewish origin contributed to their exclusion from academic and medical practice. The history of the psychoanalytic movement can thus be read as the struggle between an innovative Jewish avant-garde and a conservative Catholic medical establishment. It comes as no surprise that the Nazis burned Freud's books on public bonfires. While the rest of Freud's family was deported to concentration camps and met their deaths, Freud himself, together with his wife and children, was saved from the Holocaust at an advanced age, thanks to the intervention of his psychoanalytic disciple, the princess Marie Bonaparte.

Although questions of national and ethnic identity have always played an important role in the history of psychoanalysis, they are blatantly absent from psychoanalytical theory. Generally, psychoanalytic discourse tends to deny the importance of political and racial or ethnic questions. Conversely, only now has the history of fascist and anti-Semitic resistance against psychoanalysis begun to be written. The black feminist bell hooks rightly points out the contradictions surrounding race from the early beginnings of psychoanalysis. The Jewish doctor consciously ignored the political dangers of his society in a vain attempt to isolate science from politics (bell hooks and Childers, 1990) and thus gain some respectability for the 'science' of the unconscious.

Besides ethnicity, class also played a role in the development of psychoanalytical practice. Freud's early female patients, like Anna O. and Dora, came from well-to-do families. They introduced Freud into respectable social circles and provided him with a welcome and much-needed income, considering that he had to wait till later in his career to obtain a much-coveted chair at the university. Several of his later female patients, such as the Russian aristocrat Lou Andreas-Salomé, Hélène Deutsch, Jeanne Lampl-de-Groot and Marie Bonaparte, became practising analysts themselves. In contrast to Freud, the majority of these women did not hesitate to become involved actively in the political and social movements of their time.

The story of Anna O.

Anna O. was a pseudonym given by Freud to Bertha Poppenheim, a German-Jewish feminist who was well known at the end of the nineteenth century. Poppenheim wrote plays, contributed to the magazine *Die Frau*, and translated Mary Wollstonecraft's *Vindication of the Rights of Women* into German. She chose to remain unmarried and became involved in assistance to women in need. In 1895, the year in which her case was published, she was employed as director of the orphanage in Frankfurt. Later she became involved in social work on behalf of – mostly Jewish – prostitutes.

In 1881–82 Poppenheim underwent treatment with Freud and Breuer, because she suffered from intense neurotic disturbances. At that time hypnosis was still being used as a therapeutic method, but this technique did not seem to advance Anna O.'s cure very much. Freud therefore allowed her to talk while he took upon himself to simply listen to her 'hysterical' invented language. Anna O. called this treatment *the talking cure*, which later became the nickname for psychoanalysis itself. She was able to name the bond between the suffering patient and the assisting doctor and made it the foundation for the therapeutic situation. This foundation is what was to be called 'transference' in psychoanalysis.

Freud argues that the hysterical woman is suffering from her memories. A trauma keeps her tied to her past, which then gets expressed in dreams and hallucinations. The cure consists of releasing these memories by working backwards through the pathogenic material. The act of talking is of great therapeutical value, because the speech act creates a theatre in which the most deeply unconscious traumatic material is performed again. The shift from hypnosis to the 'talking cure' as a psychoanalytical therapy has various important implications for the status of psychoanalysis within feminist cultural studies.

In psychoanalytical practice, 'speaking' starts the process of transference. Transference indicates a mainly unconscious process through which the patient comes to identify the analyst with important figures from her or his childhood. This enables the patient to experience something of the unconscious trauma again and thus gain access to the material at the source of the psychic problem. The analyst functions as a screen for specific projections. This position allows her or him the possibility to turn the transference into a therapeutic tool. Freud was not always good at this: in the cases of both Anna O. and Dora, he mishandled the transference and, as a consequence, the therapeutic process broke down. He had to learn the hard way that transference functions both ways: the unconscious of the analyst is also mobilised in a counter-transference.

Literary critics have argued that a comparable form of transference takes place between the reader and the text. Reading, as well as interpreting, triggers off the process of transference in literary practice. The reader identifies characters in the book with important figures from her or his childhood and projects material from the unconscious onto the book. A great part of the pleasure of reading literature consists in the reactivation of unconscious desires; a comparable process of fascination is involved in cinema.

In psychoanalytical practice the illness and the symptoms become signs which need interpretation: they are caused by and connected to unconscious, sexual desires. The Freudian unconscious has its own logic far removed from conscious thought; unrecognised wishes and desires constitute the unconscious, but because they have been repressed, their content is inaccessible to consciousness. This repression can surface, however, in the form of a symptom or somatic disturbance: gestures, dreams, slips of the tongue, nervous tics, delusions and hallucinations, etc. This forms the material which psychoanalysis attempts to decipher.

In the 'talking cure' the hysterical body, with all its symptoms, becomes a text, that is to say a collection of signs which demand interpretation. The hysterical woman speaks in a language which not even she herself fully understands yet: there is a language there, but no one to speak it. The cure consists in finding adequate expression for the symptoms in everyday language. Freud explains, however, that the symptom, as an unconscious sign, cannot be translated immediately into a conscious meaning because access to it is blocked by the structure of unconscious desires. The neurotic symptom is, as it were, a text which is written without the will of the patient; interpreting the symptoms thus implies making manifest the latent meaning of the patient's behaviour. This is how bell hooks came to interpret Freud's omission of race from psychoanalytical theory as a symptom.

If the hysterical body is a text which demands a special kind of interpretation, then the body is no biological fact or anatomical essence, but a construction. Freud conceived of the body as an erotogenous surface which becomes marked by an energy which he calls 'drives'. A drive is a release of unconscious sexual energy which seeks pleasure and avoids pain. A drive is close to the instinct from which it derives its stimulus. For example, milk is the object which is sought after in order to survive; the breast – as the provider of milk – is the object of the drive and one's own mouth thereby turns to an erotogenic zone. A baby's suckling of the breast produces more than the satisfaction of a physical need; it also gives pleasure. Pleasure is the excess, or the extra bonus which the subject acquires over and above the fulfilment of her or his needs.

It is the task of a civilised society to produce subjects which have clearly defined erotogenic zones – the reproductive genitalia – and which have distanced themselves from the 'polymorphously perverse' sexuality of childhood. According to Freud, the process of acquiring adult genital sexuality is never completely finished; it is simultaneously an ideal and an illusion.

Freudian ideas about text and interpretation have strongly influenced the practice of literary criticism. Literary critics mostly employ the psychoanalytical concepts of the 'primary' and 'secondary process', which characterise the unconscious and conscious respectively, as Freud explained in *The Interpretation of Dreams* in 1900. The primary process represents the pleasure principle, in which psychical energy flows freely from one representation to another through mechanisms of condensation and displacement. In condensation, a representation is invested with all kinds of signs and associations. In a visual or verbal text this is the figure of the metaphor. In displacement, a representation is transferred by association from one sign to another. This is the figure of the metonym (Silverman, 1983). The secondary process represents the reality principle and binds the energy through memories and thoughts. It is a process of distancing and deferring fulfilment.

When a feminist literary critic includes the play of the unconscious in the analysis of metaphors and metonyms, she acquires an insight into the relationship between meaning and desire, knowledge and fantasy, interpretation and the unconscious. From a psychoanalytic perspective, every cultural activity as a whole – writing, reading, representing and interpretating – is intrinsically linked to fantasy, desire and the unconscious (Felman, 1982). I shall now further explain how female sexuality can influence the process of representation: for this purpose I will focus on Freud's famous case study of Dora.

The case of Dora

Dora's real name was Ida Bauer; she was a member of a powerful Viennese family and was brought to analysis with Freud by her father in 1901, but the treatment proved unsuccessful and she broke it off quite quickly (Freud, 1905a).

Dora told Freud that she had been seduced (read: sexually harassed) by a good friend of the family, Herr K., whose wife she adored. She knew that her father had a sexual relationship with Frau K., but Freud preferred to pursue the hypothesis that Dora was not the victim of Herr K., but was actually in love with him and, through transference, with Freud himself. Freud's problem with Dora was that he underestimated the effect of his own counter-transference; he did not recognise the way in which he projected his own unconscious self-glorification onto Dora. Consequently he did not see that Dora's neurotic conflict was caused by her unconscious desire for another woman: Frau K. As we shall see below, Dora's homosexual desire was adequately represented by Cixous in her play *Portrait of Dora*.

Dora resisted the masculinist interpretation of her case and realised that she was serving as an object of exchange between three men: her father, a womaniser who suffered from syphilis, Herr K. and Freud. Her lesbian desire, her insight and resistance have made Dora a feminist heroine. Not that this helped her pathology much: she later emigrated to New York where she entered an unhappy marriage and led an unfulfilled life.

Dora's case illustrates Freud's blind spot with respect to women. In his attempt to account for sexual traumas in the childhoods of his female patients, Freud proposed the hypothesis of the 'seduction theory'. Many female patients told him that they had been sexually approached or abused as a child by someone known to them, often their father. Although Freud was initially shocked by what he was told, he quickly doubted the truth of many of these reports. He postulated that no original seduction of the child by an adult had taken place, but that this was merely a matter of an infantile desire and fantasy. It is noteworthy therefore that in Freud's view an imaginary event can have just as great a traumatic effect as a real event.

Of course feminists have strongly criticised this idea, which was dominant within psychoanalysis for a long time. In a feminist perspective, this conversion of sexual harassment into an unconscious female desire signifies a flagrant denial of the reality of sexual violence by men, and especially of incest. Clément and Cixous (1986) state that Freud's phallocratic assumptions contributed to keeping paternal abuse hidden.

Female sexuality

Freud was the first to recognise his shortcomings: for fifteen years after the Dora case he did not publish a single case of female neurosis. In his renowned lecture *Female Sexuality* (1931) he recognised that for him female sexuality represented the 'dark continent'.

At the time of the Dora case, Freud was working on the idea that there was really only one sexual drive for both sexes; an active male libido (1905b). Twenty years later he would come to further elaborate his theory of the sexual development of both sexes (1925). At the end of the 1920s and well into the 1930s the problem of female sexuality was the subject of vehement discussion within the psychoanalytical community. In his writings Freud responded to the work of women psychoanalysts like Deutsch, Horney, Lampl-de-Groot and Klein.

Freud explained the psychological and sexual development of the young girl in analogy to that of the young boy. The process of subjectification, that is to say the way in which a girl becomes a woman and a boy becomes a man, was described by Freud as follows (1925, 1931). In the pre-Oedipal phase children of both sexes are one with their mother. In this state of 'polymorphous perversion' there is no formation yet of sexual desire; the child experiences primarily oral and anal drives. When the child separates from its mother and breaks out of the unity with her, the path for each gender differentiates. The young boy ends up in the positive Oedipus complex, which comprises a sexual desire for the mother and identification with the father: in this phase phallic or genital drives are central and the Oedipus complex comes to be broken off by a fear of castration. According to Freud, because of its visibility the penis is the most important reference in the organisation of sexuality; in contrast, the female genitalia lie hidden, which is the cause of male castration anxiety: 'the fear of nothing to see'. The young boy goes through a twofold motion: on the one hand he discovers that the young girl does not have a penis and consequently fears that the father will punish him for his forbidden love for his mother by taking away his penis, too. On the other hand, he represses his desire for his mother and forms a strong and strict super-ego.

After the pre-Oedipal stage a young girl enters the phallic stage in which she loves her mother actively, too. In this stage drives are focused on the clitoris, which is considered by Freud to be an inferior sort of penis. When the young girl makes the dramatic discovery that she has no penis she develops a castration complex, which involves self-hate and resentment towards the mother. The castration complex results in penis envy, which forces the girl to enter the positive Oedipus complex. According to Freud the girl equates the penis with a baby, in fact, for the girl the Oedipus complex involves giving up the fiercely desired penis and replacing it with the desire for a baby; to this purpose she re-directs her desire towards her father. Freud adds that only by bearing a (male) child does a woman achieve full access to mature femininity.

In the Oedipal stage, then, the young girl has to make two libidinal shifts: she replaces the erotogenic zone of the ('phallic') clitoris with the ('female') vagina, and she shifts the object of her love from the mother to the father. For the girl the psychological consequences of the Oedipus complex are permanent: penis envy gives her a sense of being castrated and therefore injured. The psychological scar of this narcissistic wound will leave the girl with a permanent sense of inferiority. Because the girl's Oedipus complex is not destroyed by castration anxiety as it is in the young boy, the Oedipal stage is never wholly resolved and as a consequence the girl has a weaker need for repression. As a result of this, says Freud, the girl scarcely develops a super-ego and remains morally defective. Repression leads the subject to the need for sublimating his/her drives, just as artists sublimate through works of art. Castration anxiety is a precondition for sublimation which, according to Freud, explains the limited participation of women in culture.

Even in Freud's time, the women psychoanalysts mentioned earlier as well as some male colleagues, like Jones, found it highly problematic that the Freudian theory about the libido led to the idea of the woman as a sign of mystery, mutilation and inferiority. Freud's view of woman as the unconscious of man, in which her own sexuality is denied, was rejected in favour of the idea of the specificity and autonomy of a female libido (Strousse, 1974).

In a feminist view, Freud's preoccupation with female sexuality provided patriarchy with an apology for male superiority. Although Freud acknowledged that becoming a woman is a painful and fragile process for girls, he still understood femininity in mainly biological terms. Later on this idea was turned into the ironic feminist slogan that *biology is destiny*. Freud thus upheld an opposition between 'natural' femininity and 'civilised' masculinity. This not only discriminated against women; it also stood in flagrant opposition to a fundamental insight of psychoanalysis. As mentioned above, the discovery of the unconscious had shifted the emphasis from human nature to the social construction of the subject as a cultural entity. However, Freud's theoy of female sexuality ended up in a biologically deterministic camp, which made him fall back on the very dualism he claimed to attack. Freud thus naturalised the inevitability of patriarchal power; following this line of thought, feminists understand Dora's resistance to Freud's interpretation of her case as a criticism of the sexist elements of psychoanalysis (Bernheimer and Kahane, 1985; Gallop, 1982).

Feminist reactions

The first systematic feminist critique of Freud was written by Simone de Beauvoir (1949). Her criticism consisted of a double rebuttal: she shattered on the one hand the biological determinist assumptions about women and on the other hand the constant subjection of women to a male model of psychological development. She disputed fiercely the concepts of penis envy, castration, the under-developed female super-ego and its inability to sublimate.

De Beauvoir argued that 'woman' functions as 'the Other' in Western culture, by which means the opposition between the man as a representative of culture and the woman as a repository of nature is maintained. Being the other, or 'difference', refers to all that which is different from and thus inferior to the male norm. For de Beauvoir the problem is that patriarchy localises the female essence in this difference; as against the psychoanalytical emphasis on *desire* she poses a political theory based on the *will* to change. The idea of social and cultural equality plays an important role in this project.

In the second feminist wave, Freud and especially psychoanalytical practice were rejected as patriarchal and oppressive. Juliet Mitchell (1974) was one of the first feminists to see psychoanalysis as a useful and potentially subversive discourse. She understood psychoanalysis as an accurate description (and not as a normative prescription) of the problematical position of women in Western culture. Another school within psychoanalysis, that is, Winnicott's object relations theory, inspired Nancy Chodorow (1978) to write a critical and psychoanalytical interpretation of motherhood, and Jessica Benjamin (1990) to develop a view of the connection between masculinity and violence.

Within women's studies in the humanities, psychoanalysis has become a method for analysing the Oedipal structure of patriarchal culture. Feminists do not understand the Oedipus complex as a universal law, but as a historical instrument in the formation of a patriarchal culture and the consequent exclusion of women. Thus Gilbert and Gubar (1979) have attacked literary history as an Oedipal struggle between established male authors (the father) and the rebellious young guard (the son). Similarly, Teresa de Lauretis (1984) has analysed the Oedipal plot of narrative structures and she proposes to extend the Oedipal structure with new versions in which the desires of the female subject are represented at last. She herself creates a different version of the Oedipal plot by reading the story from the perspective of the figure of the Sphinx.

Silverman (1988) has revised the Freudian model of the Oedipus complex for the female subject; in her view, after the Oedipal phase, the young girl enters a 'negative Oedipus complex', in which she desires the mother and considers the father to be a rival. This is 'negative' in the sense that the mother–daughter relationship as an intense love affair is scarcely represented within culture: cultural history has always been a story of fathers and sons. The recognition of sexual difference (what Freud calls the castration complex) prompts the girl to leave the negative Oedipus complex and to enter the 'positive' stage, of desire for the father and aversion from the mother. Silverman argues that heterosexual female desire is in fact structured in analogy to a homosexual desire for the mother. Female subjectivity and sexuality thus have a homosexual basis. The mother–daughter relationship is a much more complex relationship than psychoanalytical theory allows, because the mother is in fact both the object of desire and the object of identication for the daughter. Silverman concludes that the negative Oedipus complex forms the libidinal basis for feminism and that women should get more inspiration from this unconscious source.

Hirsch (1989) foregrounds the figure of the mother, Jocasta, in the Oedipus story. In both psychoanalysis and literature, the mother is traditionally represented as an object. Hirsch's project is to make the mother's voice speak specifically in relation to the daughter. To this end she analyses transformations of the mother–daughter relationship in works by female authors. In works by women the mother also appears almost exclusively as an object, if represented from the daughter's perspective. Only in texts of African-American authors does Hirsch find the mother represented as a multivoiced female subject, speaking as a mother, as a daughter and as a lover.

Hirsch praises Alice Walker's work in particular. In her essay 'In Search of Our Mothers' Gardens', Walker relates the creativity of black women explicitly to the history of their foremothers. Although the mothers' creativity was curbed by oppression and abuse, much inspiration can be found in their concealed spirituality. Their artistic bent was expressed for instance in the telling of stories, the making of quilts and the singing of songs.

A psychoanalytical reading of *The Color Purple* shows how a female author has to break open the Oedipal structure in order to establish female subjectivity. In thematising father–daughter rape Walker emphasises not so much the inevitability of Oedipal relationships as much as their violence. Patriarchal power goes so far that Celie's children can be taken away and she can be more or less 'bought' by a brutal man. Within this compulsory heterosexuality there is no room for Celie's own desires; she is in fact a 'non-subject'. The development of her homosexual desire for Shug allows Celie to unfold her specific sexuality and acquire subjectivity. Ultimately, therefore, Celie does not become the ideal Freudian subject: she refuses to adopt the position of daughter with regard to the father and shifts her desire to the mother and thus to other women, thus embodying Silverman's 'negative' Oedipal position. Celie also transposes her passive vaginal sexuality to an active clitoral sexuality; it is striking that she only really becomes a mother when she has struggled out of her position of oppressed object. It is thus not the children who make her into a subject, but her own struggle and her lesbian love for Shug.

Lacanian psychoanalysis

Juliet Mitchell (1974) turned to the French (post)structuralist psychoanalyst Jacques Lacan in order to remove the remaining traces of biological essentialism from psychoanalytic discourse. For feminists, the attraction of Lacan's theory lies in the central place he grants to language (instead of biology) as a constitutive element of subjectivity. In the period from World War II up until the 1980s, in his systematic return to Freud, Lacan developed a psychoanalytical theory with the help of structural linguistics and anthropology.

In the Lacanian view the child is initially situated in the 'imaginary', that is to say, the dimension of unconscious and conscious images. The imaginary is characterised by a dual relationship, without limits, between mother and child. In order to escape from the hold of this relationship, and to take up a position within the Oedipal triangle, a third term is needed, what Lacan describes as 'the Name of the Father'. This concept refers to the paternal law which dominates what Lacan calls the symbolic order; the latter refers to a function and not to the real or imaginary father; in this respect Lacan also uses the term 'paternal metaphor'. 'The Name of the Father' thus refers to the symbolic father.

The child enters into the symbolic order through the acquisition of language, which is a system that is regulated by symbolic structures. For Lacan language, myths, morality, family and economy are formative structures in the process of subjectification. The Lacanian 'symbolic' refers to the structuralist idea of the 'signifier', the differentiating element which in itself has no meaning but acquires meaning in relation to another element. The chain of signifiers forms a closed symbolic order dominated by the law of the father. When the subject learns to speak, the subject enters into a symbolic system which precedes her or him; Lacan even goes so far as to contend that the subject is an effect of the symbolic order, of language, and not the other way around. With the entry into language, desire arises, because language produces a distance between the self and reality. This implies that the ego has no unmediated access to reality, and from that moment, it finds itself in an existential state of loss or lack. It is significant that this moment coincides with the separation from the mother. This loss (where the child is no longer at one with the mother or with things around her) marks the birth of desire.

According to Lacan, the phallus is the transcendent signifier for this loss and thus for desire in the symbolic order, which, given its reliance on the phallus and on *logos* (language), is also known as 'phallogocentrism'. In relation to the phallus, the female subject signifies either 'too little' or 'too much': too little due to her lack of a penis; too much due to a surplus or excess on account of her sexual pleasure, or *jouissance*, that transcends the symbolic order and breaks the father's law.

Lacanian theory on the phallus is ambivalent in its constant slippage between phallus and penis. Although the phallus is the inviolable metaphor for human lack, in Lacan's work the metaphorical phallus tends to slip virtually unnoticed into the penis. The phallus can function as the privileged metaphor, because the female subject lacks a physical penis. Although, in Lacan's view, neither women nor men can be the phallus, the male subject still has an advantage because he can at least pretend to have the phallus. After the female subject has completed the Oedipus complex 'successfully', it is obvious that she can neither have nor be the phallus. Female subjectivity is thus an impossibility. She is not(hing) and she has not(hing); femininity is fundamentally emptiness. Woman only has access to the masquerade: she appears to be the phallus. Femininity knows no essence, but is a mask which covers her distressing lack. With respect to this almost bizarre game of 'being' and 'having' the phallus, Lacan speaks of the 'comedy' of heterosexuality (1977b: 289). In feminist eyes it looks more like a tragedy.

Feminist reinterpretations

Feminist criticism of Lacan began in France. Luce Irigaray, a psychoanalyst from Lacan's school who was dismissed by him after writing a critical dissertation about his work, argues that Lacan, following in Freud's footsteps, does not recognise any individual specificity for the female subject (1985a/1974). He again essentialises the feminine as a lack or excess; whether the feminine is signified as too little or too much, in both cases it refers to a symbolic absence: femininity is not represented within the symbolic order.

According to Irigaray the feminine is fundamentally unrepresentable (this does not mean that 'woman' is not represented in culture; on the contrary she is overrepresented as the 'eternal feminine'), because woman defies the phallocentric system of representation. Irigaray believes in the idea of a female symbolic order as a totally different system. The concept of 'difference' is understood here not as a sign of inferiority as in de Beauvoir, but rather as a positive source of alternative values. Irigaray's work has inspired some feminist cultural critics to look for a female aesthetic in art and literature by women.

Mitchell and Rose (1982) consider Lacanian psychoanalysis to be an adequate description of the way in which phallocentrism essentialises women as the other and elevates sexual difference into a symbolic law. Many feminists interpret the Freudian penis or the Lacanian phallus as a denial of sexual difference. As Rose puts it, the Lacanian analysis shows that anatomy is not destiny but a pretext: every male privilege based on the phallus is pure deceit. For Rose it is in fact a foregone conclusion that the female subject is not inferior but subjected.

Rose emphasises the usefulness of Lacanian psychoanalysis for feminism, because it undermines any claim to a fixed identity. This implies that women are not condemned to their gender and that femininity is a category which can be changed.

Écriture féminine

Écriture féminine is not so much a literary movement as a quest for a poetics of female writing by some very diverse French female authors. They undermine phallogocentrism with an aesthetic style of writing based on the specificity and positivity of the female libido. In the first chapter it has already been mentioned that *écriture féminine* is a text inspired by the 'female libidinal economy' (Cixous, 1986; Irigaray, 1985b/1977, 1982/1979). Moreover, the most important authors of this movement – Duras, Cixous, Irigaray, Hyvrard, Feral and others – foreground the physical self, that is sexuality and *jouissance*. They write from the body itself, the female body, and reject a phallic position within language. Where psychoanalysis speaks of loss and castration, *écriture féminine* tries to find positive terms: women's unconscious dreams, wishes and traumas form the source for their fictional work. Women writers want to liberate the female libido.

In order to gain access to the repressed feminine, a female author has to confront her images of the maternal; these do not involve the real mother but the 'archaic' Mother who is buried under the patriarchal culture. In the archaeology of the unconscious images of the maternal, women can learn to love themselves and other women. *Écriture féminine* liberates the mother–daughter relationship from the oblivion to which psychoanalysis has consigned it and gives expression to homosexual fantasies.

In the play *Portrait of Dora* Cixous allows Dora's voice to speak in a creative and humorous way. Cixous's Dora gives a different twist to the Oedipus complex and learns to voice her lesbian feelings for Frau K. In a parody of the Freudian analysis, all kinds of symbols, such as smoke, pearls, the jewellery box, acquire alternative meanings in a series of new associations. Thus Dora learns to see through and change the rules of the patriarchal order.

The female subject

As a result of internal pressure to address questions of power, history and political action in psychoanalytical discourse, the relationship between psychoanalysis and women's studies has changed over the last ten years (Brennan, 1989; Feldstein and Roof, 1989). Within feminist cultural studies, the status of psychoanalysis as a mere form of semiotics is challenged by a call for a more 'materialist' approach. Feminists are developing a psychoanalytical theory which is more historicised, politicised and contextualised, an approach which I have tried to provide in my reading of the cases of Anna O. and Dora.

An important aspect of this approach is the reconsideration of the term 'materialism' with which thinking about subjectivity is commanded in terms of the body (Braidotti, 1991). This has consequences for the feminist interpretation of the female body and female sexuality. The body is more than an erotogenous surface as suggested by psychoanalysis; the sexed body is the site where the struggle for identity and meaning takes place. It is primarily a matter of the social and cultural formation of identity in terms of power. The body is still a textual construction, but the text is no longer seen as a reflection of unconscious processes; it actively produces meanings. Female subjectivity is a continuous process in which identity is established on the basis of experience.

In their critique of the onesided definition of the female subject, black feminists build on the Lacanian idea of the instability of identity (Mohanty, 1987 and 1988; Spivak, 1987). From the experiences of black and post-colonial women, Mohanty argues that the category of the female subject should have scope for a plurality of differences. Female subjectivity can only be useful politically when it is understood as a regulating concept that acquires meaning through what it excludes as well as what it includes. The question of exclusions on the basis of race and ethnicity is central to black criticism of the way in which feminist theoreticians have looked for an unambiguous definition of the female subject on the basis of psychoanalysis. Black critics turn away from this one-sided emphasis on sexual difference. Female subjectivity is not only different from masculinity, but is also internally differentiated into age, ethnicity, sexual preference and other differences.

The representation of Celie in *The Color Purple* is a striking example of such a deconstruction of the autonomous subject. Celie represents the potential power of the decentred subject that is woman and black, lover and mother, homo- and heterosexual. In the words of Astrid Roemer quoted in Chapter 7 on theatre, Cecilia says in *Purple Blues*: 'I have a house, I have a trade, I have a husband, I have a woman lover, I have a son, I have a daughter – and most of all, you are there my sister.'

Literature for further study

Obviously the primary works of Sigmund Freud and Jacques Lacan are indispensable for a full understanding of psychoanalysis. For this purpose, see the general bibliography; the works listed here are of direct relevance to this chapter.

Benjamin, Jessica (1990) *The Bonds of Love: Psychoanalysis, Feminism and the*

Problem of Domination. An interesting analysis of power from the perspective of Winnicott's psychoanalysis and the Frankfurt School.

Brennan, Teresa (ed.) (1989) *Between Feminism and Psychoanalysis*. Anthology of articles on the theoretical debate between psychoanalytical and feminist discourses.

Chodorow, Nancy (1978) *The Reproduction of Mothering*. An important analysis of motherhood from the perspective of 'object relations' psychoanalysis. In 1989 Chodorow elaborated further on motherhood and gender in *Feminism and Psychoanalytic Theory*.

Clément, Cathérine, and Hélène Cixous (1975) *La jeune née*. Translated into English (1986) as *The Newly Born Woman*. One of the most important texts of *écriture féminine*, in which creative writing is combined with theoretical criticism.

Felman, Shoshana (ed.) (1982) *Literature and Psychoanalysis: The Question of Reading: Otherwise*. Anthology of important texts on the effect of Lacanian psychoanalysis on the practice of writing, the reading process and interpretation of texts.

Irigaray, Luce (1974) *Spéculum de l'autre femme*. Translated into English (1985) as *Speculum of the Other Woman*. In this book Irigaray provides a fundamental critique of Freud's theories on female sexuality.

Mitchell, Juliet (1974) *Psychoanalysis and Feminism*. A classic: the first attempt to develop a feminist approach to Lacanian psychoanalysis. Mitchell examines how politics can be united with a psychoanalytical approach.

Mitchell, Juliet, and Jacqueline Rose (eds) (1982), *Feminine Sexuality: Jacques Lacan and the École Freudienne*. A collection of Lacan's texts on femininity and female sexuality, with outstanding introductions by Mitchell and Rose.

Rose, Jacqueline (1983) *Sexuality in the Field of Vision*. Fascinating essays in which Rose elaborates Lacanian psychoanalysis for the field of images and representation. She focuses on the differences between Lacanian theory and 'object relations' psychoanalysis, especially the work of Chodorow.

Whitford, Margaret (1991) *Luce Irigaray: Philosophy in the Feminine*. An outstanding introduction to the most important themes in Irigaray's thought. Whitford offers an insight into feminist theory inspired by Irigaray's work.

Wright, Elizabeth (ed.) (1992) *Feminism and Psychoanalysis: A Critical Dictionary*. In this extended 'dictionary', terms, concepts and debates in the field of feminist theory and psychoanalysis are concisely presented. A reference work, but for advanced students.

Journals

Differences: A Journal of Feminist Cultural Studies. Providence: Brown University.

Les Cahiers du GRIF (Groupes des recherches et information féministe). Paris and Brussels: GRIF.

From 1978 to 1986 the British magazine *M/F* was published, containing many important articles on feminism and psychoanalysis.

Conclusion

ROSEMARIE BUIKEMA AND
ANNEKE SMELIK

In *Women's Studies and Culture* the reader has been introduced to feminist cultural studies. By explicitly making women both the object and the subject of study, a feminist perspective broadens the often one-sided representation of affairs within established academia. Moreover, within women's studies in the 1980s and 1990s it has become more common to differentiate the category of gender into ethnicity, class, age and sexual preference. In the supposedly universal culture of the West these categories have usually been treated as insignificant. The different questions and the different answers which these questions call for, however, show that the perspectives of the 'second sex', 'the stranger', the black woman, the working-class woman, the older woman or the lesbian shed a surprisingly different light on the culture in which we live and which we pretend to know so well. In *Women's Studies and Culture* we have set out to sketch a picture of the results of feminist studies in the many fields of culture, such as history, literature, linguistics, popular culture, cinema, theatre, art and music. With respect to the contributions of black and white women to Western culture, feminist cultural studies have indeed led to a rewriting of history. Women's studies have thus provided insight into the way in which 'power' works within cultural texts; knowledge of the sexist and racist structures of Western culture; an understanding of cultural representations of femininity and masculinity and of blackness and whiteness; and an appreciation of feminist cultural practices.

A feminist and anti-racist perspective signifies an enrichment not only for art and culture but also for the humanities in academic institutions. Women's studies is the academic answer of feminist scholars to the dominant white male institute of the universities in which they work. It is a field of study characterised by the link between knowledge and politics, which has far-reaching consequences for understanding the way in which knowledge is produced. For anti-racist feminists the myth of objective and detached scientific knowledge has lost most of its credibility. The subject of knowledge, that is the academic, does influence the hypotheses and interpretations that s/he formulates. Sexism and racism occur not only in cultural practices but are deeply rooted in academia and in (the production of) knowledge. The political involvement of women's studies implies, therefore, a reflection on the very structure and institution of academic knowledge.

The theoretical approach of post-structuralism is attractive for feminist cultural studies because it rethinks critically the relation between subject and language. Although an eclectic use of theories and methods is characteristic of feminist cultural studies, *Women's Studies and Culture* has put the largest emphasis on a post-structuralist perspective. Part Two has dealt in depth with post-structuralist theories and methods, such as lesbian studies, black studies, semiotics and psychoanalysis. These academic fields reveal how the subject is written into language or spoken by language, in other words how the subject is acculturated from the very beginning of its existence.

A feminist and anti-racist perspective offers insight into the way in which language, and thus culture, have given meaning to femininity and masculinity as well as to blackness and whiteness. Feminist cultural studies examine how culture produces a specific position for a female or male and a black or white subject. The post-structuralist approach has clarified the way in which the post-modern subject can occupy different (and sometimes conflicting) subject positions simultaneously. The female subject is characterised not only by her sex, but also by ethnicity, class, age and sexual preference. In feminist cultural studies, the post-modern fragmentation of subjectivity is recognised and exploited rather than regretted. This involves for example the consciousness-raising of a 'politics of place' (in the words of Adrienne Rich), i.e. an awareness in the feminist subject of all the cultural codes and conventions which to a large extent determine her (or his) subjectivity. Only then does one acquire the opportunity and the freedom to influence and transform one's subjectivity as well as one's culture.

The recognition of diverse subject positions implies a recognition of different stories. Only by knowing the different narrative traditions and distinguishing narrative structures can traditions be renewed and structures be changed. In fact, new stories can be told. This book has shown how women's studies have added a new chapter to academic knowledge. Alice Walker's work can be included in this continuing process of telling and renewing stories. Just like *Women's Studies and Culture*, *The Color Purple* is part of an ongoing story. In her later novels *The Temple of My Familiar* and *Possessing the Secret of Joy*, Walker allows characters from *The Color Purple* to return. *Possessing the Secret of Joy* features Celie's daughter-in-law Tashi, the African wife of her son Adam and friend of her daughter Olivia. In this novel Walker tells the painful story of the genital mutilation of women, a story that has still scarcely been heard in the academic world, even in women's studies.

In *The Temple of My Familiar*, Celie's granddaughter Fanny, Olivia's child, grows up in the female-dominated household of 'Big Mama Celie' and 'Big Mama Shug'. She starts teaching women's studies at the university. This looks like an enormous leap forward compared with the circumstances in which Celie grew up, but out of disappointment with an ever-pervasive racism Fanny ultimately turns her back on academic life.

The interwoven connection between sexism and racism is one of the stories that the authors in *Women's Studies and Culture* have told and investigated. Like Alice Walker they are thus contributing to the possibility to influence and change this story. In its different chapters, *Women's Studies and Culture* has told many stories. These stories are unfinished, not only because feminist cultural studies has been described in the middle of its development, but also because no single story is ever finished. It is up to women themselves, within and outside universities, to continue to investigate and tell the story of women's studies.

Afterword: forward-looking strategies

ROSI BRAIDOTTI

Introduction

I am no prophet though I do think, with Cornel West (1994), that the prophetic dimension of critical intellectual work has a great future. It has become apparent within the field of women's studies that deconstruction is a powerful and useful weapon, but that it also runs the risk of falling into a kind of scepticism or relativism of values. This is a dangerous move for marginal and oppressed peoples, because it erodes the possibility for alliances and political coalitions. To avoid the pitfall of infinite fragmentation, I follow the call of feminist theorists who put a high priority on the visionary mode of intellectuality, be it bell hooks's 'yearning' (1990) or Donna Haraway's 'ecstatic speakers' (1992). I thus call for a qualitative leap in the form of the moral reasoning of the prophetic intellectual: s/he who can move beyond critique and actually offer affirmative, new, cross-border values.

Towards a politics of diversity

One of the most promising new perspectives in feminist theory is offered by the intersection of deconstruction with black perspectives and post-colonialism (see Butler and Scott 1992). The question is: what are the points of convergence between post-structuralist critiques of identity and recent theories by women of colour to expose the whiteness of feminist theory?

One important preliminary point is that we are faced here with a question of naming. If by deconstruction we mean only the French-oriented school, then the discussion cannot go very far. The term 'deconstruction', however, is currently understood in literary and cultural studies as a more global movement. Moreover, as *Women's Studies and Culture* convincingly demonstrates, deconstruction cannot be seen as one central theory, but rather as a method of analysis. Deconstruction is a critical inquiry into the intersections of power and knowledge and the ways in which these support practices of exclusion and domination. One 'does' deconstruction and attacks certain discursive power formations, one does not 'believe' in it, like we used to believe in Marxism. In this post-face, I will make suggestions about the new phase of feminist thought, to understand deconstruction as a politics of diversity.

To begin with, some of the leading deconstructivists today are the black and post-colonial critics, especially the feminists such as Toni Morrison, Gayatri Spivak, bell hooks, and Trinh Minh-ha, as well as some of the leading male theorists such as Cornel West, Stuart Hall, Paul Gilroy, and Homi Bhabha. In some ways, black feminists have had to be deconstructivists from the start, in so far as they have had a double task to accomplish: to deconstruct simultaneously male dominance and the universalising tendencies at work within white feminism.

It is also to be noted that black perspectives have long moved beyond the phase of critique in offering alternative epistemologies and affirmative new accounts of black experience. This is an important development which is summed up beautifully by bell hooks:

> Racism is perpetuated when blackness is associated solely with concrete, gut-level experience, conceived as either opposing or having no connection to abstract thinking and the production of critical theory. (hooks 1990b: 23)

The issue of power is another important intersection between deconstruction and black and post-colonial perspectives. As clearly argued throughout *Women's Studies and Culture*, the deconstructive approach consists in unveiling the complexity and the ubiquity of masculinisation, racialisation, heterosexualisation, and classification, understood as a constant process of formation of pejorative 'others'. Here 'difference' plays a constitutive, if negative, role. 'Difference' has been colonised by power relations that reduce it to inferiority. Further, it has resulted in passing off differences as 'natural', which made entire categories of beings into devalued and therefore disposable others. The 'linguistic turn' is only another name for understanding the complexity of the intersection between power and knowledge; it assumes that no text is unambiguous. Reading a text requires a talent and a sensibility for this kind of multiple and complex effects.

Let me develop this further: a feminist post-modernist critic approaches textual analyses in terms of power and discursive formations. Discourse is about the political currency that is attributed to certain meanings, or systems of meaning, in such a way as to invest them with scientific legitimacy. Take the examples of misogyny and racism. The belief in the inferiority of women – be it mental, intellectual, spiritual or moral – has no serious scientific foundation. The same goes for racist beliefs. This does *not* prevent them from having great currency in political practice and the organisation of society. The woman or the black as 'others' – that is as both empirical referents and symbolic signs of pejoration – function discursively as shapers of meanings. That is to say that differences are organised in a hierarchical scale that divides man from woman, but also man from the animal, or non-human and the divine. The mark of difference fulfils the crucial function of dividing the subjects along a set of axes of varying degrees of 'difference'. Of dividing, so as to conquer the subversive or dangerous charge that is potentially contained in these 'others'. This is how phallogocentric order is maintained.

As a corollary of the above, the pejorative use of the feminine, or of blackness, is structurally necessary to the phallogocentric system of meaning. By being structurally embedded, these differences of gender or race become paradoxically both abstract and invisible, that is, they are perceived as 'natural'. The real-life, empirical subjects that are associated with categories of 'difference' – women and blacks – experience in their embodied existence the effects of the disqualification of the feminine and of blackness at the symbolic level.

What particularly comes under fire is the power of scientific discourse, which is singled out as the master narrative that has formalised the structural necessity for devalued difference in Western thought. The discursive approach thus makes us aware of the simplicity of the dualism of Western science, but it also reveals the disconcerting fact that the banal simplicity of dualism is also the source of its success. A deconstructivist approach to the analysis of power and discourse highlights the links between scientific truth and discursive currency. As such, it aims primarily at dislodging the belief in the 'natural' foundations of socially coded and enforced 'differences' and of the systems of value and representation which they support.

A politicised deconstructive method also emphasises the need to historicise the analysis of the formation of scientific concepts *as* normative formations. This allows us to take on the historicity of the very concepts that we are investigating. In a multicultural feminist frame, this emphasis on historicity means that the scholar needs some humility before the eternal repetitions of history and the great importance of language. We need to learn that there is no escape from the multi-layered structure of our own encoded history and language.

The implications of this are far-reaching. The logic of our system is intrinsically masculine, universalistically white, compulsorily heterosexual, favourably bourgeois and globally homicidal. The problem is that this way of thinking has also colonised the discourse of science, which implies that there is not much 'scientific discourse' that is free of this code. Thus, there is no longer a true science or true knowledge, no matter who happens to be speaking it. Nor can truth be found in experience. In other words, there is no readily accessible 'authentic' or uncontaminated voice of the oppressed, be it women, blacks or people of colour. This turns firstly into an attack on the essentialism of those who claim fixed identities of the deterministic kinds. It also undercuts any claim to 'purity' as the basis for epistemological or political alternatives. Claims to 'purity' are always suspect because they assume subject positions that would be unmediated by language and representation.

To me the crucial point is that a politics of diversity involves a political position which stresses the positivity of difference. In my view, such an approach is opposed to 'identity politics', because the counter-affirmation of oppositional identities ends up reasserting the very dualisms it is trying to undo. This kind of deconstruction is the theoretical platform for a politics of diversity, because it makes a point of carefully avoiding and even undermining any attempt at re-essentialising 'race' or 'ethnicity' as a natural given.

New strategies

This position also has interesting implications for strategy. Deconstructivists and especially black theorists open up spaces for the positive affirmation of black presence. bell hooks expresses this in terms of embodied black female genealogies. These spaces are negotiated through careful processes of undoing hegemonic discursive tendencies not only in the dominant discourse, but also within critical feminist theory itself.

Politicised deconstruction is the means of achieving possible margins of affirmation by subjects who are conscious of and accountable for the paradox of being both caught inside a symbolic code and deeply opposed to it. The point is that, willingly or not, we are complicitous with that which we are trying to deconstruct. Being aware of one's complicity lays the foundation for a radical politics of resistance, which would be mercifully free of claims to purity, but also of the luxury of guilt. Learning the lesson of black feminist theory, we need to learn to think the simultaneity of potentially contradictory social and textual effects. Thus we can cut across established ways of thinking and dualistic, essentialised 'natural' oppositions.

This simultaneity is not to be confused with easy parallels or arguments by analogy. That gender, race, class and sexual choice may be equally effective power variables does not amount to flattening out any differences between them. An account of feminist theory and practice which gives the impression that simultaneity is merely a multi-layered version of one-directional thinking is inadequate. Thus, the sequence equality/difference/deconstruction is not supposed to infuse a sense of unitary teleological purpose to the development of feminist theory. It only marks some of the moments in a process of continuous undoing of the power relations with which these categories are shot through. As has emerged from reading this volume, these stages are not hierarchically ordained, nor are they dialectically opposed; rather, they are different facets of a multi-layered struggle.

I could sum up deconstructivist strategies by saying that all deconstructions are equal, but some are more equal than others. Whereas the deconstruction of masculinity and whiteness is an end in itself, the non-essentialistic reconstruction of black perspectives, as well as the feminist reconstruction of multiple ways of being women, also have new values to offer. In other words, some notions need to be deconstructed so as to be laid to rest once and for all: masculinity, whiteness, classism, heterosexism, agism. Others need to be deconstructed only as a prelude to offering positive values and effective ways of asserting the political presence of newly empowered subjects: feminism, diversity, multiculturalism, environmentalism. We need to fight passionately for the simultaneous assertion of positive differences by, for and among women, while resisting essentialisation and claims to authenticity.

Both poles of the gender dualism need to be deconstructed. I think that masculinity can only be effectively extricated from the phallus by men, if they choose to become politically involved. This position rests on a point that I consider to be crucial, namely the dissymetrical power differentials between men and women, white and black. Men and women, as empirical referents for the respective social and symbolic institutions of masculinity and femininity, are in a dissymetrical relationship to each other. Power differentials make their positions incomparable, though patriarchy would like them to be complementary to each other. If feminist-minded men take on the issue of masculinity, they also have to confront the question of power relations and the extent to which they structure women's entire way of living. The recognition of this dissymetry is a fundamental moment in the process of deconstructing phallic power and of men's coming to consciousness.

I think the same dissymetrical relationship applies to the white/black divide. Like masculinity, whiteness is invisible in the symbolic order because it is conflated with the universal. That 'universal' is in fact a pseudo-universal in that it carries within itself the whole package deal of masculinity, whiteness and heterosexuality, which all pass themselves off as natural. To go on deconstructing it, new strategies are needed. I would like to suggest that, while priority is given to opening up concrete spaces for black women in scientific discourse and academic institutions, it is also extremely important to itemise 'whiteness' as a target of analysis. We need to tear down whiteness so as to show the knots of contradiction and violence that make it tick. We need to do this not instead of but alongside the negotiation for spaces of affirmation of black perspectives.

In order to bring about this affirmative phase of deconstruction, new alliances are necessary, especially between post-colonialism and post-structuralism. Such an alliance can reveal the critique of Western logic as part of the decentering of colonial hegemony. Cornel West is especially careful to demolish any dualistic opposition between allegedly Eurocentric theories and black deconstructive movements. West states:

> If one is talking about critiques of racism, critiques of patriarchy, critiques of homophobia, then simply call it that. Eurocentrism is not identical with racism. So, you deny the John Browns of the world. You deny the anti-racist movement in the heart of Europe. Eurocentrism is not the same as male supremacists. Why? Because every culture we know has been patriarchal in such an ugly way and that you deny the anti-patriarchal movements in the heart of Europe. And the same with homophobia. Demistify the categories in order to stay attuned to the complexity of the realities. (West, 1994: 20)

I think this kind of questioning corresponds to a new interdisciplinary dialogue. It offers a constructive answer to the quest for new intersections between the field of cultural studies and social policy and social thought. It also provides some grounding for a form of accountability for a feminist position that works outside the reference to a universal, coherent and stable self and yet is still committed to political accountability, methodological accuracy and academic excellence.

Towards new universals

As the authors of *Women's Studies and Culture* have argued, gender is used as a category to both conceal and express a fundamental sense of common humanity. The critiques of universalism proposed by deconstructivist feminists and other critical theorists rest on the assumption that the old universal was a 'pseudo-universal'.

As Naomi Schor (1995) acutely remarks, however, this implies that there is or even that there should be such a thing as a 'good' or an adequate form of universalism. In Schor's analysis, the rejection of white universalism on the emancipatory model of the European Enlightenment does not amount to abandoning universal values altogether. It rather calls for their radical redefinition. Just as previously marginalised peoples have gained access to socio-symbolic agency, the point is not to overthrow the universal, but to historicise it, radicalise it so as to propose a more inclusive understanding of it (also see Scott 1995).

Nowhere is this problem felt more strongly than in the feminist classroom. In *Teaching to Transgress* (1994b), bell hooks defends a pedagogical practice that has emerged 'from the mutually illuminating interplay of anticolonial, critical and feminist pedagogies' (p. 10). Adapting from Paulo Freire, she calls for 'conscientization', or the process of critical awareness and engagement. This produces simultaneously a strategic form of essentialism and a call for new universals:

> A critique of essentialism that challenges only marginalized groups to interrogate their use of identity politics or an essentialist standpoint as a means of exerting coercive power leaves unquestioned the critical practices of other groups who employ the same strategies in different ways and whose exclusionary behavior may be firmly buttressed by institutionalized structures of domination that do not critique or check it. (hooks 1994b: 82)

While rejecting essentialism, bell hooks warns against hasty dismissals of foundations for alternative knowledge claims and identities. Similarly, she argues against the 'authority of experience', replacing it with 'the passion of experience' which encompasses some shared sense of suffering (p. 90).

This is the challenge of our immediate future: how to avoid the pitfalls of relativism (dismissing the universal as redundant) and of essentialism (nostalgic reassertion of essentialised identities), while asserting accountability for our gender. It is not an easy challenge, but as the material gathered in this volume shows, there is no nostalgia or fear that will keep critical and visionary intellectuals from constructing viable alternatives. In this process, the women's studies classroom functions as the site of an on-going experimentation about new ways of learning that can respond to the complexity of our age, while staying tuned to the experiences of women.

This process is in no way nostalgic. Instead it is forward-looking. It does not aim at the glorification of the feminine, but rather at its actualisation as a political project of alternative female subjectivities. Its object is not to recover a lost origin, but to bring about modes of representation that take into account the sort of women whom we have already become.

I am grateful to Gloria Wekker for her extensive commentary on earlier versions of this text. I have also benefited from conversations with Evelynn Hammonds, Joan Scott, Judith Butler and Naomi Schor.

Glossary of key terms

Words in *italic* can be found as glossary entries.

black Political term which does not literally refer to skin colour, but to a marginalised social position on the basis of ethnicity. From the black perspective, white ethnicity coincides with dominance and hegemony in Western culture.

castration complex In Freudian psychoanalysis the central point of this concept is the castration fantasy, a fantasy that enables the child to explain the riddle of the anatomical distinction between the sexes. The child explains this difference by believing that the girl has been deprived of the penis. In young girls this would give rise to penis envy and in young boys to castration anxiety. Feminists give a broader meaning to these terms: penis envy indicates women's outrage with regard to the privileged cultural and social position of men; castration anxiety indicates the inability of men to accept and value sexual difference positively. In Lacanian psychoanalysis, the concept of castration indicates the loss or lack which each subject experiences on her or his entry into the *symbolic order*. This experience of loss shapes *desire*.

deconstruction Deconstruction is a way of reading texts by revealing their logocentrism, i.e. their dichotomic and hierarchical structures of meaning, and in doing so subverting their power. Central to the philosophy of deconstruction is the notion that there is nothing outside the text. This should be understood not as a denial of reality, but as a recognition of the fact that reality is mediated through language and is therefore discursive. The method of deconstruction is interesting for feminist theory because of the possibility of separating sexual difference from biological sex or social group. Instead, sexual difference can be understood as an effect of language. In both the study and practice of literature, art and popular culture, feminists use the deconstructive strategy to undo conventional meanings of femininity and masculinity.

desire The loss that the subject experiences upon her or his entry into the *symbolic order* gives rise to desire. For Lacan, desire in fact denotes more than sexual desire; it is a general human desire for unity and harmony.

discourse The concept of discourse comes from Michel Foucault and – in contrast to *ideology* – transcends the opposition between representation and reality. Instead, the concept of discourse emphasises the simultaneity of representation and reality, of text and effect. Power, subjectivity, ethnicity and gender are included in these textual effects. Texts, historical events and institutions can all be forms of discourse.

écriture féminine Experimental practice of writing by women which started in France during the 1970s. It aims at exploring the feminine in language. This feminine writing will express and represent whatever has become marginalised, repressed and unsaid within the *phallogocentric culture*.

essentialism In feminist theory this term is used to indicate the biological or psychological essence of 'woman' and the feminine. An essentialist view would imply that female subjectivity stands outside historical or social change.

focalisation A term from narratology (narrative theory) indicating which agent (narrator, character) observes (seeing, hearing, feeling, tasting, thinking) a narrated event. A useful instrument for analysing the relation between who sees and what is seen, who speaks and what is said in texts.

the gaze A term from film theory. The concept of 'the gaze' or 'the look' derives from an analysis of the way in which cinema stimulates scopophilia, the pleasure of looking. In classic Hollywood cinema the gaze is mostly linked to male voyeurism. The movie involves a triple look; the look of the camera, the look of the male character at the female character; and the look of the spectator who, through the look of the camera, identifies her/himself with the main character (see also *focalisation*).

gender Within feminist theory this term initially referred to the distinction between biological sex and a social role. In current feminist theory it refers primarily to sexual identity as the effect of historical, social and cultural processes. Unconscious processes do not play a significant role in these views of the construction of gender. To a certain extent, feminist thinking in terms of gender conflicts with thinking in terms of *sexual difference*.

ideology There are two views of ideology in feminist cultural theory. In the first place there is the view developed by the Marxist and structuralist Louis Althusser: ideology as the imaginary relationship of the subject to her or his real conditions of existence (see also *discourse*). In this view there is no escape from ideology. Ideology precedes the subject and determines the way in which it perceives the world. In a feminist framework ideology refers to the myths of a culture and to the way in which these myths (about women, for example) appear as natural and unproblematic. The Althusserian concept of ideology is a reaction to an earlier view in which ideology was experienced as 'false' compared with a 'true' insight into conditions of existence. Within early feminist cultural theory this concept of ideology led to the notion of patriarchy as a system of false practices and representations of gender.

the imaginary This Lacanian term denotes the first phase of a child's development, in which the child observes no distinction between itself and her or his surroundings. The child experiences a unity with its mother whom s/he does not yet recognise as the Other. This separation originates in the *mirror stage*.

libidinal economy This psychoanalytical concept comprises a dynamic (non-biological) view of the unconscious. The term refers to the idea that sexual energy circulates within social and political structures and maintains these. Authors within *écriture féminine* resist the way in which women function as objects of exchange among men and call for an investment of sexual energy in women themselves in order to liberate the female libidinal economy.

mirror stage In this stage the child breaks through its unity with the mother by recognising the mother as an image, as the Other. By identifying with her or his own image the child experiences itself as simultaneously 'self' and 'other'; this is the beginning of the formation of the ego. The ego ideal is by definition an image, that is imaginary, and therefore does not collapse with the experience of the self.

Oedipus complex In the classic Freudian view, the Oedipus complex means the whole of sexual desires which the young child feels for the parent of the other sex and the hostile feelings for the parent of the same sex who is experienced as a rival. In this psychic complex the child gives meaning to sexual difference and establishes her or his gendered identity.

phallogocentrism This term combines phallocentrism and logocentrism and is sometimes also described as phallologocentrism. These monolithic systems respectively privilege the *phallus* as signifier of sexuality and *logos* (the word) as the signifier of truth.

phallus A symbolic concept in Lacanian psychoanalysis, not to be confused with the physical penis. The phallus signifies the relations of desire between the sexes, in the sense that men and women occupy different positions with regard to the phallus: respectively a position of 'having' and of 'being'. In the Lacanian view, men cannot really possess the phallus either. Nevertheless, a phallic position indicates the power to signify reality, and within the symbolic order that position is male.

post-modernism We here distinguish post-modernism as a philosophical discourse, as a cultural and artistic practice and as a historical period. As a philosophy, post-modernism turns away from the philosophy of Enlightenment (modernism) in which an optimistic view of human reason led to the idea of a manageable and rational society. In contrast, post-modern philosophy emphasises uncontrollable forces in society. With the rejection of universal truth that lies at the basis of the rational world view, post-modern philosophy opens the way to theorising and to representing fragmentation and discontinuity. As a cultural and artistic practice post-modernism is in the first place eclectic. This is expressed by the combination of elements from different genres, trends, media, styles and techniques. Post-modernism also undermines the clear division between high and low culture. It is not easy to designate a clear-cut period for post-modernism; the term was already used in 1917 to indicate an architectural movement. However, the term is mostly reserved for the period after 1970, with the loss of modernism in art and the emergence of post-industrial culture.

post-structuralism Post-structuralism rejects the *structuralist* view that unchanging, fundamental and universal structures lie at the basis of the world of phenomena, texts, social systems, etc. In contrast post-structuralism focuses more on problematising structures by studying their discursive construction, their function and their power.

representation Within feminist theory this term refers to the construction of verbal and visual texts. It may refer especially to the image of the feminine and the masculine, black and white, as constructions.

sexual difference The term sexual difference refers to psychoanalytic ideas of sexual identity and sexuality. More specifically, the notion of sexual difference is linked to a debate which has primarily taken place in French theory. Theories of sexual difference start from the fact that a *subject* is born with a female or male body, and develops a related psycho-sexual identity. Where *gender* theorists understand the construction of femininity and masculinity as more determined by cultural and social processes, sexual difference theorists understand it as more determined by (unconscious) intra-psychological processes.

sign A sign is something which stands to somebody for something in some respect or capacity. According to a Saussurian view of the sign, it consists of the 'signifier', the material carrier of meaning and 'signified', that which is referred to.

structuralism Structuralism was initiated by the linguist de Saussure. In his structural linguistics he studied language as a system of differences. Lévi-Strauss then developed a structuralist anthropology. He studied so-called primitive cultures and showed that a sort of grammar, a structure, also lays the foundations of human culture. Structuralist theory conceives systems of meaning as products of an underlying structure. This structure would correspond to the way in which the human mind works and gives meaning to reality. See also *post-structuralism*.

subject The concept of subject does not coincide with the concepts of 'individual' or 'person'. This term is used in theoretical discourses which have rejected the idea of an autonomous individual who dominates/ed her or his own history. In a general sense the concept of subject allows for changeability in human development. Someone can take up diverse subject positions, not only in the course of her or his own life, but also simultaneously. The *post-modern* feminist subject undermines the idea of stability, unity and self-determination, but emphasises nevertheless the ability of subjective agency (in contrast to an object).

symbolic order According to Lacan, after the *imaginary* phase, the child enters the symbolic order with the acquisition of language. The gain for the subject is to speak; the loss is the break with the unity of oneself with the mother and the surrounding. The symbolic order is based on the *phallic* law.

text The structure and organisation of a cultural product or of a representation; a novel, a painting, a film or an advertisement can be analysed as text.

Student assignments

The assignments can help to process the material in this book as well as serve as suggestions for papers and/or oral presentations. Please use the recommended literature which is listed at the end of each chapter. Complete bibliographical information can be found in the Bibliography below. The assignments are numbered accordingly to the chapters in this book.

1 Feminist theory

Read *The Color Purple* and the chapter on feminist theory and then try to situate the ideas on femininity and subjectivity as expressed in the novel within the three distinct feminist positions of equality, difference and deconstruction. Illustrate your argument with extracts from the novel.

2 History

1A. Look for a slave narrative (for example, *Our Nig* by Harriet Wilson) and compare it with *The Color Purple*. Pay attention to similarities of theme, style, narrative structure and details. Then find out when and how the slave narrative in question was first published. Collect information about the history of writings by (liberated) slaves in the United States. For this purpose, use the bibliographies of bell hooks (1990a) and Jacqueline Jones (1985).

1B. Collect information about slavery in a Caribbean country. Compare what you have found with information about slavery in the United States. Make a list of differences and similarities in the position of women in slavery in the Caribbean and in the United States.

2. A question like 'Did women have a Renaissance?' can also be asked about other great events in world history. Take World War II in your country, for example, and collect evidence to show whether it meant something different for women than for men. Look in a library for texts which were written after the war as well as 'primary sources', that is to say texts which came into being in the period 1940–45. Try to find not only texts about women but also texts written by women.

Use both academic and popular texts as well as literary novels about the war. You can write a report of your research in the form of a discussion between people supporting and contradicting the hypothesis. This discussion can of course also be brought to life in class by role play.

3 Literary theory

1. Read Toni Morrison's *Playing In The Dark: Whiteness in the Literary Imagination*. Make an outline of her method of reading. Then choose a novel by a white author (male or female) and try to identify 'Africanism' and the function of 'black figurations'. Compose a written analysis of your findings.

2. (Re)read Alice Walker's *The Color Purple*. Then read bell hooks's critical essay 'Writing the Subject; Reading *The Color Purple*' in *Yearning* (1990). Write an (imaginary) letter to bell hooks, explaining carefully where and how you agree or disgree with her. Make it an open and personal letter while you try to put into writing how your reading process may be linked up with your situatedness in life (male/ female; black/of colour/white; gay/straight; lower/middle/upper-class; other aspects which might have influenced your reading process). Defend your own reading experiences.

3A. Sexism in a text (or film) does not necessarily produce a sexist text. Whether a text 'is' sexist depends on the way in which misogyny (for example of characters) is embedded and presented. Try to find one text with embedded sexism (that is, a text in which sexism is a motif while the text *as a whole* takes a more enlightened stand), as well as an example of an unabashed sexist text. Explain through a detailed textual analysis how the difference between sexism in these texts is produced. For your analysis you may want to use concepts from narrative theory (e.g. Mieke Bal's *Narratology*, 1985).

3B. Sometimes it may be difficult to decide which position the text takes or which interpretation it allows. Read Brett Ellis Easton's *American Psycho* as an example of this problem. *American Psycho* can easily be read as a profoundly misogynist novel: feminists Tammy Bruce, Gloria Steinem and Kate Millett predicted that the *American Psycho* murders would soon be imitated in real life. Yet, this same book can also be read as a protest against male sexual terrorism. The Dutch feminist writer Renate Dorrestein, for example, commented: 'Ellis was able to write this book because the world in which we live is already scattered with dead women's bodies.' She continues:

> His representation of slaughter is the symbol of a society which allows daily violence against women. Obligatory reading, especially for feminists I would say. We can observe Man at his Worst here. ... I do not think that *American Psycho* is a monument of Hatred against Women. If Elfriede Jelinek had written exactly the same book critics would probably have called it a monument of Hatred against Men. There would have been an outcry then against the way in which Man is portrayed in this book: as a horrifying beast. Read it, and judge for yourself. (Dorrestein, in a column entitled 'Korte metten' in the Dutch feminist journal *Opzij*, June 1991: p. 15)

What do you think? Organise a discussion by dividing the class in two groups. The first group defends Ellis Easton's book, and Dorrestein's position, i.e. that the representation of violence against women in *American Psycho* can be read as a radicalising exposure of the problem and that the book is therefore useful. The other group argues in line with Bruce, Steinem and Millett, i.e. that the novel is a misogynist representation which induces violence against women and that the book is therefore dangerous.

Is it of any help for your opinion and argumentation that *American Psycho* was intended to be a critical work? (If you collect interviews with its author you will become acquainted with his interpretation.) In your view, how (un)important is the author's voice in this debate?

4 Linguistics

1. Make a study of racist and sexist presuppositions in several editions of the standard dictionary of your own language. Look at the entries for 'man' and 'woman', 'black' and 'white', and some relevant themes as well (for example, entries related to household, work, sexuality, children, education, expertise). Pay special attention to the intersection of ethnicity and gender. Describe the changes and evaluate the present state of affairs.

2. Collect graffiti from public places, some of which are primarily frequented by women and some primarily by men. Analyse them according to linguistic, thematic, political and sexual views and compare and contrast them.

3. Make video recordings of several instalments of a TV soap opera. Describe the characters according to the following characteristics: gender, estimated age, socio-economic status, level of education, as well as the types of relationship between the characters (parent, child, lover, marriage partner, acquaintance, employer/employee, etc.). Analyse the pronunciation in the dialogues (e.g. 'coarser', 'more correct'), the use of words (e.g. swear words) and the way characters address each other

(e.g. 'formal', 'familiar'), etc. Examine whether there is a connection between the differences in linguistic performance and the type of dialogue, with specific attention to the speaker's gender and ethnicity.

5 Media studies

1. Feminist cultural critics take different positions with regard to the female reader. Sometimes the critic sets herself up as the ideal reader; sometimes she refers to contexts beyond the experience of the individual female reader; and sometimes she is primarily concerned with the effect of a specific popular genre on the lives of women.

Compare, for example, how Germaine Greer (1970) writes about the effect of pulp fiction on women readers, how Cora Kaplan (1986) writes about her own reading experiences and how Mary-Ellen Brown (1990) sees the relationship between the feminist critic and the female reader. Try to formulate your own opinion on the ideal position of the feminist critic. Can her reading experience be examplary for other reading experiences? If so, why? If not, why not?

2. Ethnographic research is an important source of information about the meanings that popular culture has for its public, that is to say that the desired information is acquired by means of qualitative interviews with women readers or viewers.

Choose a popular cultural genre which you know well (for example, romantic fiction, a soap opera or a magazine) and define the meanings of that genre for yourself. Then try to discover what meanings other women assign to that genre by interviewing other consumers. Try to formulate open-ended questions in your interviews, so as to gather as much information as possible from the interviewees. Report your findings in class and discuss possible interpretations of the data. Also discuss whether your own views influenced the interviews.

6 Film studies

Choose a contemporary film or video clip in which a woman plays a leading role. Make sure that the film or clip is available on video for you to see several times.

1A. To what extent does the female character acquire subjectivity? You can answer this question by making a detailed analysis of the narrative structure. Does this character have an autonomous desire at the beginning of the story; this can be an erotic desire or an ambition? Does she focus on an object (man, work, career)? Does her desire structure the narrative and does she obtain the desired object? Pay attention to the role that the male character (if there is one) plays in the development of the female character. Does the female character reach a position other than the conventional ones of death or romance at the end of the film?

1B. Analyse how the cinematic means, such as camera work, editing and mise-en-scène, give subjectivity to the female character. Are there situations in which the female subject is the object of the gaze? Does the film stimulate or subvert a voyeuristic gaze on the female character? Which visual and other signs are used to represent femininity (and possibly masculinity)? Think of photography, lighting, costume, make-up, gestures, etc.

1C. On the basis of your data from this analysis, write an interpretation in which you answer the question of whether the female character acquires subjectivity. Do you think the film you have chosen conveys a traditional or a feminist representation of women?

2. Choose a film by a woman director.

2A. View it once and immediately write down your first response. View the film several more times and produce the same type of analysis as in assignment 1. Here, concentrate on the moments where the film deviates from a conventional narrative structure, where the voyeuristic gaze is deconstructed and where conventional signs of femininity are changed. In films by women there is often a play with images-within-the-image, such as a television, video, camera, photo, painting; does that happen in the film you chose, and if so what does it signify? Pay particular attention to the way in which the female body is visually represented; does this deviate from conventional imagery?

2B. Now return to your initial viewing experience. Can you answer the question of cinematic address, that is, did the film address you as a female spectator? If so, how? If not, why not?

You can find female film-makers and titles of women's films in *The Women's Companion to International Film* by A. Kuhn and S. Radstone (1990).

7 Theatre studies

1. Take a drama text and analyse the ways in which the point of view on one or more female characters is represented in both the 'main' and 'additional' texts (the dialogue and the stage directions respectively). Use the concept of focalisation (see Bal 1985). Although traditional plays do not have a narrator, the information from the additional text can be understood as a form of external focalisation.

2. Go to a performance of a classic play. Make a semiotic analysis of

the representation of the female main character. What theatrical means are used in this representation? Do these means also function to express the point of view of the female character? What means are used in order to provide a view of the female character?

You could extend this assignment by studying in articles and reviews how the representation of the female main character has changed in historical performances within a certain period. Try to find out from historical reviews what theatrical means were used to give expression to that representation.

8 Art history

1. Feminist women artists and critics have debated the possibilities for feminist strategies in the production of art. They wonder which strategies can best be used and what possible effects these have on the public. Read the following three articles about this debate:

—Angela Partington, 'Feminist Art and Avantgardism' in: Robinson, *Visibly Female* (1987)
—Judith Barry and Susan Flitterman, 'Textual Strategies: The Politics of Artmaking' in Parker and Pollock, *Framing Feminism* (1987)
—Mary Kelly, 'On Sexual Politics and Art', ibid.

Compare these articles by explaining the different viewpoints. Then formulate your own position.

2 Visit an art gallery or museum which owns or shows many works by women in its collection, or visit a relevant exhibition if there happens to be one. Study the works by women artists closely and extensively. Do these works of art reflect any of the strategies from the literature you studied. Can you say something about the effect of these strategies? Write a paper about your research.

3. How does Pollock (1988) outline the position of women in the Paris of the Impressionists, in her essay 'Modernity and the Spaces of Femininity'? What did this mean for women artists like Morisot and Cassatt? In what ways can a differentiated view of the female position be recognised in their paintings?

9 Music studies

1. Read Chapter 1 ('Introduction') and Chapter III ('Sexual Politics in Classical Music') of Susan McClary's *Feminine Endings: Music, Gender, and Sexuality*.

In the third chapter McClary compares two very different compositions, the opera *Carmen* by Bizet and Tchaikovsky's Fourth Symphony, and finds a similarity in both works. The narrative structure and the diverse constructions of femininity and masculinity which McClary observes in *Carmen*, she also recognises in the Fourth Symphony. Although McClary gives a historical dimension to her argument (Tchaikovsky would be influenced by Bizet's opera), her reading is primarily the result of a deconstructive reading/listening strategy.

Attempt to formulate an answer to the following questions (using the two chapters mentioned from McClary's book):

1A. According to McClary, which musical features belong to the *different* representations of femininity and masculinity in both compositions?

1B. What can be understood by McClary's deconstructive reading/listening strategy?

2. Chapter 9 in this book states that 'in [the] second phase of feminist musicology there is no feminist movement of theoreticians and composers claiming specific developments in music on [the term *écriture féminine musicale*] or comparable terms'.

This implies that a form of *écriture féminine musicale* may still be conceivable. In her essay 'Recovering *Jouissance*: An Introduction to Feminist Musical Aesthetics' (in Pendle, 1991: 331–40), Renée Cox indicates a number of trends in music where a specifically female voice may be heard. She refers to feminist folk music, popular music and music from non-Western cultures as fields where some research has already been carried out. She sees possibilities for further research in composers like Laurie Anderson, Pauline Oliveros and Ellen Taafe Zwillich.

3A. Read Cox's essay very thoroughly. Pay attention to the telling epigraph: '*Wa-oh-oh-oh* ..., The Ronettes'.

3B. Choose one of Cox's examples or use an example you have found yourself (perhaps from non-Western music). Examine carefully the reasons why your example can be connected with the concept of *écriture féminine*, using the literature to which Cox refers.

10 Lesbian studies

1. Literary texts and films written and made before the late 1960s/early 1970s – before either the feminist or the sexual revolution had taken place – generally dealt with sexuality in implicit if not actually coded terms. This holds particularly true for novels or films whose focus is on the 'unspeakable' subject of lesbian sexuality. Choose a novel, a short story or film of the pre-revolutionary period that has as

one of its thematic focuses female friendship, or female same-sex intimacy. Carefully trace the textual representation of this friendship: you could, for instance, concentrate on its setting(s); the specific ways in which the characters are portrayed, both in themselves and in relation to each other; how the bond between the characters informs the text's narrative development; and/or metaphors or patterns of imagery that convey the particular nature of this friendship. On the basis of your findings, decide whether you would be willing to define the novel, story or film as a lesbian text (even if does not mention the word 'lesbian' itself). Drawing on textual and contextual evidence alike, set up an argument in favour of or against the text's inclusion in a lesbian canon. If possible, check the validity and persuasiveness of your arguments by presenting it to someone, preferably a fellow-student or teacher/tutor, who, in the first instance, takes a contrary view on the question to your own.

If you have difficulty finding a suitable text, seek inspiration in one of various feminist critical studies focusing on sisterhood, female friendship, and/or women's communities, e.g., Janeway 1975; Smith-Rosenberg 1975; Auerbach 1978; Todd 1980; Faderman 1985/1981; Raymond 1984. For films you can look at catalogues of International Gay and Lesbian Film Festivals.

2. Virginia Woolf's *Mrs Dalloway* (1925) and Sylvia Plath's *The Bell Jar* (1962) have long been established as important contributions to a (Eurowestern) female/feminist canon. While individual readings of these – very different – novels may vary, mainstream feminists on the whole place the problematics of sexual difference (as woman's difference from man) at their respective critical/thematical centres. Select a novel by a female author of similar canonical stature (if you cannot think of one, pick either Woolf's or Plath's), adopt a consciously lesbian perspective, and subject the text to a critical analysis in which not the problematics of sex/gender but differences in terms of sexuality stand at the centre of attention. Show how such a reading may (or may not) add significantly to mainstream feminist appreciations of the text, and/or to what extent reading the text 'as a lesbian' may actually undermine previous feminist readings.

11 Black studies

1. Examine your own perspective by reading (or viewing) a black/ethnic text of your own choice. What is your reading position? Pay attention to colour/ethnicity (don't forget that white is also an ethnic category), class, gender, sexual identity, religion, age and whatever else

is important to you. With what and with whom do you identify when reading (or viewing) and with whom or with what do you not identify? Then try to put into words why this identification comes about. Has it something to do with the subject, with the narrative style, with the narrator and/or with your reading (viewing) position?

2. Read a novel, visit a performance or view a film which is written or made by a black/ethnic woman in a white context. Try to point out references to a collective experience, history and the search for identity. Indicate where you can find 'blackness' or 'ethnicity' in the text. If you can find nothing, or very little, explain why you would still call the text a black female text, or why you would not.

12 Semiotics

1. Comparisons or similarities play an important role in the creation of characters in literature. In *The Color Purple*, look for comparisons in the letters from Celie and Nettie; indicate whether they are iconic or indexical and illustrate your answer. In this respect are there differences between Celie's and Nettie's letters?

2. Read the first chapter of *The Color Purple* carefully and describe in detail how the author gives a negative picture of the stepfather in Celie's letters. Examine to what extent your own knowledge of the world or your own moral views about people plays a part in the evaluation of this character.

3. Think of three situations in which your being a woman or a man matters, and indicate where this significance is located. Then think of three situations in which, although formally your being a woman or a man does not matter, you still feel uncomfortable, because your gender seems to play a role. Finally think of three situations in which your being a woman or a man does not matter, and describe how these situations are connected to your view of yourself.

13 Psychoanalysis

1. Read Freud's *Fragment of an Analysis of a Case of Hysteria* ('Dora'; 1905a). Analyse Freud's rhetoric and observe how his interpretation of Dora is constructed. For that purpose you can ask a number of questions, e.g., to whom does Freud address his case study? Which passages in the text reveal Freud's role as a representative of a patriarchal order? What information about Dora's history does he withhold in his report?

2. Read *Portrait of Dora* by Hélène Cixous. Describe the ways in which Cixous puts Freud in his place and analyse the role she assigns

to the female body. You can also consider an interpretation of Cixous's text by way of performing extracts from the play in class.

For these assignments you may want to consult the book *In Dora's Case,* edited by Charles Bernheimer and Claire Kahane (1985).

Bibliography

A supplementary bibliography on Alice Walker and *The Color Purple* follows the main bibliography.

Abbott, Sidney and Barbara Love (1973/1972) *Sappho Was a Right-On Woman: A Liberated View of Lesbianism.* New York: Stein & Day.

Abelove, Henry, Michèle Aina Barale and David M. Halperin (1993) *The Lesbian and Gay Studies Reader.* New York: Routledge.

Alexander, Karen, (1991) 'Fatal Beauties: Black Women in Hollywood', in Christine Gledhill (ed.), *Stardom: Industry of Desire*. London and New York: Routledge, 45–54.

Ang, Ien (1985) *Watching Dallas*. London: Methuen.

Armstrong, Nancy (1987) *Desire and Domestic Fiction: A Political History of the Novel*. Oxford: Oxford University Press.

Auerbach, Nina (1978) *Communities of Women: An Idea in Fiction*. Cambridge, Mass.: Harvard University Press.

Bad Object Choices (ed.) (1991) *How Do I Look? Queer Film and Video*. Seattle: Bay Press.

Bailey, Lee Ann, and Leonora A. Timm (1976) 'More on Women's – and Men's – Expletives', in *Anthropological Linguistics* 18, 438–49.

Baker, Houston Jr (1984) *Blues, Ideology and Afro-American Literature: A Vernacular Theory*. Chicago: University of Chicago Press.

Bal, Mieke (1985) *Narratology: Introduction to the Theory of Narrative.* Trans. by Christine van Bohememen. Toronto: University of Toronto Press.

— (1988) *Verkrachting Verbeeld: Seksueel geweld in cultuur gebracht*. Utrecht: HES.

Banks, Olive (1981) *Faces of Feminism: A Study of Feminism as a Social Movement*. Oxford: Basil Blackwell.

Barta, Ilsebil, Zita Breu and Daniela Hammer-Tugendhat (eds) (1987) *Frauen. Bilder. Männer. Mythen. Kunsthistorische Beiträge*. Berlin: Dietrich Reimer.

Baym, Nina (1981) 'Melodramas of Beset Manhood: How Theories of American Fiction Exclude Women Authors', in Elaine Showalter (ed.), 63–81.

Beauvoir, Simone de (1960, first edn 1949), *The Second Sex: Facts, Myths and Lived Reality*. Original title: *Le deuxième sexe*.

Benjamin, Jessica (1990) *The Bonds of Love: Psychoanalysis, Feminism and the Problem of Domination*. London: Virago.

Benstock, Shari (1990) 'Expatriate Sapphic Modernism: Entering Literary History' in Karla Jay and Joanne Glasgow (eds), *Lesbian Texts and Contexts: Radical Revisions*. New York: New York University Press, 183–203.

Berger, Renate (1982) *Malerinnen auf dem Weg ins 20. Jahrhundert: Kunstgeschichte als Sozialgeschichte*. Cologne: DuMont.

Berger, Renate and Daniela Hammer Tugendhat (1985) *Der Garten der Lüste: Zur Deutung des erotischen und sexuallen bei Künstlern and ihren Interpreten*. Cologne: Du-Mont.

Bernheimer, Charles, and Claire Kahane (eds) (1985) *In Dora's Case: Freud, Hysteria, Feminism*. London: Virago.

Bernikow, Louise (ed.) (1974) *The World Split Open: Women Poets 1552–1950*. London: The Women's Press.

Betterton, Rosemary (1987) *Looking On: Images of Femininity in the Visual Arts and Media*. London: Routledge.

Blau Du Plessis, Rachel (1985) *Writing beyond the Ending: Narrative Strategies of Twentieth Century Women Writers*. Bloomington: Indiana University Press.

Blok, H. Josine (1995) *The Early Amazons: Modern and Ancient Perspectives on a Persistent Myth*. Leiden: Brill.

Bloom, Harold (1973) *The Anxiety of Influence: Theory of Poetry*. New York: Oxford University Press.

Bobo, Jaqueline. See supplementary bibliography below.

Bodine, Ann (1975) 'Sex Differentiation in Language', in Barrie Thorne and Nancy Henley (eds), *Language and Sex: Difference and Dominance*. Rowley: Newbury House Publishers, 130–151.

Bosch, Mineke (1987) 'Women's Culture in Women's History: Historical Notion or Feminist Vision?', in M. Meijer and J. Schaap (eds), *Historiography of Women's Cultural Traditions*. Dordrecht: Foris Publications, 35–52.

Bowers, Jane and Judith Tick (eds) (1986) *Women Making Music: The Western Art Tradition 1150–1950*. Urbana and Chicago: University of Illinois Press.

Braidotti, Rosi (1991a) *Patterns of Dissonance: A Study of Women in Contemporary Philosophy*. Cambridge: Polity Press.

— (1991b) 'Introduction: Dutch Treats and Other Strangers – Reading Dutch Feminism', in Joke J. Hermsen and Alkeline van Lenning (eds), *Sharing the Difference: Feminist Debates in Holland*. London and New York: Routledge, 1–22.

— (1993) 'An Editorial Introduction: Women's Studies at the University of Utrecht', in *Women's Studies International Forum* 16 (4), 311–324.

— (1994) *Nomadic Subjects: Embodiment and Sexual Difference in Contemporary Feminist Theory*. New York: Columbia University Press.

Brennan, Teresa (ed.) (1989) *Between Feminism and Psychoanalysis*. London and New York: Routledge.

Brett, Philip, Gary Thomas and Elizabeth Wood (1993) *Queering the Pitch: The New Lesbian and Gay Musicology*. New York: Routledge.

Briscoe, James R. (ed.) (1987) *Historical Anthology of Music by Women*. Bloomington: Indiana University Press.

Broude, Norma and Mary D. Garrard (1994) *The Power of Feminist Art: The American Movement of the 1970s, History and Impact*. New York: Abrams Inc.

Brouwer, Dédé (1989) *Gender Variation in Dutch: A Sociolinguistic Study of Amsterdam Speech*. Dordrecht: Foris Publications.

— (1991) 'Feminist Language Policy in Dutch: Equality rather than Difference', in *Working Papers on Language, Gender and Sexism* 1 (2), 73–82.

Brouwer, Dédé, Marinel Gerritsen and Dorian de Haan (1979). 'Speech Differences between Women and Men: On the Wrong Track?', in *Language in Society* 8, 33–50.

Brouwer, Dédé and Dorian de Haan (eds) (1987) *Women's Language, Socialization and Self-Image*. Dordrecht: Foris Publications.

Brouwer, Liesbeth (1990) 'Beyond Limits: Boundaries in Feminist Semiotics and Literary Theory: An Introduction', in L. Brouwer, P. Broomans and R. Paasman (eds), *Beyond Limits: Boundaries in Feminist Semiotics and Literary Theory*. Groningen: Rijksuniversiteit Groningen, 11–22.

Brown, Mary-Ellen (1990) *Television and Women's Culture*. London: Sage Publications.

Brügmann, Margret (1990) 'Marilyn Monroe meets Cassandra: Women's Studies in the Nineties', in V. Zürcher and T. Langendorff (eds) *The Humanities in the Nineties*. Amsterdam and Lisse: Swets & Zeitlinger, 257–77.

Butler, Joan and Joan Scott (1992) 'Introduction', in *Feminists Theorize the Political*, New York: Routledge.

Butler, Judith (1994) *Bodies That Matter: On the Discursive Limits of 'Sex'*. New York: Routledge.

Cameron, Deborah (1985) *Feminism and Linguistic Theory*. London and Basingstoke: Macmillan.

Carby, Hazel V. (1984) 'White Women Listen! Black Feminism and the Boundaries of Sisterhood', in *The Empire Strikes Back: Race and Racism in the 1970s*. Boston and London: Hutchinson.

— (1987) *Reconstructing Womanhood: The Emergence of the Afro-American Woman Novelist*. New York and Oxford: Oxford University Press.

Carson, Diane, Linda Dittmar, and Janice R. Welsch (eds) (1994) *Multiple Voices in Feminist Film Criticism*. Minneapolis and London: University of Minnesota Press.

Case, Sue-Ellen (1985) 'Classic Drag: The Greek Creation of Female Parts', in *Theatre Journal* 37, 317–27.

— (1988) *Feminism and Theatre*. London/Basingstoke: Macmillan.

— (ed.) (1990) *Performing Feminisms: Feminist Critical Theory and Theatre*. Baltimore and London: Johns Hopkins University Press.

Chicago, Judy (1977) *Through the Flower: My Struggle as a Woman Artist*. New York: Anchor Press.

— (1979) *The Dinner Party: A Symbol of our Heritage*. New York: Anchor Books.

Chodorow, Nancy (1978) *The Reproduction of Mothering: Psychoanalysis and the Sociology of Gender*. Berkeley: University of California Press.

— (1989) *Feminism and Psychoanalytic Theory*. Oxford: Polity Press.

Christian, Barbara (1985) 'Trajectories of Self-Definition: Placing Contemporary Afro-American Women's Fiction', in *Black Feminist Criticism: Perspectives on Black Women Writers*. New York: Pergamon Press, 171–86.

Citron, Marcia J. (1990) 'Gender, Professionalism and the Musical Canon', in *Journal of Musicology* 8 (1), 102–17.

— (1993) *Gender and the Musical Canon*. Cambridge: Cambridge University Press.

Cixous, Hélène (1976) 'The Laugh of the Medusa', trans. Keith Cohen and Paula Cohen, in *Signs* 1 (1), 875–899. Original title (1975) 'Le rire de Medusa'.

— (1983) *Portrait of Dora*, trans. Sarah Burd, in *Diacritics*, (Spring), pp. 2–32. Another translation by Anita Barrows, in *Benmussa Directs*, London: Calder, 1979; Dallas: Riverrun Press, 1979. Original title (1979) *Portrait de Dora*.

Clément, Cathérine (1988) *Opera, or the Undoing of Women*. Trans. Betsy Wing. Minneapolis: University of Minnesota Press. Original title (1979) *L'opéra ou la défaite des femmes*.

Clément, Cathérine and Hélène Cixous (1986). *The Newly Born Woman*. Minneapolis: University of Minnesota Press. Original title (1975) *La jeune née*.

Coates, Jennifer (1986) *Women, Men and Language: A Sociolinguistic Account of Sex Differences in Language*. London and New York: Longman.

Coates, Jennifer and Deborah Cameron (eds) (1989) *Women in Their Speech Communities: New Perspectives on Language and Sex*. London and New York: Longman.

Collins, Patricia Hill (1990) *The Social Construction of Black Feminist Thought: Knowledge, Consciousness, and the Politics of Empowerment*. Boston: Unwin Hyman.

Comrie, Bernard and Gerald Stone (1978) 'Sex, Gender and the Status of Women', in *The Russian Language Since the Revolution*. Oxford: Clarendon Press, 159–171.

Coward, Rosalind, and John Ellis (1977) *Language and Materialism: Developments in Semiology and the Theory of the Subject*. London: Routledge & Kegan Paul.

Crosby, Faye and Linda Nyquist (1977) 'The Female Register: An Empirical Study of Lakoff's Hypotheses', in *Language in Society* 6, 313–322.

Cudjoe, Selwyn R. (1990) 'Maya Angelou: The Autobiographical Statement Updated', in Gates (ed.) (1990), 272–306.

Culler, Jonathan (1981) *The Pursuit of Signs: Semiotics, Literature, Deconstruction*. Ithaca: Cornell University Press.

— (1983) *On Deconstruction*. London: Routledge & Kegan Paul.

Cutler, Anne and Donia R. Scott (1990) 'Speaker Sex and Perceived Apportionment of Talk', in *Applied Psycholinguistics* 11, 253–72.

Daly, Mary (1978) *Gyn/Ecology: The Metaethics of Radical Feminism*. Boston: Beacon Press.

Dame, Joke (1992a) 'Rocky Times: Feminist Musicology in the 1990s', *Muziek & Wetenschap* 2(1), 25–31.

— (1992b) 'Stimmen Innerhalb der Stimme – Genotext und Phänotext in Berios *Sequenza III*', in Freia Hoffmann and Eva Rieger (eds) *Von der Spielfrau zur Performancekünstlerin: Auf der Suche nach einer Musikgeschichte der Frauen*. Kassel: Furore, 144–157.

— (1994a) 'Unveiled Voices: Sexual Difference and the Castrato', in Philip Brett, Elizabeth Wood and Gary Thomas (eds), *Queering the Pitch: The New Gay and Lesbian Musicology*. New York: Routledge, 139–153.

— (1994b) 'The Female Voice as Fetish. Occurrences in the Practices of Psychoanalysis and Music', in Mieke Bal and Inge Boer (eds), *The Point of Theory*. Amsterdam: Amsterdam University Press, 260–270.

Davidoff, Lenore and Catherine Hall (1987) *Family Fortunes: Men and Women of the English Middle Class, 1780–1850*. Chicago: University of Chicago Press.

Davis, Natalie Zemon (1980) 'Gender and Genre: Women as Historical Writers, 1400–1820', in Patricia H. Labalme (ed.), *Beyond Their Sex: Learned Women of the European Past*. New York and London: New York University Press, 153–82.

Diamond, Elin (1985) 'Refusing the Romanticism of Identity: Narrative Interventions in Churchill, Benmussa, Duras', in *Theatre Journal* 37, 133–54. Reprinted in Case (ed.) (1990).

Diawara, Manthia. See supplementary bibliography below.

Doane, Mary Ann (1987) *The Desire to Desire: The Woman's Film of the 1940s*. Bloomington: Indiana University Press.

— (1991) *Femmes Fatales: Feminism, Film Theory, Psychoanalysis*. New York and London: Routledge.

Dolan, Jill (1988) *The Feminist Spectator as Critic*. Ann Arbor: University of Michigan Press.

Duby, Georges, and Michelle Perrot (eds) (1991–1994) *History of Women in the West* (five volumes). Cambridge, Massachusetts: Harvard University Press.

Dudovitz, Resa L. (1990) *The Myth of Superwoman: Women's Bestsellers in France and the United States*. London and New York: Routledge.

d'Eaubonne, Françoise (1977) *Histoire de l'art et lutte des sexes*. Paris: Editions de la Différence.

Eco, Umberto (1976) *A Theory of Semiotics*. Bloomington: Indiana University Press.

Edwards, Viv (1989) 'The Speech of British Black Women in Dudley, West Midlands', in Jennifer Coates and Deborah Cameron (eds) *Women in Their Speech Communities: New Perspectives on Language and Sex*. London and New York: Longman, 33–50.

Erens, Patricia (ed.) (1990) *Issues in Feminist Film Criticism*. Bloomington: Indiana University Press.

Essed, Philomena (1991) *Understanding Everyday Racism: An Interdisciplinary Theory*. London: Sage Publications.

Faderman, Lilian (1985/1981) *Surpassing the Love of Men: Romantic Friendship and Love between Women from the Renaissance to the Present*. London: The Women's Press.

Feldstein, Richard, and Judith Roof (eds) (1989) *Feminism and Psychoanalysis*. Ithaca and London: Cornell University Press.

Felman, Shoshana (1975) 'Women and Madness: The Critical Phallacy', in *Diacritics*, 2–11.

— (ed.) (1982 orig. 1977), *Literature and Psychoanalysis: The Question of Reading: Otherwise*. Baltimore and London: Johns Hopkins University Press.

Felperin, Howard (1990) *The Uses of the Canon: Elizabethan Literature and Contemporary Literature*. Oxford: Clarendon Press.

Fetterley, Judith (1978) *The Resisting Reader: A Feminist Approach to American Fiction*. Bloomington: Indiana University Press.

Fischer, Lucy (1989) *Shot/Countershot: Film Tradition and Women's Cinema*. Princeton: Princeton University Press.

Fishman, Pamela M. (1983) 'Interaction: The Work Women Do', in Thorne, Kramerae and Henley (eds), 89–101.

Flitterman-Lewis, Sandy (1990) *To Desire Differently: Feminism and the French Cinema*. Urbana and Chicago: University of Illinois Press.

Forster, Jeanette H. (1985/1956) *Sex Variant Women in Literature*. Tallahassee: Naiad Press.

Fox-Genovese, Elizabeth (1988) *Within the Plantation Household: Black and White Women in the Old South*. Chapel Hill and London: University of North Carolina Press.

Freud, Sigmund (1900) *The Interpretation of Dreams*, in *Standard Edition of the Complete Psychological Works* (SE), translated and edited by James Strachey, 1953, London: Hogarth, Vols. IV and V.

— (1905a) *Fragment of an Analysis of a Case of Hysteria*, in SE, VII: 3–122.

— (1905b) *Three Essays on the Theory of Sexuality*, in SE, VII: 125–245.

— (1925) *Some Psychical Consequences of the Anatomical Distinction between the Sexes*, in SE, XIX: 243–258.

— (1931) *Female Sexuality*, in SE, XXI: 223–243.

Freud, Sigmund and Josef Breuer (1895) *Studies on Hysteria*, in SE, II.

Friedan, Betty (1963) *The Feminine Mystique*. London: Penguin Books.

Frye, Marilyn (1983) *The Politics of Reality: Essays in Feminist Theory*. Trumansburg: Crossing Press.

Fuss, Diana (ed.) (1991) *Inside/Out: Lesbian Theories, Gay Theories*. New York: Routledge.

Gaines, Jane (1988) 'White Privilege and Looking Relations: Race and Gender in Feminist Film Theory', in *Screen* 29 (4), 12–27.

Gal, Susan (1978) 'Peasant Men Can't Get Wives: Language Change and Sex Roles in a Bilingual Community', in *Language in Society* 7, 1–16.

Gallop, Jane (1982) *The Daughter's Seduction: Feminism and Psychoanalysis*. Ithaca: Cornell University Press.

— (1985) *Reading Lacan*. Ithaca, New York: Cornell University Press.

Gamman, Lorraine, and Margaret Marshment (eds) (1988) *The Female Gaze: Women as Viewers of Popular Culture*. London: The Women's Press.

Gates, Henry Louis Jr (ed.) (1984) *Black Literature and Literary Theory*. New York and London: Methuen.

— (ed.) (1986) *'Race' Writing and Difference*. Chicago: University of Chicago Press.

— (ed.) (1990) *Reading Black, Reading Feminist: A Critical Anthology*. New York: Meridian.

Geraghty, Christine (1991) *Women and Soap Opera: A Study of Prime Time Soaps*. Cambridge: Polity Press.

Gever, Martha and Nathalie Magnan (1991/1986) 'The Same Difference: On Lesbian Representation', in Tessa Boffin and Jean Fraser (eds), *Stolen Glances: Lesbians Take Photographs*. London: Pandora, 67–75.

Gilbert, Sandra, and Susan Gubar (1979) *The Madwoman in the Attic: The Woman Writer and the Nineteenth Century Literary Imagination*. New Haven and London: Yale University Press.

— (1985) *The Norton Anthology of Literature by Women: The Tradition in English*. New York and London: Norton.

Goodwin, Marjorie Harness (1980) 'Directive-response Speech Sequences in Girls' and Boys' Task Activities', in Sally McConnell-Ginet, Ruth Borker and Nelly Furman (eds), 157–173.

Gouges, Olympe de (1979) *The Declaration of the Rights of Woman*, in: trans. and ed. by Darlene Gay Levy, Harriet Branson Applewhite, and Mary Durham Johnson, *Women in Revolutionary Paris, 1789–1795, Selected Documents*. Urbana: University of Illinois Press. Original title (1791) *Déclaration des droites de la femme et de la citoyenne*.

Graddoll, David, and Joan Swann (1989) *Gender Voices*. Oxford: Blackwell.

Graves Miller, Judith (1989) 'Contemporary Women's Voices in French Theater', in *Modern Drama* 32 (1), 5–23.

Green, Gayle, and Coppélia Kahn (eds) (1985) *Making a Difference: Feminist Literary Criticism*. London and New York: Methuen.

Greenblatt, Stephen (1989) 'Towards a Poetics of Culture', in H. Aram Veeser (ed.), *The New Historicism*. New York and London: Routledge, 1–15.

Greer, Germaine (1970) *The Female Eunuch*. London: MacGibbon & Kee.

Grever, Maria (1995) '"Scolding Old Bags and Whining Hags": Women's History and the Myth of Compatible Paradigms in History', in Mary O'Dowd and Sabine Wicherts (eds), *Historical Studies: Women's History*. Dublin: Irish committee of Historical Sciences, 23–41.

Grier, Barbara (ed.) (1981) *The Lesbian in Literature*. 3d edn Tallahassee: Naiad Press.

Griffin, Gabriele (1993) *Heavenly Love? Lesbian Images in Twentieth-century Women's Writing*. Manchester: Manchester University Press.

Hamer, Diane and Belinda Budge (eds) (1994) *The Good, the Bad and the Gorgeous: Popular Culture's Romance with Lesbianism*. London: Scarlett Press.

Hannerz, Ulf (1970) 'Language Variation and Social Relationships', in *Studia Linguistica* 24, 128–151.

Haraway, Donna (1991) 'Ecce Homo, Ain't (Ar'n't) I a Woman, and Inappropriate/d Others: The Human in a Post-Humanist Landscape', in Judith Butler and Joan W. Scott (eds), *Feminists Theorize the Political*, New York and London: Routledge, 86–100.

Hart, Lynda (ed.) (1989) *Making a Spectacle: Feminist Essays on Contemporary Women's Theater*. Ann Arbor: University of Michigan Press.

Haskell, Molly (1987/1973) *From Reverence to Rape: The Treatment of Women in the Movies*. Rev. edn, Chicago and London: University of Chicago Press.

Hermes, Joke (1995) *Reading Women's Magazines: An Analysis of Everyday Media Use*. Cambridge: Polity Press.

Herrmann, Anne (1989) 'Travesty and Transgression: Transvestism in Shakespeare, Brecht and Churchill', in *Theatre Journal* 41 (2), 133–54. Reprinted in Case (ed.) (1990).

Hinding, Andrea (ed.) (1979) *Women's History Sources: A Guide to the Archives and Manuscript Collections in the United States* (two parts). New York and London: R. R. Bowker.

Hirsch, Marianne (1989) *The Mother/Daughter Plot: Narrative, Psychoanalysis, Feminism*. Bloomington: Indiana University Press.

Hite, Molly See supplementary bibliography below.

Hoogland, Renée C. (1994) *Elizabeth Bowen: A Reputation in Writing*. New York: New York University Press.

hooks, bell (1981) *Ain't I a Woman: Black Women and Feminism*. Boston: South End Press.

— (1984) *From Margin to Center*. Boston: South End Press.

— (1989) *Talking Back: Thinking Feminist, Thinking Black*. Boston: South End Press.

— (1990a) See supplementary bibliography below.

— (1990b) *Yearning: Race, Gender and Cultural Politics*. Boston: South End Press.

— (1992) *Black Looks: Race and Representation*. Boston: South End Press.

— (1994a) *Outlaw Culture: Resisting Representations*. New York and London: Routledge.

— (1994b) *Teaching to Transgress: Education as the Practice of Freedom*. New York: Routledge.

hooks, bell, and M. Childers (1990) 'A Conversation About Race and Class', in Marianne Hirsch and Evelyn Fox Keller (eds), *Conflicts in Feminism*. London and New York: Routledge.

Horton, James (1986) 'Freedom's Yoke: Gender Conventions among Antebellum Free Blacks', in *Feminist Studies* 12.

Irigaray, Luce (1982) 'And the One Doesn't Stir Without the Other', trans. Hélène Vivienne Wenzel, *Signs* 7 (1), 60–67. Original title (1979) 'L'une ne bouge pas sans l'autre'.

— (1985a) *Speculum of the Other Woman*. Trans. Gilliann C. Gill, Ithaca: Cornell University Press. Original title (1974) *Spéculum de l'autre femme*.

— (1985b) *This Sex Which Is Not One*. Trans. Catherine Porter with Carolyn Burke. Original title (1977) *Ce sexe qui n'en est pas un*.

Janeway, Elizabeth (1975) *Between Myth and Morning: Women Awakening*. New York: William Morrow & Co.

Jespersen, Otto (1922) 'The Woman', in *Language, Its Nature, Development, and Origin*. London: Allen & Unwin, 237–54.

Johnson, Barbara (1984) 'Metaphor, Metonymy and Voice in *Their Eyes Were Watching God*', in Gates (ed.), (1984), 209–19.

— (1994) *The Wake of Deconstruction*. Oxford and Cambridge: Blackwell.

Johnston, Claire (1973) 'Women's Cinema as Counter Cinema', in *Notes on Women's Cinema*. London: SEFT. Reprinted Glasgow: Screen (1991).

Jones, Jacqueline (1985) *Labor of Love, Labor of Sorrow: Black Women, Work and the Family from Slavery to the Present*. New York: Basic Books.

Kaplan, Cora (1986) *Sea Changes: Culture and Feminism*. London: Verso.

Kaplan, E. Ann (1983) *Women and Film: Both Sides of the Camera*. New York and London: Methuen.

— (1987) *Rocking Around the Clock: Music Television, Postmodernism and Consumer Culture*. New York and London: Routledge.

— (1988) *Postmodernism and its Discontents: Theories, Practices*. London and New York: Verso.

Kearns, Martha (1976) *Käthe Kollwitz: Woman and Artist*. New York: The Feminist Press.

Keenan, Elinor (1974) 'Norm-makers, Norm-breakers: Uses of Speech by Men and Women in a Malagasy Community', in Richard Bauman and Joel Sherzer (eds), *Explorations in the Ethnography of Speaking*. London: Cambridge University Press, 124–143.

Kelly-Gadol, Joan (1976a) *Women in European History*. Boston: Houghton Mifflin Company.

— (1976b) 'The Social Relations of the Sexes: Methodological Implications of Women's History', in *Signs: Journal of Women in Culture and Society* 1 (4), 809–824.

— (1987, orig. 1976) 'Did Women Have a Renaissance?', in Renate Bridenthal, Claudia Koonz, Susan Stuard (eds), *Becoming Visible*.

Key, Mary Ritchie (1975) *Male/Female Language*. With a Comprehensive Bibliography. Methuen: Scarecrow Press.

Kingsbury, Martha (1973) 'The Femme Fatale and Her Sisters', in Thomas B. Hess and Linda Nochlin (eds), *Women and Sex Object*. London: Penguin.

Koch, Gertrud (1989), 'Warum Frauen ins Männerkino gehen', in *'Was ich erbeute sind Bilder': Zum Diskurs der Geschlechter im Film*. 125–36. Frankfurt am Main: Stroemfeld/Roter Stern.

Koedt, Annette, Ellen Levine, and Anita Rapone (eds) (1973) *Radical Feminism*. New York: Quadrangle Books.

Koonz, Claudia (1987) *Mothers in the Fatherland: Women, the Family and Nazi Politics*. New York: St. Martin's Press.

Koskoff, Ellen (ed.) (1987) *Women and Music in Cross-Cultural Perspective*. New York: Greenwood Press.

Kristeva, Julia (1981) *Desire in Language: A Semiotic Approach to Literature and Art*. Edited by Leon S. Roudiez. Oxford: Basil Blackwell. Original title (1979) *Semiotikè: Recherches pour une sémanalyse*.

— (1986) *Tales of Love*. Trans. Léon S. Roudiez. New York: Columbia University Press. Original title (1983) *Histoires d'Amour*.

— (1991) *Strangers To Ourselves*. Trans. Leon S. Roudiez. New York: Columbia University Press. Original title (1988) *Étrangers à nous-mêmes*.

Kuhn, Annette (1982) *Women's Pictures: Feminism and Cinema*. London: Routledge & Kegan Paul.

Kuhn, Annette and Susannah Radstone (1990) *The Women's Companion to International Film*. London: Virago.

Künstlerinnen der Russischen Avantgarde: 1910–1930 (1979). Cologne: Galerie Gmurzynska.

Labov, William (1972a) *Language in the Inner City: Studies in the Black English Vernacular*. Philadelphia: University of Pennsylvania Press.

— (1972b) *Sociolinguistic Patterns*. Philadelphia: University of Pennsylvania Press.

Lacan, Jacques (1977a) 'The Mirror Stage as Formative of the I', in *Écrits: A Selection*. New York and London: W.W. Norton & Co: 1–7. Original title (1966) 'Le stade du miroir comme formateur de la fonction du Je', in *Écrits I*.

— (1977b) 'The Signification of the Phallus', in *Écrits: A Selection*. New York and London: W.W. Norton & Co: 281–91. Original title (1966) 'La signification du phallus', in *Écrits II*.

Lakoff, Robin (1975) *Language and Woman's Place*. New York: Harper & Row.

Lauretis, Teresa de (1984) *Alice Doesn't: Feminism, Semiotics, Cinema*. Bloomington: Indiana University Press.

— (1987) *Technologies of Gender: Essays on Theory, Film and Fiction*. Bloomington: Indiana University Press.

— (1991) 'Queer Theory: Lesbian and Gay Sexualities, An Introduction', in *Differences* 5 (2), iii-xviii.

— (1994) *The Practice of Love: Lesbian Sexuality and Perverse Desire*. Bloomington: Indiana University Press.

Lauter, Paul (ed.) (1990) *The Heath Anthology of American Literature*. Lexington, Mass.: D. C. Heath and Co.

Lenz, Carolyn, *et al.* (1980) *The Women's Part: Feminist Criticism on Shakespeare*. Urbana: University of Illinois Press.

Lindner, Ines, Sigrid Schade, Silke Wenk and Gabriele Werner (eds) (1989) *Blick-Wechsel: Konstruktionen von Männlichkeit und Weiblichkeit in Kunst und Kunstgeschichte*. Berlin: Dietrich Reimer.

Lippard, Lucy (1976) *From the Center: Feminist Essays on Women's Art*. New York: Dutton.

Lorde, Audre (1984) *Sister Outsider: Essays and Speeches by Audre Lorde*. New York: Crossing Press.

Maltz, Daniel, and Ruth Borker (1982) 'A Cultural Approach to Male–Female Miscommunication', in John Gumperz (ed.), *Language and Social Identity*. Cambridge: Cambridge University Press.

Marcus, Jane (1987) 'Still Practice: A/Wrested Alphabet', in Shari Benstock (ed.), *Feminist Issues in Literary Scholarship*. Bloomington: Indiana University Press, 79–97.

Marks, Elaine (1979) 'Lesbian Intertextuality', in Elaine Marks and Geroge Stambolian (eds), *Homosexuality and French Literature*. Ithaca: Cornell University Press, 353–77.

Martyna, Wendy (1978) 'What Does He Mean – Use of the Generic Masculine', in *Journal of Communication* 28, 131–8.

Mayne, Judith (1990) *The Woman at the Keyhole: Feminism and Women's Cinema*. Bloomington: Indiana University Press.

McClary, Susan (1991) *Feminine Endings: Music, Gender, and Sexuality*. Minneapolis: University of Minnesota Press.

Meijer, Maaike (1988) *De lust tot lezen: Nederlandse dichteressen en het literaire systeem*. Amsterdam: Sara/Van Gennep.

Mellencamp, Patricia (1990) *Indiscretions, Avant-Garde Film, Video and Feminism*. Bloomington: Indiana University Press.

Miller, Casey, and Kate Swift (1977) *Words and Women*. London: Gollancz.

Millett, Kate (1969) *Sexual Politics*. London: Sphere Books.

Mills, Sara, Lynn Pearce, Sue Spaull, Elaine Millard (eds) (1989) *Feminist Readings, Feminists Reading*. New York and London: Harvester Wheatsheaf.

Milroy, Lesley (1980) *Language and Social Networks*. Oxford: Blackwell.

Mitchell, Juliet (1974) *Psychoanalysis and Feminism*. London: Penguin.

Mitchell, Juliet, and Jacqueline Rose (eds) (1982) *Feminine Sexuality: Jacques Lacan and the École Freudienne*. London: Macmillan.

Modleski, Tania (1984) *Loving with a Vengeance: Mass-produced Fantasies for Women*. London: Methuen.

— (1986) 'Feminism and the Power of Interpretation: Some Critical Readings', in Teresa de Lauretis (ed.), *Feminist Studies: Critical Studies*. Bloomington: Indiana University Press, 121–39.

Mohanty, Chandra Talpade (1987) 'Feminist Encounters: Locating the Politics of Experience', in *Copyright* 1, 30–44.

— (1988) 'Under Western Eyes: Feminist Scholarship and Colonial Discourse', in *Feminist Review* 30, 60–86.

Moi, Toril (1985) *Sexual/Textual Politics: Feminist Literary Theory*. London: Routledge.

Moraga, Cherrie, and Gloria Anzaldúa (eds) (1981) *This Bridge Called my Back: Writing by Radical Women of Color*. New York: Kitchen Table, Women of Color Press.

Morrison, Toni (1992) *Playing in the Dark: Whiteness and the Literary Imagination*. Cambridge: Harvard University Press.

Mortagne, Marie-José (1981) 'Fonctions feminines, fonctionnement du feminin', *Rapports* 51, 11–28.

Mulvey, Laura (1975) 'Visual Pleasure and Narrative Film', reprinted in (1989) *Visual and Other Pleasures*. London: Macmillan Press.

Munt, Sally (ed.) (1992) *New Lesbian Criticism: Literary and Cultural Readings*. New York: Harvester Wheatsheaf.

Myron, Nancy and Charlotte Bunch (eds) (1975) *Lesbianism and the Women's Movement*. Baltimore: Diana Press.

Neal, Larry (1975) 'The Black Arts Movement', in Gayle Addison (ed.), *The Black Aesthetic*. New York: Anchor Books.

Neuls-Bates, Carol (ed.) (1982) *Women in Music: An Anthology of Source Readings from the Middle Ages to the Present*. New York: Harper & Row.

Newton, Esther (1989/1984) 'The Mythic Mannish Lesbian: Radclyffe Hall and the New Woman', in Martin Bauml Duberman, Martha Vicinus, and George Chauncey Jr. (eds), *Hidden from History: Reclaiming the Gay and Lesbian Past*. London: Penguin, 281–93.

Nichols, Patricia C. (1980) 'Women in Their Speech Communities', in Sally McConnell-Ginet, Ruth Borker and Nelly Furman (eds), *Women and Language in Literature and Society.* New York: Praeger.

Nilsen, Alleen Pace, Haig Bosmajian, H. Lee Gershuny, Julia P. Stanley (eds) (1977) *Sexism and Language.* Urbana: National Council of Teachers of English.

Nochlin, Linda (1973) 'Why Have There Been No Great Women Artists?', in V. Gornick, and B. Moran (eds), *Woman in Sexist Society: Studies in Power and Powerlessness.* New York, 1–44.

— (1991) 'Women, Art and Power', in N. Bryson, M. Holly and K. Moxey (eds), *Visual Theory: Painting and Interpretation.* Cambridge: Cambridge University Press.

Ostriker, Alicia (1986) *Stealing the Language: The Emergence of Women's Poetry in America.* London: The Women's Press.

Parker, Rozsika (1984) *The Subversive Stitch.* London: The Women's Press.

Parker, Rozsika and Griselda Pollock (1981) *Old Mistresses: Women, Art and Ideology.* London: Routledge.

— (1987) *Framing Feminism: Art and the Women's Movement 1970–1985.* London: Routledge.

Pendle, Karin (ed.) (1991) *Women and Music: A History.* Bloomington: Indiana University Press.

Penley, Constance (1989) *The Future of an Illusion: Film, Feminism and Psychoanalysis.* Minneapolis: University of Minnesota Press.

Penley, Constance and E. Lyon, L. Spigel and J. Bergstrom (eds) (1991) *Close Encounters: Film, Feminism and Science Fiction.* Minneapolis: University of Minnesota Press.

Perry, Gillian (1979) *Paula Modersohn-Becker: Life and Work.* Amsterdam: Sara.

Peterson, Karen, and J. J. Wilson (1976) *Women Artists: Recognition and Reappraisal – From the Early Middle Ages to the Twentieth Century.* New York and London: Harper & Row.

Philips, Susan U., Susan Steele and Christine Tanz (eds) (1987) *Language, Gender and Sex in Comparative Perspective.* Cambridge: Cambridge University Press.

Pisan, Christine de (1983) *The Book of the City of Ladies.* Trans. Earl Jeffrey Richards; foreword by Marina Warner. London: Pan Books. Original title (1405) *Le Livre de la Cité des Dames.*

Pollock, Griselda (1988) *Vision and Difference: Femininity, Feminism and the Histories of Art.* London and New York: Routledge.

Pomata, Gianna (1987) 'La storia delle donne: una questione di confina', in *Gli strumenti della ricerca. Vol. II* Firenze, 1434–1469.

— (1993) 'History, Particular and Universal: On Reading Some Recent Women's History Textbooks', in *Feminist Studies* 19 (1), 7–49.

Press, Andrea (1990) 'Class, Gender and the Female Viewer: Women's Responses to *Dynasty*', in M. E. Brown, *Television and Women's Culture.*

Pribram, E. Deidre (ed.) (1988) *Female Spectators: Looking At Film and Television.* London and New York: Verso.

Pryse, Marjorie, and Hortense J. Spillers (eds) (1985) *Conjuring: Black Women, Fiction and Literary Tradition*. Bloomington: Indiana University Press.

Purvis, June (1992) 'Using Primary Sources When Researching Women's History from a Feminist Perspective', in *Women's History Review* 1 (2), 273–306.

Radicalesbians (1973) 'The Woman Identified Woman', in Anne Koedt, Ellen Levine, and Anita Rapone (eds), *Radical Feminism*. New York: Quadrangle, 240–245.

Radway, Janice (1984) *Reading the Romance: Women, Patriarchy and Popular Literature*. Chapel Hill and London: University of North Carolina Press.

Raymond, Janice (1984) *A Passion for Friends: Toward a Philosophy of Female Affection*. Boston: Beacon Press.

Reinelt, Janelle (1989) 'Feminist Theory and the Problem of Performance', in *Modern Drama* 32 (1), 48–57.

Rich, Adrienne (1986) 'Compulsory Heterosexuality and Lesbian Existence', in *Blood, Bread, and Poetry: Selected Prose 1979–1985*. New York: Norton.

Rieger, Eva (1980) *Frau und Musik*. Frankfurt am Main: Fischer Taschenbuch Verlag.

— (1981) *Frau, Musik und Männerherrschaft: Zum Auschluss der Frau aus der deutschen Musikpädagogik, Musikwissenschaft und Musikausübung*. Frankfurt am Main: Ullstein.

— (1984) 'Weibliches Musikschaffen – weibliche Ästhetik?', in *Neue Zeitschrift für Musik* 145 (1), 407.

Robinson, Hilary (ed.) (1987) *Visibly Female: Feminism and Art Today*. London: Camden Press.

Roof, Judith (1991) *A Lure of Knowledge: Lesbian Sexuality and Theory*. New York: Columbia University Press.

Rosaldo, Michelle (1980) 'The Use and Abuse of Anthropology: Reflections on Feminism and Cross-cultural Understanding', in *Signs: Journal of Women in Culture and Society*, 5 (3), 389–417.

Rose, Jacqueline (1983) *Sexuality in the Field of Vision*. London: Verso.

Rubin, Gayle (1975) 'The Traffic in Women: Notes Toward a Political Economy of Sex', in Reina Rayter (ed.), *Toward an Anthropology of Women*. New York: Monthly Review Press, 157–210.

— (1993) 'Thinking Sex: Notes for a Radical Theory of the Politics of Sexuality', in Henry Abelove, Michèle Aina Barale, David M. Halperin (eds), *The Lesbian and Gay Studies Reader*. New York: Routledge, 3–44.

Rule, Jane (1975) *Lesbian Images*. Freedom: The Crossing Press.

Russell, Joan (1982) 'Networks and Sociolinguistic Variation in an African Urban Setting', in Suzanne Romaine (ed.), *Sociolinguistic Variation in Speech Communities*. London: Edward Arnold, 125–140.

Said, Edward W. (1978) *Orientalism*. New York: Vintage.

Sato, Hiroko (1972) 'Under That Harlem Shadow: A Study of Jessie Fauset and Nella Larsen', in Arna Bontemps (ed.), *The Harlem Renaissance Remembered*. New York: Dodd Mead & Co.

Sayers, J. (1991) *Mothering Psychoanalysis*. London: Hamish Hamilton.

Schor, Naomi (1995) 'French Feminism is a Universalism', forthcoming in *Differences*.

Scott, Joan Wallach, (1986) 'Gender: a Useful Category of Historical Analysis', in *American Historical Review* 91 (4), 1053–75.

— (1988) 'American Women Historians, 1884–1984', in *Gender and the Politics of History*. New York: Columbia University Press, 28–49.

— (1995) *Women Who Only Have Paradoxes To Offer*. Cambridge: Harvard University Press.

Sebeok, Thomas A. (1986) *Contributions to the Doctrine of Signs*. Bloomington: Indiana University Press.

Seiter, Ellen, Hans Borchers, Gabriele Kreutzner and Eva-Maria Warth (1989) 'Don't Treat Us Like We're So Stupid and Naive', in *Remote Control: Television, Audiences and Cultural Power*. London and New York: Routledge, 223–47.

Shepherd, John (1987) 'Music and Male Hegemony', in Richard Leppert and Susan McClary (eds), *Music and Society: The Politics of Composition, Performance and Reception*. Cambridge: Cambridge University Press, 151–72.

Showalter, Elaine (1977) *A Literature of Their Own: British Women Novelists from Brontë to Lessing*. London: Virago.

— (1985) 'Representing Ophelia: Women, Madness and the Responsibilities of Feminist Criticism', in Patricia Parker and Geoffrey Harman (eds), *Shakespeare and the Question of Theory*. New York: Methuen, 77–94.

— (ed.) (1986 orig. 1985) *The New Feminist Criticism: Essays on Women, Literature and Theory*. London: Virago.

— (1987) 'Critical Crossdressing: Male Feminists and the Woman of the Year', in A. Jardine and P. Smith (eds), *Men in Feminism*. New York: Methuen, 116–33.

Shuy, Roger W. (1969) 'Sociolinguistic Research at the Center for Applied Linguistics: the Correlation of Language and Sex', in *Giornate internazionali di sociolinguistica*. Roma: Palazzo Baldasini, 849–857.

Silveira, Jeanette (1980) 'Generic Masculine Words and Thinking', in Cheris Kramarae (ed.), *The Voices and Words of Women and Men*. Oxford: Pergamon Press, 165–78.

Silverman, Kaja (1983) *The Subject of Semiotics*. New York and Oxford: Oxford University Press.

— (1988) *The Acoustic Mirror: The Female Voice in Psychoanalysis and Cinema*. Bloomington: Indiana University Press.

Smelik, Anneke (1993) 'And the Mirror Cracked: Metaphors of Violence in the Films of Marleen Gorris', in *Women's Studies International Forum* 16 (4), 349–636.

Smith, Barbara (1977) 'Toward a Black Feminist Criticism', in Elaine Showalter (ed.), *The New Feminist Criticism: Essays on Women, Literature and Theory*. New York: Pantheon, 168–85.

— (1990) 'The Truth That Never Hurts', in Joanna M. Braxton, and Andrée Nicola McLaughlin (eds), *Wild Women in the Whirlwind: Afro-American*

Culture and the Contemporary Literary Renaissance. London: Serpent's Tail, 213–46.

Smith, Bonnie (1984a) 'Women's Contribution to Modern Historical Scholarship, 1750–1940', in *American Historical Review* 89 (3), 709–32.

— (1984b) 'Seeing Mary Beard', in *Feminist Studies* 10 (3), 399–416.

Smith-Rosenberg, Carroll (1975) 'The Female World of Love and Ritual: Relations Between Women in Nineteeth-Century America', in *Signs* 1 (1) 1–29.

Snitow, Ann, Christine Stansell, Sharon Thomson (eds) (1984/1983) *Powers of Desire: The Politics of Sexuality*. London: Virago.

Solie, Ruth (1992) 'Whose Life? The Gendered Self in Schumann's *Frauenliebe* songs', in S.P. Scher (ed.), *Music and Text: Critical Inquiries*. Cambridge: Cambridge University Press.

— (ed.) (1993) *Musicology and Difference: Gender and Sexuality in Music Scholarship*. Berkeley: University of California Press.

Spender, Dale (1980) *Man Made Language*. London: Routledge & Kegan Paul.

Spivak, Gayatri Chakravorty (1987) *In Other Worlds: Essays in Cultural Politics*. New York: Methuen.

Stacey, Jackie (1987) 'Desperately Seeking Difference', in *Screen* 28 (1), 48–61.

Stimpson, Catherine R. (1984) 'Women as Knowers', in Diane Fowlkes and Charlotte McClure (eds), *Feminist Visions: Toward a Transformation of the Liberal Arts Curriculum*. Alabama: Habama Press.

— (1985/1981) 'Zero Degree Deviancy: The Lesbian Novel in English', in *Where the Meanings Are: Feminism and Cultural Spaces*. New York: Methuen.

— (1990) 'Afterword: Lesbian Studies in the 1990s', in Karla Jay and Joanne Glasgow (eds), *Lesbian Texts and Contexts: Radical Revisions*. New York: New York University Press, 377–382.

Strousse, Jean (ed.) (1974) *Women and Analysis: Dialogues on Psychoanalytic Views of Femininity*. Boston: G. K. Hall & Co.

Tannen, Deborah (1990) *You Just Don't Understand: Women and Men in Conversation*. New York: William Morrow & Co.

Tate, Claudia (ed.) (1983) *Black Women Writers at Work*. New York: Continuum.

Thorne, Barrie, and Nancy Henley (eds) (1975) *Language and Sex: Difference and Dominance*. Rowley: Newbury House.

Thorne, Barrie, Cheris Kramerae and Nancy Henley (eds) (1983) *Language, Gender and Society*. Rowley: Newbury House.

Tickner, Lisa (1988) 'Feminism, Art History and Sexual Difference', in *Genders* 3, 92–129.

Todd, Alexandra D., and Sue Fischer (1988) 'Theories of Gender, Theories of Discourse', in Todd and Fischer (eds), *Gender and Discourse: The Power of Talk*. Norwood: Ablex Publishing Corporation, 1–16.

Todd, Janet (1980) *Women's Friendship in Literature*. New York: Columbia University Press.

Trudgill, Peter (1983) 'Language and Ethnic Group', in *Sociolinguistics: An Introduction to Language and Society*. Harmondsworth: Penguin, 51–77.

Tuchman, Gaye (1978) 'Introduction: The Symbolic Annihilation of Women by the Mass Media', in Tuchman, Kaplan and Benet (ed.), *Hearth and Home: Images of Women in the Mass Media*. New York: Oxford University Press, 3–38.

Vetterling-Braggin, Mary (ed.) (1981) *Sexist Language: A Modern Philosophical Analysis*. Totowa: Littlefield, Adams.

Walker, Alice (1983) *In Search of Our Mothers' Gardens: Womanist Prose*. See supplementary bibliography below.

— (1986, orig. 1983) *The Color Purple*. See supplementary bibliography below.

Wallace, Michele (1990) *Invisibility Blues: From Pop to Theory*. London and New York: Verso.

— (1993) 'Race, Gender, and Psychoanalysis in Forties Film', in Manthia Diawara (ed.), *Black American Cinema*. New York and London: Routledge, 257–271.

Weedon, Chris (1987) *Feminist Practice and Poststructuralist Theory*. Oxford and New York: Basil Blackwell.

Weisweiller, Eva (1981) *Komponistinen aus 500 Jahren*. Frankfurt am Main: Fischer.

West, Cornel (1993) *Race Matters*, New York: Vintage Books.

— (1994) *Prophetic Thought in Postmodern Times*, Monroe: Common Courage Press.

Whitford, Margaret (1991) *Luce Irigaray: Philosophy in the Feminine*. London and New York: Routledge.

Wiesen Cook, Blanche (1992/1979) '"Women Alone Stir My Imagination": Lesbianism and the Cultural Tradition', in Wayne R. Dynes and Stephen Donaldson (eds), *Studies in Homosexuality*, Vol. VII *Lesbianism*. New York: Garland Publishing, 42–62.

Willis, Susan (1987) *Specifying: Black Women Writing the American Experience*. London: University of Wisconsin Press.

Wilson, A. (1989) 'History and Hysteria: Writing the Body in *Portrait of Dora* and *Signs of Life*', in *Modern Drama* 32 (1), 73–88.

Wilson, Harriet E. (1985; originally 1859) *Our Nig, or Sketches from the Life of a Free Black*. With an introduction by Alice Walker and an afterword by H.L. Gates. New York: Random House and Vintage Books.

Wittig, Monique (1992) *The Straight Mind and Other Essays*. Boston: Beacon Press.

Wittig, Monique and Sande Zeig (1979) *Lesbian Peoples: Material for a Dictionary*. New York: Avon.

Wolfram, Walter A. (1969) *A Sociolinguistic Description of Detroit Negro Speech*. Washington: Center for Applied Linguistics.

Wolfson, Nessa, and Joan Manes (1980) 'Don't "Dear" Me', in Sally McConnell-Ginet, Ruth Borker and Nelly Furman (eds), *Women and Language in Literature and Society*. New York: Praeger, 79–92.

Women: A Cultural Review 3/1 (1992) Women and Music: Opera Now/Music and Aesthetics. Oxford: Oxford University Press.

Woolf, Virginia (1928) *A Room of One's Own*. London: Penguin Books (1945 edn).

Wright, Elizabeth (ed.) (1992) *Feminism and Psychoanalysis: A Critical Dictionary*. Oxford: Blackwell.

Zimmerman, Bonnie (1983) 'Exiting from Patriarchy: The Lesbian Novel of Development', in Elizabeth Abel, Marianne Hirsch, and Elizabeth Langland (eds), *The Voyage In: Fictions of Female Development*. Hanover and London: University Press of New England, 244–257.

— (1990) *The Safe Sea of Women: Lesbian Fiction 1969–1989*. Boston: Beacon Press.

Zimmerman, Don H., and Candace West (1975) 'Sex Roles, Interruptions and Silences in Conversation', in Thorne and Henley (eds) (1975), 105–29.

Literature about *The Color Purple*

Bobo, Jacqueline (1988) '*The Color Purple*: Black Women as Cultural Readers', in E. D. Pribram (ed.), (1988), 90–109.

Bobo, Jacqueline, and Ellen Seiter (1991) 'Black Feminism and Media Criticism: *The Women of Brewster Place*', in *Screen* 32 (3), 286–302.

Butler, Cheryl (1991) '*The Color Purple* Controversy: Black Woman Spectatorship', in *Wide Angle* 13 (3 & 4).

Diawara, Manthia (1988) 'Black Spectatorship: Problems of Identification and Resistance', in *Screen* 29 (4), 66–76.

Hite, Molly (1990) 'Romance, Marginality and Matrilineage: *The Color Purple* and *Their Eyes Were Watching God*', in Gates (ed.), (1990), 431–54.

hooks, bell (1990a) 'Writing the Subject: Reading *The Color Purple*', in Henry Louis Gates Jr. (ed.), *Reading Black, Reading Feminist: A Critical Anthology*. New York: Meridian, 454–70.

Kaplan, Cora (1986) 'Keeping the Color in *The Color Purple*', in *Sea Changes: Culture and Feminism*. London: Verso.

Stuart, Andrea (1988) '*The Color Purple*: In Defence of Happy Endings', in Gamman and Marshment (eds), 60–75.

Wallace, Michele (1990) 'Blues for Mr Spielberg' (67–76) and 'Negative Images: Towards a Black Feminist Cultural Criticism' (241–255), in *Invisibility Blues*. London and New York: Verso.

Publications by Alice Walker

Poetry

1973 *Revolutionary Petunias*. London: The Women's Press.

1976 *Once*. London: The Women's Press.

1984 *Horses Make a Landscape Look More Beautiful*. London: The Women's Press.

1984 *Good Night, Willie Lee, I'll See You in the Morning*. London: The Women's Press.

1990 *Her Blue Body Everything We Know: Earthling Poems 1965–1990*. London: The Women's Press.

Narrative anthologies

1970 *In Love and Trouble*. London: The Women's Press.
1981 *You Can't Keep a Good Woman Down*. London: The Women's Press.

Novels

1970 *The Third Life of Grange Copeland*. Washington: Square Press/New York: Simon & Schuster.
1976 *Meridian*. Washington: Square Press/New York: Simon & Schuster.
1983 *The Color Purple*. Washington: Square Press/New York: Simon & Schuster.
1989 *The Temple of My Familiar*. Washington: Square Press/New York: Simon & Schuster.
1992 Possessing the Secret of Joy. Washington: Square Press/New York: Simon & Schuster.

Essays

1983 *In Search of Our Mothers' Gardens: Womanist Prose*. London: The Women's Press.
1988 *Living by the Word: Selected Writings*. London: The Women's Press.

Forthcoming

The Same River Twice: Honoring the Difficult: A Meditation on the Making of the Film The Color Purple Ten Years Later.

Index